World Food

HONG KONG

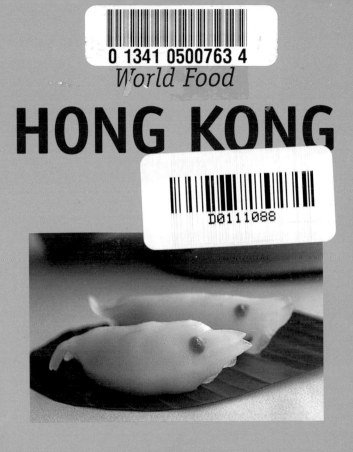

200501 - 000

Richard Sterling
Elizabeth Chong
Lushan Charles Qin

WORLD FOOD Hong Kong
   1st edition

Published by
   Lonely Planet Publications Pty Ltd ABN 36 005 607 983
   90 Maribyrnong St, Footscray, Victoria 3011, Australia

Lonely Planet Offices
   Australia Locked Bag 1, Footscray, Victoria 3011
   USA 150 Linden Street, Oakland CA 94607
   UK 10a Spring Place, London NW5 3BH
   France 1 rue du Dahomey, 75011 Paris

Photography
   Many images in this guide are available for licensing from
   Lonely Planet Images. email: **lpi@lonelyplanet.com.au**

   Front cover: *Lee Kum Kee Premium Oyster Sauce*

   Back cover: *A young Chinese family get snapped in front of the ruins of Saint Paul, Macau.*

Published
   April 2001

Although the author and publisher have tried to make the information as accurate as possible, they accept
no responsibility for any loss, injury or inconvenience sustained by any person using this book

   ISBN 1 86450 288 6

   text & maps © Lonely Planet Publications Pty Ltd, 2001
   photos © photographers as indicated 2001
   LONELY PLANET and the Lonely Planet logo are trade marks of
   Lonely Planet Publications Pty. Ltd.

Printed by
   The Bookmaker International Ltd
   Printed in China

MAP KEY

▬O Place to Eat & Drink	— · — · Provincial Border	⊢—◦—⊣ Railway, Station
Pedestrian Mall	——— Freeway	—◦— MTR, Station
Building	Primary Road	– – ◦ – – Tram, Station
Park, Garden	Secondary Road	⊢⊢⊢⊢⊢ Escalator
Sports Ground	Tertiary Road	🏛 Museum
Urban Area	▪▪▪▪ Tunnel	● Point of Interest
	❼ Route Number	O Town

About the Authors

Richard Sterling is known as the Indiana Jones of Gastronomy for his willingness to go anywhere and court any danger for the sake of a good meal. His other books include *Dining with Headhunters*; *The Fearless Diner*; and the award winning *Travelers' Tales: A Taste of the Road*. He has been honoured by the James Beard Foundation for his food writing, and by the Lowell Thomas awards for his travel literature. His lifestyle column 'Maitre d' appears monthly in *San Francisco* magazine. Though he lives in Berkeley, California, he is very often politically incorrect.

Richard wishes to thank Diana Budeman, Steven Wong, Mandy Lo and Nevin Lim of the Hong Kong Tourist Association. Their assistance, advice and knowlege made the writing richer and the research process an absolute joy. Special thanks to Patsy Chan, just for being Patsy Chan. And to that clutch of delightful soaks on Lamma Island who made us promise not to mention Lamma Island in this book.

Elizabeth Chong wrote the *Eat Your Words* language section. She is an author, freelance writer, prolific public speaker, teacher and Chinese cooking consultant based in Melbourne, Australia. She is both a frequent visitor to Hong Kong and an avid fan of the city's cuisine. Elizabeth wishes to thank the ever-diligent Peter Guberek for his research and assistance.

Lushan Charles Qin of Chin Communications contributed to the *Eat Your Words* language section. He has been assisting with Lonely Planet publications for a number of years. He has also worked as a translator and interpreter, and conducts language and culture training programs. Charles wishes to thank Kate Richie and Clara Yim who assisted greatly with this project.

About the Photographer

A food and travel photographer, Oliver works from Bondi Beach, Sydney, where he lives with Tina and two surf-crazed kids, Halley and Billy. This is his third World Food guide. He has photographed for many food and wine books, and is a regular contributor to a number of Australian and international magazines.

Oliver wishes to thank Stephen Wong and Mandy Lo of the Hong Kong Tourist Association, Nevin Lim for being his guide in Hong Kong, Mr Fung Kam Hung of Fook Ying Hot Pot Seafood Restaurant, Chow Teddy the snake handler, Tony Chan of Tung's restaurant, Patsy Chan, Christine Smith-Mann, Lamey Chang, Kelly Sum and Carole Klein of the major hotels in Hong Kong. In Macau Oliver wishes to thank Nicki Keegan and Teresa Costa Gomes of the Macau Government Tourist Office, Restaurante Litoral, Ivo Estorninho and Derek Fong Chi Kuong of The Westin Resort, Catherine Kong of the Hyatt Regency, Fernando's restaurant and everybody at the Macau Mandarin Oriental. And finally, all the chefs restaurant and club staff, as well as market vendors who were so helpful; making the photographic research so much fun.

From the Publisher

This first edition of *World Food Hong Kong* was edited by Patrick Witton and designed by Brendan Dempsey of Lonely Planet's Melbourne office. Natasha Velleley mapped, Lara Morcombe proofed. Lyndal Hall oversaw the book's production and indexed.

The language section was compiled by Elizabeth Chong and Lushan Charles Qin, and was edited by Fleur Goding. Peter D'Onghia oversaw the language section's production.

Valerie Tellini, of Lonely Planet Images, coordinated the supply of photographs, Glenn Beanland assessed and Brett Pascoe managed the pre-press work on the images.

Sally Steward, publisher, developed the series and Martin Hughes, former series editor, assisted with pre-production.

Warning & Request

Things change; markets give way to supermarkets, prices go up, good places go bad and not much stays the same. Please tell us if you've discovered changes and help make the next edition even more useful. We value all your feedback, and strive to improve our books accordingly. We have a well-travelled, well-fed team that reads and acknowledges every letter, postcard and email and ensures that every morsel of information finds its way to the appropriate people.

Each correspondent will receive the latest issue of Planet Talk, our quarterly printed newsletter, or Comet, our monthly email newsletter. Subscriptions to both are free. The newsletters might even feature your letter so let us know if you don't want it published.

If you have an interesting anecdote or story to do with your culinary travels, we'd love to hear it. If we publish it in the next edition, we'll send you a free Lonely Planet book of your choice.

Send your correspondence to the nearest Lonely Planet office:

Australia Locked Bag 1, Footscray, Victoria 3011
UK 10a Spring Place, London NW5 3BH
USA 150 Linden St, Oakland CA 94607
France 1 rue du Dahomey, Paris 75011

Or email us at: talk2us@lonelyplanet.com

contents

HONG KONG & MACAU

Guangdong

Pearl River Mouth

Shekou

Nim Wan

Qiao Island

Lingding Island

Lung Kwu Chau

Zhuhai Special Economic Zone

HONG KONG SPECIAL ADMINISTRATIVE REGION

Tung Chung

Zhuhai

Tai O

Ngong Ping

Lantau Is

Shek Pik Reservoir

Macau

MACAU SPECIAL ADMINISTRATIVE REGION

Soko Islands

Taipa

Taipa Island

Lantau Channel

Coloane Island

Coloane

Hengqin Island

South China Sea

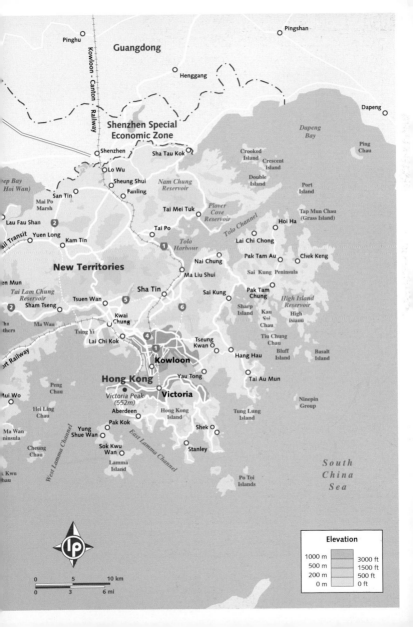

Hungry for the flavours of the world? Want to eat up all of China, with perhaps a side order of Portugal? You'll find that whole nations and former empires are on the table in Hong Kong. As emporium to the world, Hong Kong is also restaurateur to the world. It's a portal to nearly any cuisine you could desire. If you're craving Chinese for breakfast, Nepali for lunch, or Cajun for dinner, all you have to do is place yourself in the middle of Hong Kong and follow your stomach. It's all within reach. Nowhere in the world is there such a dense concentration of the world's culinary heritages. Sure there are cities in the world that can offer you a wide range of cuisines. But none, we think, offer as much as Hong Kong.

This cultural and culinary diversity wasn't always part of the plan. Hong Kong was designed to be a transit point on a trade route to riches. But over time this road to riches changed course and followed other avenues of commerce: from tea to textiles to finance and information. And all the while the people came from around the globe to make Hong Kong their home. At first British and Cantonese, then people from all over mainland China. And then from everywhere. And with them they all brought their traditions and tastes. The result of this flavourful mix can now be seen, and sampled, in Hong Kong's home kitchens, **dai pai dong** (food stalls) and banquet halls.

Here on the estuary of the Pearl River you will also encounter cuisines that are unique, to be found nowhere else. The Hakka, a wandering people whose odyssey brought them finally to Hong Kong, tease out all possible goodness from the humblest fare. Take a short ferry ride to Macau you will be seduced by Macanese cookery, a culinary melding of Chinese, Portuguese and Portugal's colonies; the true cuisine of an empire. And the culinary variety extends to the glass. Thirsty for wine? Microbrew? Want to learn to become a Tea Master? Hong Kong will quench any desire. So whether you want a five-star banquet or a five-minute meal of **juk** (rice porridge) it's all right here: the people, the cultures, the cuisines. The world on your table. Care to order?

the culture of
hong kong cuisine

Hong Kong is more than a Special Administrative Region, it is a process in which things are changed, enriched, even sundered. It is style, attitude, flair. Geographically, at best, it is a transit point on the road to wealth. Gastronomically it is a shape-shifting chimera, a microcosm of the world. You could call it culinary sophistication or gluttony; confusion or variety; east meeting west, or never the twain. And in every case you would be right.

Hong Kong presents perhaps one of the oddest jumbles in the whole world. It is neither fish, flesh, fowl, nor good red herring. The government and principal people are English, the population are Chinese, the police are Indian, the language is bastard English mixed with Cantonese, the currency is the Mexican dollar, and the element no more amalgamate than the oil and vinegar in a salad.

Lord Redesdale (1837-1916)

Lanterns painted with slogans and well wishes

Hong Kong will not be defined by its cuisine, because it has none. And yet it has all. There is no indigenous cookery, no special Hong Kong dishes, nothing that a person can point to and say, "ah, that's from Hong Kong". And despite the coming together of many styles and cultures, let any thoughts of 'fusion cuisine' be banished from your mind. There is none of that here either. All this is so because Hong Kong is not really a place. Not really. As a clever person once observed, Wales is not a state but a state of mind. Hong Kong is neither country nor culture, but a conduit through which pass people, goods, appetites, energies and ideas.

Unlike most of the great cities of the world, Hong Kong did not spring from the soil. It did not begin as a village, grow into a town and then mature into a city. It was invented. It was purpose built, custom made, to do exactly what it does: create wealth by whatever means. At first it was the tea trade, then general trade, then manufacturing, now finance and information. So as the means of creation change over time, Hong Kong reinvents itself. Its current form has nothing to do with the handover in 1997. It started in the 1980s. And gastronomically speaking, this is the best Hong Kong yet. This is the World's Fair of Food.

Wanna buy a bird? Visit the bird market off Prince Edward Road, Hong Kong Island

History

The story of Hong Kong cuisine began with a great historic collision of two empires; one new and insatiable, the other ancient and complaisant. When these two tectonic plates of east and west drove into each other, they threw up this astonishing promontory that came to be called Victoria, or Hong Kong. Before that seismic event it was a backwater in every sense. It had been long inhabited by humble fishermen, farmers and a lesser breed of pirate. They had eked out a living for centuries, the world passing by unheeding. In the 16th century, across the mouth of the Pearl River, the Portuguese established themselves in what is now Macau, and any of the world's attentions in the region were paid there. But then came that collision in the form of the Opium Wars (see Tea in the Drinks chapter). And almost overnight, in historic terms, the invention was up and operating.

This did not instantly bring good dining. The British brought their own provisions, and in this far corner continued to eat their gammon and sausage and wash it down with beer. Wealthy settlers brought French chefs to Hong Kong, and they have been there since, upholding the finer traditions of Europe. The Chinese opportunity seekers who flowed in with the British brought their traditions, for the most part Cantonese, considered by many to be the acme of Chinese cookery. But there was no Promethean spark in the Hong Kong kitchen. No one ever said: let's go to Hong Kong for the food. But there began a slow building of the foundation of Hong Kong's culinary culture.

It was fortunate, for diners, that the Crown Colony had come to rely on the mainland city of Guangzhou (Canton) for its survival, as it provided food, labour, building materials, water, and cooks. For mainland cooks, pay was always better in Hong Kong, as it is today. People say that the best cooks in China come from Guangzhou. And the best of Guangzhou go to Hong Kong. And so for many decades Hong Kong was 'the real Guangzhou', because they had the money and the acumen to always strive for the best, the most exotic, the new. There were other Chinese people in Hong Kong, such as the Hakka, but their culinary contribution would wait.

Hong Kong was ready for the long-awaited Promethean spark when it came in 1949. With the declaration of the People's Republic of China, floods of immigrants came to Hong Kong from all over the mainland. Many chefs among them. From Shanghai, Sichuan, Hunan and Beijing (Peking) they came, looking for safety, succour and a new life. These uprooted people established themselves in Hong Kong. And their cooks opened restaurants for them. For though they would never see their home-lands again, they could at least nourish themselves on their memories. They could keep their birthplaces alive in the hearth and at the table.

CULTURE

Fishing village in Sam Mum Chai, New Territories

And they thrive there to this day. Though they eat each other's fare, they do not blend them. They maintain their culinary identity. Hong Kong is not an amalgam of Chinese cookery, it is a focus.

And now it is also a focus for the rest of the world's cookery. Though there were always non-Chinese restaurants in Hong Kong, it was in the 1980s that they began to be important. Before then, foreign food was for the most part British, and not the best of that (although the fish and chips were always of the highest quality). There were only two Italian restaurants, for example, in the whole territory. As the British troops departed, though, new entrepreneurs moved in. And they demanded the best. Anglophones, Europeans, Japanese, Taiwanese, Indians, and a great number of Hong Kongers who had lived and studied abroad and acquired Catholic tastes, began to converge on Hong Kong. And they all called for good eats. And they had more money than the soldiers ever did. One effect of which is that there are now enough Italian restaurants in town to support an Italian Restaurant Association.

CULTURE

THE SOJOURNER – Faces of Gastronomy

I had never visited Hong Kong before I moved here in 1993. I am Chinese-American, and had lived my whole life in areas of the United States with the highest Chinese populations, first in Los Angeles' Monterey Park, then in San Francisco and Manhattan. But Chinatowns in the United States had not prepared me for the sights and smells of The Territory, as it was known before the British returned it to Chinese rule in 1997.

Chinese-style fast food and drink, Mong Kok, Kowloon

Most of the food I'd grown up eating was Cantonese – it's what my mother and grandmother cooked, what we ate when we dined at Chinese restaurants, and what I cooked after I left home. When I came to Hong Kong, I found the diversity of Chinese cuisine exhilarating. My friends and relatives introduced me to earthy Hakka and Chui Chow dishes, rich and flavourful Shanghainese and Taiwanese dishes, and spicy but well-balanced Sichuan dishes. I went on an eating frenzy, trying to taste as many of these unfamiliar flavours as I possibly could.

At first, I bought my meals from illegal street vendors who sold their wares from carts that were always ready for a quick getaway. Snails simmered in their shells (you could still see their antennae), **tong yuen** (glutinous rice flour balls) served in a sweet-spicy ginger broth and **chiau deo fu** (stinky tofu; you can smell it blocks away). It's difficult nowadays to find this food being sold by street vendors: the government has waged a serious and fairly successful campaign against them.

CULTURE

Ill-fated fish in a Hong Kong restaurant

My friends took me to seafood restaurants where you could peer into tanks and choose which creatures would make up your meal. Although I was very familiar with the Cantonese emphasis on freshness, this was an eye-opener. The fish vendors would call to passing customers, bragging that they had the freshest seafood. But it was all fresh – row upon row of tanks filled with crawling, swimming fish, lobsters, shrimp, crabs, scallops, mussels, cuttlefish. The variety was endless. The vendor would scoop what you wanted from the tank, weigh it, and it would be taken to the restaurant of your choice. There the cook would dispatch it (out of sight) and prepare it to your specifications – do you want it steamed, deep fried, stir fried or boiled? With garlic and ginger, perhaps, or maybe black beans and chilli? The main expense was in the price of the seafood; the charge for cooking and serving being so minimal.

Hong Kong is a 24-hour city, and you can find something to eat whenever you're hungry. Of course you might be eating at hastily wiped tables under bright fluorescent lights, or even at a folding table on the footpath. In fact all kinds of people eat at these places, from street cleaners grabbing a quick bite during their break, to couples in evening dress who have danced all night.

When people find out that I'm a food editor, I know without a doubt that their first question is going to be: what's your favourite restaurant? But it's an impossible question to answer, without narrowing things down a bit. What kind of cuisine? If Chinese, what kind of Chinese? Casual or formal? Is it for a date or with a large group? Cheap or expensive? In which area? The permutations are endless, but fortunately, Hong Kong always satisfies.

Susan Jung is the food editor for the South China Morning Post

CULTURE

Hong Kong Flavours

There isn't any Hong Kong dish. There isn't any Hong Kong sauce. Even **hou yau** (oyster sauce), which is so strongly associated with Hong Kong, is originally from Guangzhou. There is only the Hong Kong style, the Hong Kong way of doing, and doing it better than anybody else. Or at least doing it different. Hong Kong chefs pride themselves on innovating, experimenting, improvising and creating. They will instantly seize upon a new ingredient and find ways to use it. Asparagus is a vegetable unknown in most of China. But Hong Kong chefs serve it every day, and take it for granted. In the Dynasty Restaurant in the Renaissance Harbour View Hotel, Chef Tam coats baby abalone with olive oil before serving. At the Shang Palace in the Kowloon Shangri-La, Chef Ip combines caviar with Chinese preserved eggs. A **dai pai dong** (food stall) cook in the Temple Street night market uses ketchup in his stir-fry sauce. And it is delicious. Another uses mayonnaise.

Even more than the willingness to try new ingredients is the willingness to do new things, practice new techniques. This is the crux of Hong Kong style. To refine, to push the envelope, to extract the maximum possibility from a recipe. A Hong Kong technique known as velveting is a good example: meats are marinated in spices whipped into a froth of egg white, giving the meat a soft and pleasing texture. The use of yeast or baking powder in deep-fry batters produces a crispier product.

Heat is an important factor in Hong Kong cooking. Very high heat. In most parts of China claypots are traditionally used for slow cooking, but in Hong Kong they are placed over a blast of high heat to quickly infuse flavours into the dish. And even more importantly, Hong Kong chefs hew to the concept of **wok chi**. The Mandarin term in common usage across China refers to what could be called a hot wind that roars off a super-heated wok. This can only be achieved with a powerful fire burner that covers the entire underside of the wok, not just the small ring of fire to be found on the common cooker. This produces a fire so hot that home kitchens cannot use it. The insulation needed for a wok chi stove would take up all the space in a home kitchen. And wok chi takes a great deal of fuel, hence a lot more money. So you won't find it much on the mainland. But Chef Kwong of the Tang Court in the Great Eagle Hotel is so wedded to wok chi that he has to replace his woks every three months. This cooking technique sears and cabonises the outer surfaces of foods sealing-in flavour. Although debate surrounds the benefits of wok chi (see the boxed text The Innovator later in this chapter) the general consensus is positive. It is said that high heat imparts natural iron to the food being cooked. You'll taste the difference immediately.

Vibrant neon on the streets of Kowloon

Regional Influences

Despite Lord Redesdale's remarks, Hong Kong is a Chinese city. Or at least it's more Chinese than anything else. Yet it's less Chinese than any city in China. Or more, depending on how you look at it. Virtually all of Chinese gastronomy is to be found here. It is China on a plate. Yet the people are the most cosmopolitan of China. They are the most outward looking, the most adventurous. They are citizens of the world. So Hong Kong is also the world on a plate, albeit a smaller plate. Let's look at the larger picture, at the styles that make up Hong Kong's Chinese culinary heritage.

Boats heading towards the Pearl River through the Kap Sui Mun straits

Guangzhou (Canton)

Cantonese cuisine has the largest collection of specialised dishes in the whole of China and is characterised by elaborate preparation and the use of an infinite variety of ingredients. Subtle flavours are combined with a light touch of soy sauce and ginger, enhancing the freshness of the ingredients. Flavours are delicate and well balanced – neither salty nor greasy, and are obtained through cooking techniques such as quick stir frying and steaming.

It was from the cuisine's hometown of Guangzhou, capital of the province of Guangdong (formerly Kwangtung) that the main bulk of Chinese emigrants went abroad. Consequently Cantonese cuisine established itself as 'Chinese cuisine' in the western world. Favourites of the Cantonese kitchen include **xiu ab** (roast duck, seasoned on the inside with spices, sewn up securely, then basted in a mixture of honey, soy and vinegar), **dung gua tong** (winter melon soup; see the recipe in the Banquet chapter) and, of course, **yum cha** (see the boxed text).

CULTURE

YUM CHA & DIM SUM

Although found throughout the world, yum cha is best experienced in Hong Kong. Essentially, yum cha is a meal of snacks called dim sum, which is taken from mid-morning to late afternoon, and served at Cantonese restaurants and yum cha houses. Yum cha translates as 'to drink tea', and dim sum literally means 'to touch the heart lightly', and the vast array of delectable steamed or fried dumplings and small dishes do just that. Teapots are replenished constantly (without extra charge) as tea and little heart dishes go together like love and marriage. Yum cha is a Cantonese institution, and is undoubtedly Hong Kong's favourite lunch (see Yum Cha Houses in the Where to Eat & Drink chapter).

Serving dim sum in the Hoover Restaurant, Kowloon

A Dim Sum Selection

Cha Xiu Bao – Barbecued Pork Bun
Barbecued and seasoned sweet roast pork wrapped inside a soft dough and steamed to make a soft fluffy bun.

Xi Jap Fung Zao – Chicken Feet in Black Bean Sauce
Deep fried then steamed chicken feet in a black bean and chilli sauce.

Jin Dui Zei – Combination Deep-Fried Dumpling
An egg-shaped dumpling made from glutinous rice flour.

Daan Tad – Egg Tart
A baked, tart-shaped puff pastry containing a smooth-as-silk egg custard filling, always served warm from the oven.

Hedgehog buns (steamed egg custard cream), Shang Palace, Kowloon

Jade coral dumplings (steamed shrimp & asparagus), Shang Palace, Kowloon

Lin Yung Bao – Lotus Seed Dumpling
A sweet bun filled with a paste made of mashed lotus seeds.

Mong Guo Bou Ding – Mango Pudding
A fresh mango puree set into a smooth mousse-like dessert.

Ma Lai Gou – Malay-Style Sponge Cake
A steamed egg sponge cake.

Ha Gao – Prawn Dumpling
A bonnet-shaped dumpling with a thin translucent dough made from Chinese wheat starch and potato flour. Crisp succulent prawns nestle inside this steamed favourite.

Cheung Fen – Rice Noodle Roll
Shrimp, pork or beef filling encased by fresh rice noodles, forming a soft roll that is lightly steamed and served with a dressing of soy sauce and sesame oil.

Chun Guen – Spring Roll
The Cantonese like finely shredded chicken or pork, mushrooms, bean sprouts and sometimes a few bean thread noodles in their spring rolls. Always deep fried until golden and crisp.

Steamed shrimp rice roll, Fook Ying Hot Pot seafood, Hong Kong Island

Xiu Mai – Steamed Dumpling
A small dumpling made by steaming won ton wrappers that are filled with a delicately seasoned mixture of minced pork, prawns, water chestnuts and bamboo shoots.

Xi Jap Jing Pai Gwat – Steamed Spareribs in Chilli & Black Bean Sauce
Pork spareribs chopped into bite-size pieces, marinated then steamed with the sauce.

Noh Mei Gei – Sticky Rice Dumpling
A dumpling made of glutinous rice steamed in lotus leaves with Chinese pork sausage and other delicacies.

Wu Gok – Taro Dumpling
A deep-fried egg-shaped dumpling made of mashed and grated taro and filled with a sweet pork mixture.

Silver silk baby octopus (deep fried turnip dumplings), Shang Palace, Kowloon

Chargor (glutinous cakes steamed on leaves), Mong Kok, Kowloon

Shantou (Chui Chow)

The Chui Chow people originate from the area around the seaport of Shantou, in the east of Guangdong. Although part of that province, the cuisine of the Chui Chow people is distinctive enough to be identified as a special regional cuisine of its own. Birds' nests gathered on cliffs of the south seas are a speciality. These are in fact nests made from the saliva of swiftlets, which contains semi-digested seaweed. Other Chui Chow dishes reflect a love of seafood, including **hai ji yu chi tong** (shark's fin soup).

Chui Chow cuisine differs from Cantonese, in so far as there is more emphasis on accompanying sauces. There is a wonderful garlic and vinegar dip for the famous **chui jau lou sui ngoh** (Chui Chow soyed goose) and cumquat jam flatters **tim suen hung xiu ha kau** (deep-fried shrimp balls with sweet & sour sauce). A distinctive sauce known as **chin jiu** is made from a skilful blend of spices including wild peppercorn, pepper and chillies, and is an integral component of many Chui Chow dishes.

Other Chui Chow specialities include **chui jau yi min** (pan-fried egg noodles served over chives) and **chui jau yu tong** (aromatic fish soup). And no Chui Chow meal is complete without two thimble-size cups of strong, bitter **Ti Kwan Yu** (Iron Goddess Tea), one to be swallowed before the meal, one after (see Tea Types and the boxed text Tea Treasure in the Drinks chapter).

East China: Shanghai, Yangzhou, Hangzhou, Nanjing

The food of China's eastern coastal provinces are the most diverse of all China's regional cuisines. The extensive coastline ensures that seafood is an eastern joy, and the network of irrigation canals running from the mighty Yangzi River gives rise to a lush and fertile soil.

Although diverse, east coast dishes are not considered sophisticated enough for elegant banquets, that honour having been reserved for Beijing and Cantonese cuisine. Dishes flavoured with sugar and vinegar are characteristic of this region. Ginger, garlic and pepper are prevalent players, with any resulting saltiness balanced by sweeter flavourings such as sugar. Red-cooked or soyed dishes are favourites both in east Chinese and Shantou cooking. Popular dishes include **tim suen pai gued** (sweet & sour pork), **hung xiu ju sau** (red simmered knuckle of pork) and **jing saam xin** (finely shredded ham, chicken and pork with bamboo shoots).

The food of Shanghai tends to be a little more greasy, sugary and strongly flavoured, with stewing, frying and braising being the principal cooking techniques. Shanghai winters are cold and, as in north China, bread, dumplings, and noodles are staples. During summer, people prefer cooling foods such as soy bean products, fish, shrimp and mushrooms.

CULTURE

Sichuan

Proudly different from other cooking styles of China, Sichuan cuisine bespeaks the independent mindset of the people in the country's west. Good, home-style Sichuan food consists of peppery, hot, chilli-laden dishes, but the Sichuan cooks do not rely on this one spice. Sichuan's own wild peppercorns, ginger, garlic, vinegar and broad-bean paste are just some of the taste enhancers that create such exciting tastes.

Sichuan food aims for a perfect blend of five key flavours: sweet, sour, salty, peppery and, of course, chilli hot; a good example is **suen laat tong** (hot & sour soup). The food is highly fragrant, and the contrast in textures almost defies description. This is a result of intricate cooking methods. Stir-fried dishes, for instance, are firstly deep fried, then returned to the wok and cooked to the point where juices are almost entirely reduced. The results are chewy yet tender, dry yet flavoursome.

The Sichuan speciality **jeung cha ab** (duck smoked in camphor tea) is a serious contender to Peking duck. The duck is seasoned with ginger, orange peel, cinnamon, peppercorns and coriander, then marinated in Chinese rice wine. After an initial steaming, the duck is smoked over a charcoal fire sprinkled with chips of camphorwood and red tea leaves. Served with fluffy white steamed buns, the final result is heavenly blend of flavours.

Protein-rich tofu in all its forms is another of Sichuan's treasures. **Ma po deo fu** (grandmother's tofu; tofu with beef, garlic, chilli, soy sauce, rice wine, peppercorn and spring onion) is proudly Sichuanese, but is cooked and eaten all over China and beyond.

A LANGUAGE OF FOOD

Have you eaten rice?	The typical greeting.
The time it takes to drink a cup of tea/eat a bowl of rice	A few minutes.
You are breaking my rice bowl!	You are destroying my livelihood!
I have an iron rice bowl	I have a job for life.
Going vegetarian	To take vows of chastity.
He's a hairy crab	Hairy crabs are kept trussed in a water tank in restaurants until they are needed in the kitchen. A stock trader is called a hairy crab when all his money is in low value shares that he can't sell. It's all tied up with no place to go.

North China: Beijing, Shandong, Hebei

Beijing inevitably acquired a cosmopolitan cuisine through the presence and influence of the imperial court, which encouraged the development of a wonderful range of dishes originating from every province of China.

The food of north China can be identified by the extensive use of oils such as sesame oil and chilli oil, coupled with ingredients such as vinegar, garlic, spring onions, bean pastes and dark soy sauce. The cool climate in which Beijing shivers for six months of the year undoubtedly reflects the desire for stronger tastes and oilier textures. Wheat products, such as dumplings, noodles and buns often replace rice as a staple. Noodle-making is a special skill of northern chefs, hand-pulled noodles being a star attraction in many restaurants.

The cuisine of north China is marked by Mongolian influences, such as the passion for game, mutton and goat – reminders of a nomadic age. A Mongolian-influenced favourite is **da bin lou** (hotpot, fire kettle or steamboat). It's a bit like fondue. Picture a hollow metal cone about 30cm (12 inches) high and 7 1/2cm (3 inches) across at the base. Fitted to the outside about half way up is a metal moat, the shape of a bagel or donut split in half. Inside the cone is a fire, and in the moat is soup stock. Beside the hotpot are platters of goodies (meat, tofu, vegetables, noodles) placed in the bubbling broth and cooked to taste.

The city of Beijing is immortalised by elaborate Imperial dishes from the bygone era of the royal palace. The Imperial banquet lists 365 dishes, the most famous being **bak ging tin ab** (Peking duck), which is revered not only in China, but in culinary circles throughout the world.

Card playing in Rear Lakes, near Beihai Park, Beijing

CULTURE

HAKKA – HONG KONG'S FIRST PEOPLE

The Hakka people were originally a rural, nomadic group from the northern reaches of China – Hakka literally means 'guest people'. Moving steadily into the southern provinces of China, the Hakka eventually settled in Hong Kong, where they could go no further. The Hakka people are sometimes referred to as the gypsies of China, and have made an art of salting and preserving ingredients, as well as developing tasty dishes from whatever cheap produce was available. Offal features in many different ways, an example being **ja dai cheung** (deep-fried intestines), much enjoyed by folk other than Hakka. Clever use is also made of tofu and preserved vegetables. Arguably the signature dish of the Hakka people is **yim guk gei** (salt-baked chicken; see Fowl in the Staples & Specialities chapter). Also look out for **tong sui** (sweet soup), which is made with some peculiar ingredients (see The Bold Palate chapter).

Another Hakka speciality is **poon choy** (literally, dinner in a bucket). Into a wood or metal basin the cook places seven different foods, in layers: vegetables on the bottom, meat on the top. All the diners eat from the basin, layer by layer. This dish has the great virtue of providing a meal for a whole family while producing only one dirty dish.

The cuisine is similar to Cantonese in its preference for contrasting flavours and the willingness to cook anything. However there is an earthiness and simplicity that has led to this style being called peasant food.

Sadly, Hakka restaurants are disappearing, and the Hakka being so frugal, there just isn't much profit margin. So they continue to decline. But you should avail yourself of Hakka cuisine while you can. It's the least expensive kind of dining in proper restaurants, and some of the most satisfying. The hard part is finding the Hakka restaurants. They tend not to be listed in dining guides. So we have no compunction about telling you of our own particular favourite: The Hakka Gourmet at 67B Waterloo Rd, Kowloon. Try salt-baked chicken. You'll go back again.

Row boats near the fishing village of Sam Mum Chai, New Territories

How Hong Kongers Eat

It should come as no surprise that Hong Kong folk like to eat five times a day: breakfast, lunch, afternoon tea, dinner and a late night snack. Afternoon tea and a late night snack are not considered meals, however. That's just filling up space. A proper meal comprises rice (or other cereal food) and something else such as garnish. Afternoon tea might consist of savouries and sweets, fruits and nuts, or even bits of steamed seafood or a dish of tofu braised in spicy sauce. And the tea taker might stagger from the table. But he has not had a meal. However, if in the morning he sits down to a bowl of **juk** (congee; rice porridge) with a bit of dried shrimp and a few mung bean sprouts, then our man has had a meal.

Breakfast is usually taken at home for children and stay-at-home parents. Workers might breakfast at home or in a small restaurant specialising in breakfast foods such as juk, taken plain or with a multitude of garnishes.

Lunch downtown will often be a set lunch consisting of one to four courses at a fixed price. However, lunch can also be a bowl of noodle soup with slices of roast duck, or a **rice plate** (a stir-fried dish or a few smaller servings on a bed of rice). It might be something more elaborate at one of the hotel dining rooms, or a buffet. There is a popular foreign restaurant chain in Hong Kong that serves a very inexpensive set lunch; the 'happy meal'. Purists might gag at the thought of stopping for some grease-on-the-run, in Hong Kong diversity reigns supreme and chowing down on fast food is just a part of modern life.

Afternoon tea in Hong Kong is especially popular on weekends at the good hotels. This can be an elaborate affair, a traditional English high tea (replete with scones jam and cream), or a dim sum tea. It might be at the office and comprise little more than tea and candies or a steamed bun. At home the tenant might invite her neighbour over for tea and melon seeds, or a plate of sesame crisps. Labourers will stop for a few short minutes to pour steaming hot tea from their thermos, and snack on rice crackers before getting back to work.

Dinner is a big event every day, especially dinner in a restaurant. The great majority of Hong Kong people live in very small apartments with very small kitchens. Dining in such cramped quarters every day and every night would rob life of some of its savour. Furthermore, Hong Kong people are too busy to cook every night. Everybody works at least a five-and-a-half-day week. Many people have two, even three jobs. Not only do they lack time to cook, they lack sufficient time to socialise. Dining out together solves both problems. This is one reason Hong Kong's restaurants are always so noisy. This is where people are communing with each other, catching up on all the gossip, making plans, telling jokes and just enjoying life. Life happens around the Hong Kong table.

CULTURE

RULES AT THE CHINESE TABLE

Do feel free to shovel in the rice by putting the bowl to your mouth like everyone else. Trying to pick at individual grains is a fool's errand.

Do say thanks if someone picks up a piece of food and puts it in your bowl. This is a gesture of high courtesy.

Do stand up and lean over the table if a particularly tasty morsel is on the other side. Asking someone to pass the sauce is not the norm.

Do put your chopsticks horizontally down on the table or the plate rather than on top of the bowl.

Do cover your mouth when you pick your teeth.

Eating out in the Temple Street night market, Kowloon

Don't start eating until everyone is ready, particularly in a formal or banquet setting. Once all are seated and ready, the head of the table might say **seck fan** (literally, eat rice) or he or she might just start eating.

Don't be afraid to spit out the bones or shells onto the table when eating fish or shellfish. That's what your fellow diners will be doing!

Don't hold your chopsticks pointing straight up, or pointing at anyone. According to Chinese tradition, misfortune will ensue.

Don't try to help to clear the dishes while someone else is still eating, even in someone's home. It suggests that you are impatient.

Some things are common in restaurants throughout Hong Kong: cigarettes, pets and mobile phones. The whole territory smokes, and there is very little sympathy for the non-smoker. Restaurants that seat 200 or more are required to set aside a non-smoking section, and roughly 25% of restaurants fall into that category. At the time of writing there is a move in the legislature to reduce the seating requirement to 100, but there is fierce opposition. Hotel restaurants tend to be a little better at accommodating the non-smoker. What will save you from asphyxiation is the fact that all restaurants are air-conditioned and the machines run nonstop.

Many Hong Kong people have lap dogs. Given the size of Hong Kong homes that's about the only kind of dog they could have. Do not be surprised to see a table full of richly bejewelled **tai tais** (ladies who lunch) feeding their Fidos with chopsticks and making goo goo noises at them and just spoiling them rotten. Fortunately they do not treat their children so.

THE INNOVATOR – Faces of Gastronomy

Innovation and the eagerness to try something new, to think 'outside the box' is the essence of Hong Kong's culinary magic. Few people are as eager and innovative as Cecilia J Au-Yeung, one of Hong Kong's best known authors and most popular cooking teachers. In 1971 Cecilia estab lished the Chopsticks Cooking Centre in Kowloon where she offers training to those who want to pursue a culinary occupation, and day-long seminars and classes for those who simply want to improve their kitchen savvy. Her students range from homemakers to well-known chefs looking to expand their repertoires. She has trained so many Hong Kong chefs that if you spend any time in the city you will likely be served by one of her graduates.

"Contrary to public opinion", she lectures, "I do not believe that Chinese cooking is very healthy. At least not as it is practised by most people". It would be difficult for someone of less stature to say such a thing in public. "For example, the high heat used by so many causes the formation of carcinogens. Do you want to eat cancer? And all the oil. My goodness! And it isn't even very healthy oil." Less than thirty seconds into her lecture, Cecilia has established her credentials as an iconoclast. "I recommend much greater use of olive oil, and at lower temperature." To this a confused student asks, "But isn't olive oil very expensive?"

"Ha!" Cecilia retorts. "How much is your life worth? I also recommend German-made stainless steel cooking pans and woks. They require less heat. Yes, they are more expensive, but they save money at the Doctor's." She also demonstrates techniques and strategies for

And then there is the ubiquitous and damnable mobile phone. Even children carry them, electronic apron strings that never let them out of mother's reach. For adults they're more of an umbilical cord, the severing of which would result in quick social and commercial bleeding to death. You will hear mobile phones chirping everywhere. If there are more than six people in your field of vision, at least one of them will be chatting away into the ether. As diners approach a table the ritual is always the same. Set down any purses or briefcases, take out mobile phones and set them on the table, to your right. Take seats. No need to apologise for telephonic interruptions to the conversation. We are astonished that Chinese people, whose regard for food and the culinary art approaches reverence, would tolerate this kind of distraction at the table. But then the mobile phone is still a status symbol. We look forward to the day when mobile phones cease to be glamorous and are seen to be nothing more than the ball and chain of middle management.

---

saving time in the kitchen. This is important as working hours are long in Hong Kong. However she does draw the line. "This is quick and easy. But you can't be too quick and easy. I'm not saying you're lazy, but if this is not fast enough for you then you should resort to fast food. There's nothing more I can do for you." We are humbled.

In somewhat more familiar terrain we are shown how to cut, slice and dice vegetables in the proper Chinese manner. As we do, Cecilia gives us a running commentary on the healthful benefits of each ingredient. "Hearts of bamboo are good for reducing cholesterol. Add a pinch of sugar to counter the salt." She shows us how to slice chillies with a knife and fork so as not to touch the hot little nubbins with our bare hands. She demonstrates her way of blanching tofu before cooking it in order to improve the smell, get rid of scummy content and firm the stuff up before frying. And she stresses the importance of practising in the kitchen. "You can only learn so much from books. Even my books. You have to observe, over and over again. Look. You can see through the shrimp dumpling. That's the way. You need patience."

In the class today we are producing a buffet lunch. The buffet is yet another western adaptation. It even includes finger sandwiches. But when our ox tongue with garlic sauce looks a bit tired she makes it clear that she will not interfere with the traditional Chinese art of presentation. She quickly remakes it. And it looks like edible jewellery. "There!" she says. "Always make it look shimmering and luscious. It won't be Chinese if you don't."

See the Recommended Reading & Contacts list for Chopsticks Cooking Centre details.

CULTURE

CHOPSTICKS IN TRAINING

There was a sinking feeling in the pit of my stomach. I was in China and I didn't know how to use chopsticks. I'd tried, but success escaped me. Now I was climbing the stairs of one of the oldest yum cha houses in Hong Kong and there wasn't a fork in sight. Resplendent in his Mandarin robes, Nevin, our Chinese guide, seated us at a large round table and began preparing tea. I rallied a bit knowing I could handle a teapot. That wasn't to be the case. Nevin prepared the jasmine tea in a small bowl, covered it, let it seep, and then with a flourish, pushed back the floating tea leaves with the lid and poured the hot liquid into a small delicate cup. My turn, tea in, cover on, tilt it back, pour, mostly on the table. I watched in dismay as the tea stain spread slowly across the crisp, white tablecloth. Nevin, deep in conversation with Richard about dim sum, didn't seem to take notice and began to order a variety of those tasty delights nestled in their steam baskets.

Now the moment of truth. "Nevin, I don't know how to use chopsticks", I said with my best smile. He looked at me, not unkindly, and replied, "This is not a problem". Reaching into his robe he brought out a rubber band and wrapped it tightly around the ends of the chopsticks. Then taking a match from the table, he broke it and put the two halves between the sticks making a fulcrum. "Try this", he said. Gingerly I picked them up and behold, I managed to capture one of those slippery delights. Well, not perfectly. Bits and pieces kept falling off and sometimes the paper doily at the bottom of the basket came up with the dim sum. At the end of the meal, the table area was far from tidy. Noticing my embarrassment, Nevin said quietly, "Don't worry. We Chinese are not so concerned with table manners, we just want the food to taste good". Thank you, Nevin, and I promise always to carry rubber bands and matches in my pocket.

Gina Comaich is an Oakland teacher known for enthralling her students with colourful travel tales.

staples
& specialities

What are the specialities of a place that produces nothing, but imports and consumes everything? Is asparagus a staple when it has to be flown in from France? Hong Kongers eat it by the ton. Is dairy food a staple for a people whose adults are lactose intolerant, yet can't get enough ice cream and yoghurt? Do sandwiches count? Wine is frequently on the table, alongside the green tea. Abalone doesn't grow anywhere near Hong Kong, but it is sought after by everyone.

It is no easy task to list the staples and specialities of a people who are both willing and eager to eat anything and everything. No list could be complete. And any would seem too long. And once drawn up the Hong Kongers would be off on some new culinary quest, developing new tastes, seeking new gustatory thrills. You'll find the foods from every region of China, and every other region in the world as well. The best we can do is tell you what you will find most of in Hong Kong, and advise you to keep an eye out for more. Most, of course, will be of the Chinese school. But do not think that this is the sum.

Shopping in the Mong Kok Market, Kowloon

Rice

It is almost trite to say that rice is the indispensable staple of most Hong Kongers. But it is true. It accompanies almost every Chinese-style meal. Even those meals that incorporate a dish of fried noodles will still turn on a bowl of rice. These days, among the affluent, it has been losing its mystique. In a restaurant they order it, but then might ignore it, preferring to feed on delicacies and exotica to the exclusion of the wholesome grain. But the newly rich are wont to do such things. And you will see many newly rich in Hong Kong.

Wing Wo General Store, Hong Kong

But the Chinese revere rice, not only as the staff of life, but for its aesthetic value. Its mellow aroma is not unlike bread. Its texture when properly done – soft yet offering something to the teeth – sets off the textures of the foods that surround it, their shimmering colours the more vivid for their rice's whiteness. Flavours are brought into better focus by its simplicity. Rice is the unifier of the table, bringing all the dishes into harmony.

Cooking rice used to be a delicate balancing act performed over a charcoal fire. Nowadays everybody in Hong Kong has an electric rice cooker in their kitchen. The rice – long grain being the preferred variety – is washed thoroughly, then transferred to the rice cooker and covered with water to depth up to the first knuckle of the index finger. The lid is then closed and the machine does its thing.

There are many ways to eat rice; white, fluffy and from a small bowl being the most popular. There is fried rice. But this is little more than the Chinese version of hash or bubble and squeak. And while we might enjoy fried rice from time to time, we do not seek it out in one of the great gastronomic centres of the earth. There is glutinous rice dumplings made of sticky rice that is wrapped in bamboo leaves and steamed – standard fare at the dragon-boat races. And then there is **juk** (congee). This is little more than rice porridge, but unlike fried rice we do not disparage it. This is comfort food par excellence. Hong Kong is famous for its juk and rightly so. It takes hours to make. You may have it plain or dressed for the fair with meats, fish, croutons, condiments, toasted garlic, bean sprouts. It's a culinary canvas waiting for you to paint.

CONGEE CRAVINGS

When I asked restaurant owner, art critic, curator and friend, Kin Wai to name his favourite **dai pai dong** (food stall), he said it entirely depended on what we wanted to eat. Here for beef noodles, there for won ton, and of course Sang Gai in Sheung Wan for **juk** (congee; rice porridge).

My own answer would have been more complicated. I go into a long explanation of how I need a 'total experience' involving ambience and atmosphere. And then I end up eating juk in Sang Gai with Kin Wai. Now it is my favourite place.

I know that juk is not complicated to make, but I also know that it is hard to get a good bowl. Juk is all about standing and stirring for a couple of hours, and few people are prepared to put in the time. Some restaurants use rice powder, other fail to cook the grains until they've all softened into a porridge like consistency. But not at Sang Gai.

I always order juk with fish balls, stirred in with shredded lettuce then seasoned up with spring onion and ginger shreds in soy sauce. Kin Wai takes his with fish balls and beef. We never eat the accompanying **yauh ja gwai** (fried baguettes), as we can't even get through the bowl of juk.

Taking 10 minutes to throw back some food really is not my style, but for when that craving hits, there's nothing like stopping at Sang Gai for juk. It's just a pity they're not still serving at midnight.

Sang Gai is located at 7-9 Burd St, Sheung Wan.

Annabel Jackson has been a food & wine author, consultant and Hong Kong resident for 12 years.

Juk

Basic juk is simplicity itself. Once it is made, like oatmeal or pasta, you can add almost anything to it. Some people like their juk thick, some like it thin. Adjust the proportions of rice and water to your liking.

Ingredients

½ cup long-grain rice (some people mix three parts long grain to one part glutinous)
6 cups water
  salt to taste

Wash the rice thoroughly. Place it in a pot with the water. Be mindful that juk can boil over easily, so use a deep pot. Bring the water and rice to a boil. Reduce the heat to low and simmer until the mixture begins to thicken into a porridge (about two hours). Stir occasionally to prevent the rice sticking to the bottom. Add the salt. If you want your juk to be creamy, beat it with an egg beater.

Serves 2

The cook at Sang Kee Congee, Kowloon

Popular Additions to Juk

Add any or all of these to the juk about three minutes before serving: 100g (3¹/₂oz) minced beef; 1 thinly sliced spring onion; 1 tsp dry sherry or rice wine; 1 tsp soy sauce; a few drops of sesame oil; a pinch of sugar. Whisk in a raw egg immediately before serving.

or

200g (7oz) thinly sliced fish fillets ¹/₂ tsp minced ginger; 2 minced spring onions; 1 Tbs light soy sauce; 2 tsp dry sherry or rice wine; 1 Tbs oil; a pinch of salt and sugar.

Combine all ingredients and let stand for 15 minutes. Transfer the mixture to individual serving bowls and pour the hot juk over it. The fish will cook in less than a minute.

Breakfast time at Sang Kee Congee, Kowloon

Noodles

Noodles are thought to have originated in north China during the Han dynasty (206 BC to AD 220) when the Chinese developed techniques for large-scale flour grinding. Not only were noodles nutritious, cheap and versatile, they were portable and could be stored for long periods. Their popularity quickly spread throughout Asia and beyond via the packtrains of traders and larders of immigrants. Legend credits Marco Polo with having brought noodles to Italy in 1295. Legend also credits him with bringing the kiss to China. Leave it to an Italian to either do it or at least take credit for it. At any rate, with the surging popularity of Italian food in Hong Kong, pasta seems to have made the round trip.

Chinese like to eat noodles on birthdays and on the new year, because their long thin shape symbolises longevity. That's why it's bad luck to break noodles before cooking them. You may be shortening more than you think!

Various regions of China, and elsewhere in Asia, claim certain kinds of noodles as their own. The Hong Kong people don't care. They eat them all. Thin, translucent strands made from mung bean starch are called **fen xi** (cellophane noodles or bean threads). They are used most often in South-East Asian dishes, and are usually cooked in soups or deep fried. **Haw fun** are wide, white, flat, slippery rice noodles, and are usually pan fried.

STAPLES

De Farinna VA Heng noodle shop, Macau Peninsula

The Cantonese word for noodle is **mein**, and **chow mein** is probably the noodle dish most people think of when they think of takeaway Chinese cuisine. There are a many variations on this dish, but most often the thin noodles are fried crisp. The story goes that in the 19th century a certain Chinese cook was employed by the railroad. When frying noodles one day for the boss, the lazy fellow fell asleep and when he woke the noodles were burnt to a crisp. As he had no more noodles he served them to the boss and hoped for leniency. But the boss, never having had chow mein before, pronounced them tasty and demanded that they be served every day.

De Farinna VA Heng noodle shop, Macau Peninsula

La mein (pulled noodles) look almost like toffee when they are in the making. The noodle puller repeatedly stretches a piece of wheat-flour dough, folding it over and stretching again, until a network of noodle strands materialise. These noodles are thick, and when cooked they are softer in texture than most noodles, almost gooey. Pulled noodles are a Beijing speciality and some restaurants, like Peking Garden, station the noodle puller in the dining room so you can watch the show. Sort of like watching your pizza being tossed.

The art of making noodles in the Peking Gardens restaurant, Hong Kong Island

Thin, translucent noodles made from rice flour are called **gon hoh fen** (rice sticks). Vietnamese cooks use these extensively in all kinds of dishes. And the excellent Vietnamese restaurants of Hong Kong are the best places to enjoy these noodles.

Won ton are not exactly noodles, more noodle packets, similar to ravioli. Normally no wider than a watch face, they are filled with meat, seafood or vegetables and can be fried, steamed or added to soup (see Won Ton Soup later in this chapter).

Tofu

The pressed curd of the soybean is also known as bean curd, or even 'poor man's meat'. Tofu contains all the essential amino acids, is low in calories and is devoid of cholesterol. It is mainly used for its texture and goes well with any other ingredients. You can do absolutely anything with tofu: deep fry, saute, steam, bake, simmer, broil or puree. It comes in three textures: soft or silken, which is added to soups or steamed dishes where cooking time is brief; semi-soft, which is used in stir-fry dishes; and firm, which is used for stuffing and deep frying.

Other tofu products include tofu skin, which is the skin that forms when the soybeans are being boiled. It is used to add texture to stir-fry dishes and to wrap up meat and fish balls. You will also find marinated tofu sold in jars, the taste of which can be extremely strong, but not as strong as **chiau deo fu** (stinky tofu), which is made from fermented tofu (see The Bold Palate chapter).

Tofu is also used to make **nam yu** (pressed tofu cubes fermented in salt, spices and rice wine until red in colour) and **ji juk** (cream-coloured sticks of dried tofu that have a nutty flavour).

Deep frying tofu

Meat

The people of Hong Kong consume more protein per capita than any other group in the world. Of course some of that is tofu, but this is far and away the meat-eatingest city in all of China. Our guess is that only Argentina eats more. Pork is the premier meat, as it is anywhere in China. Even the dour communists of the Chinese Revolution recognised the importance of the transcendentally tasty swine. It was no less a personage than the Great Helmsman himself, Mao Zedong, who proclaimed that one of the goals of the revolution was to see to it that every family owned a pig.

But you'll find every other four-legged critter available for food here as well. Beef is big, and steak houses are increasingly popular. Chinese-style barbecue is a long-standing staple. Lamb is not as common, but look for it at northern Chinese, Lebanese and Italian restaurants. Having a Big Mac attack? They got that too.

Beef Dishes

Ho Yau Ngau Yug (Sliced Beef with Oyster Sauce)
A simple but popular beef dish; slices of tender beef are stir-fried and seasoned with a savoury oyster sauce.

Suan Jap Au Lei (Beef Tongue with Garlic Sauce)
A tasty dish flavoured with ginger, star anise, Tabasco and garlic (see the recipe in the Banquet chapter).

Xi Jui Cao Pai Gued (Spareribs in Black Bean Sauce)
Made by sauteing marinated rib pieces and sliced onion and capsicum in a pungent black bean sauce. This dish can also be made with pork spareribs.

Pork Dishes

Xiu Yu Ju (Roast Suckling Pig)
A banquet dish often ordered for special occasions. A whole pig is marinated then roasted over hot coals resulting in a golden crackling skin and a rich, sweet, fatty meat. It can be served on its own, or with small pancakes or buns, and eaten in the manner of Peking Duck (see Peking Duck later in this chapter). Roast pork is sold in pieces from takeaway sections of many Cantonese restaurants.

Tim Suen Pai Gued (Sweet & Sour Pork)
This dish needs no introduction as it's so famous outside of China. Tender pork pieces are marinated, coated in an egg and flour mixture, deep fried until golden, then mixed with a few vegetables and pickles. The ingredients are then bathed in a fruity sweet & sour sauce made from a judicious blend of vinegar and sugar.

Roast pork with rice from the Fook Ying Hot Pot seafood restaurant, Hong Kong Island

Cha Xiu (Barbecued Sweet Roast Pork)

A dish made of thick strips of barbecued pork that have been marinated in spices and seasonings, including five-spice powder and **hoisin sauce** (see Hoisin Sauce later in this chapter). It is often eaten sliced as a cold entree or can be combined in cooked dishes such as noodles or stir-fried vegetables.

Hung Xiu Pai Gued (Braised Spareribs)

These are made by deep frying the ribs until they are brown and crisp, then braising them in a sauce made of tomato ketchup, sweet vinegar and sugar until the ribs are tender and the sauce is reduced to a sticky sweet glaze.

Hung Xu Ju Sau (Red Simmered Knuckle of Pork)

This is a typically rich Shanghai pork dish, prepared with liberal use of sugar and soy sauce. This dish goes well with plain rice and vegetables.

Ma Ngei Seung Xu (Ants Climbing a Tree)

This is the name for a dish of cellophane noodles braised with seasoned minced pork. The combined textures of pork and slippery noodles create an interesting tension, and the appearance of the dish justifies its title.

Mui Choi Kau Yug (Double Cooked Steamed Pork & Pickled Cabbage)

Preserved, salted cabbage, chopped and steamed with thick slices of fried belly pork.

Xi Ji Tau (Stewed Meatballs)

This is a popular home-cooked dish, often called lion's head casserole because the large pork meatballs are thought to look like lion's heads with the accompanying cabbage resembling manes. The pork, sometimes mixed with crabmeat, is seasoned with spring onion, ginger, salt and wine before being made into meatballs. Cabbage is laid across the bottom of a casserole with the meatballs on top. They are then covered with more cabbage then simmered in stock until the meatballs are melt-in-the-mouth tender.

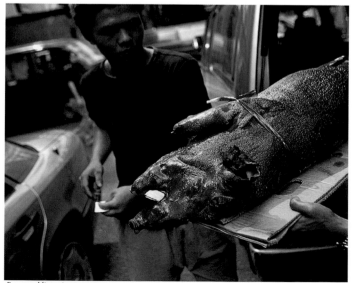

Roast suckling pig au go go

Fish & Seafood

With China's long coastline and many rivers and lakes, it is no wonder that fish has always been important to the Chinese people. In Chinese, the word for fish is **yu**. Pronounced with a slightly different inflexion, yu also means plenty or abundance. So a traditional final dish at a formal dinner banquet is often a whole fish, signifying to the guests that although many courses have already been consumed, there is plenty more to eat if they so desire.

When the catch is landed, from sea, river or pond, it must be cooked immediately. It is vital to capture the freshness of the fish in the wok – a maxim held by chefs from every Chinese kitchen. In fact Cantonese chefs have an insistence bordering on obsession for freshness, so it is common to see fish tanks in many restaurants in Hong Kong.

Abalone

A highly prized mollusc native to the north Pacific Ocean. In the east Pacific they grow to be as much as 30cm (12 inches) across. But the variety preferred in Hong Kong is the Japanese abalone, which taste somewhat like scallop.

Carp

Brought into Hong Kong from south China, carp is used extensively in claypot cooking. You won't often find carp on menus as it's not considered refined enough for the restaurants of Hong Kong.

Fish Maw

Is it a flavouring agent? Is it a protein supplement? A dish by itself? Well, it's all of the above. It is the dried stomach lining of a fish. If you know tripe, you'll know what this is like. It has to be rehydrated before cooking, which causes it to expand three fold. Usually fish maw is deep fried then chopped up into soup.

Grouper

Coral trout and rock cod are members of this family. It is a very popular fish in Hong Kong and is brought in from Indonesia, Malaysia, the Philippines and Australia. Grouper is delicious steamed and served whole (see the recipe Steamed Whole Fish in the Celebrating with Food chapter).

Lobster

A Hong Kong favourite. In **xi jap lung ha** (lobster & black bean sauce) the lobster is chopped in sections with the shell, deep fried, then returned to the wok and tossed with black beans, ginger and garlic. Chicken stock is then added to the wok and the lobster is gently braised. This dish can also be made with prawns.

THE KING OF ABALONE – Faces of Gastronomy

Looking at the unassuming facade of The Forum Restaurant in Causeway Bay and at its understated interior, you wouldn't guess that this is one of the most expensive restaurants in the city. You would not guess that in business and commercial circles it is looked upon with awe for its power to generate mighty rivers of liquid asset. Neither would you guess that this establishment is held in high regard by members of the world's most prestigious gastronomical societies. And you wouldn't guess that in his youth the master of the kitchen faced starvation.

Chef and owner of The Forum, Yeung Koon Yat (known as Ah Yat) was born on the mainland in Guangdong province. During the Japanese war he and his two sisters were separated from their parents, and in the tumultuous years of upheaval they suffered privation. One of Ah Yat's sisters died in his arms from starvation. At the end of the war he came to Hong Kong to start over. He worked menial jobs, and saved what he could. He had a vision of himself as an entrepreneur, so typical of people in this city of opportunity. And he was determined not to suffer again as he and his family had in the war.

It took him many years to acquire the wherewithal, and in 1974 he and some partners opened The Forum, yet another Cantonese restaurant. Initial success then began to turn sour and his partners left one by one, he buying them out. By 1977 he was the restaurant's sole owner and chef. It was not the best year in the restaurant business and many houses were doing what they could to lower prices and attract more customers. Ah Yat saw his chance. He would not lower his prices. He would make it one of the most expensive by specialising in those rare and costly foods so loved by Chinese in general and Hong Kongers in particular, especially a tiny variety of abalone brought from Japan.

30,000 Hong Kong dollars worth of abalone, Forum restaurant, Causeway Bay

He had to invest heavily just for enough abalone with which to learn to prepare it and to develop his own recipes. His colleagues thought he had gone off the deep end. But his vision was spot on. Hong Kongers can't resist a bit of conspicuous consumption, especially if it's something of super high quality. Almost immediately the famous, the rich and the famously rich were staking out their regular tables at The Forum. Ah Yat has since become known throughout China as the King of Abalone. Even the late Deng Xiaoping proclaimed, upon tasting the Ah Yat's viands, that the then new Chinese policy of open exchange was justified by the ability to eat this dish.

The 'King of Abalone'

And as to his esteem among the culinary lights of the world. He is one of the most decorated chefs anywhere in the world. He holds among other awards, the Star of Excellence from La Chaine des Rotisseurs, the Medaille d'Honneur de Vermeil, and most significantly he is one of three current holders of the Gold Medal from the Club des Chefs des Chefs. His fellow honourees are the chef to a president of France and another who was chef to five presidents of the USA. Perhaps most telling is that he was invited to address the French Parliament and then to prepare them a meal. High honours indeed.

Do not think that you cannot dine at The Forum. There are several items on the menu within the means of the average traveller. Ah Yat remembers he was once poor and hungry. Many fish dishes are on offer and vegetable dishes are especially tasty. Unlike most Chinese restaurants the kitchen is open to view. You may even glimpse the master at work. You'll note that unlike most Cantonese chefs he seldom uses the wok. He prefers the casserole, and a much lower heat. No wok chi here. He believes it is better for the delicate flavours of the foods he prepares. Who could argue with the King?

Oysters
These are the key ingredient in the Hong Kong speciality, **jin hou beng** (oyster omelette), which is made with fresh oysters, spring onion and coriander (see Dai Pai Dong in the Where to Eat & Drink chapter).

Pike
A slender fish with flaky white flesh, used primarily for making fish balls and fish cake.

Prawns
In Hong Kong, prawns are enjoyed as **baak cheuk ha** (steamed fresh prawns), which are served with a dip made by heating a little peanut oil until smoking and pouring it immediately over a small dish of soy sauce.

Salmon
Imported from Scotland, Norway and parts of the Pacific, salmon is used mainly in western cooking. However it is gaining popularity in modern Chinese cuisine.

Shark
Caught in nearby waters, shark is used for making seafood soups including the coveted shark's fin soup. An expensive but popular shark dish is **hung xiu yu chi** (braised shark's fin) in which a whole shark's fin is slow-cooked until soft and gelatinous, steamed with pork and chicken, then braised and served in a superior stock. Another costly dish, **hai ji yu chi tong** (shark's fin soup with crab roe sauce) requires elaborate preparation. The prepared shark's fins are added to superior chicken stock and the crab roe is stirred in at the last minute to create a rich soup.

There is good reason, however, to resist eating shark, not only for its rarity (almost no edible sharks exist in the South China Sea any more) but for the cruelty in how they are caught, the fins are torn off, and they are pushed in the sea to drown.

Sole
This is an excellent fish for steaming, which commands a fairly high price at restaurant tables. Sometimes called dragon's tongue, it is mainly brought in from Macau.

Yellow Croaker
This fish is a favourite of Shanghai cuisine, and is the preferred fish for making deep-fried **tim suen yu** (sweet & sour fish).

Fowl

They are batty for birds in Hong Kong. Chickens, ducks, geese, pigeons; anything with wings except an aeroplane will find its way to the Hong Kong table. One of the greatest collective traumas to Hong Kong was when avian flu swept through the feathered population in the late 1990s. As a precaution, millions of chickens had to be destroyed. Most people think that the government went too far in its efforts at hygiene, but at least you know you won't get sick. Chicken appears at almost every meal, in the form of stock, which is one of the most important flavouring agents in the Chinese kitchen. And of course chicken is fried, stewed and roasted as well. Ducks and geese are generally roasted. And also roasted are pigeons, a great Hong Kong favourite. Restaurants famous for pigeon don't even ask how many people will be dining, they just ask "How many pigeons?"

Bak Ging Tin Ab (Peking Duck)

The original recipe for Peking Duck was scribed some 300 years ago and ran for more than 15,000 words! Ducks are specially bred for this dish, and consequently there is a prosperous duck industry in Beijing. The ducks are generously fed so they are quite big and plump by the time they are ready for market. The preparation of this dish is lengthy and complicated, and there are specialist Peking Duck chefs who are highly trained in this art.

First, air is pumped into the body between the skin and the flesh, in much the same way a balloon is inflated. The neck is then tightly tied with string, so that the duck remains inflated. Next the bird is blanched in boiling water several times, then left to dry in a cool draughty place for five hours. A mixture of malt honey, cornflour and vinegar is brushed over the skin and then it is hung to dry for a further four to five hours, before a second coating is applied. The duck is then roasted in a hot oven to make the skin crisp, after which the heat is lowered and cooking continues for one hour.

The serving of Peking Duck is quite theatrical. It is ceremoniously wheeled out to the table on a trolley by the chef, resplendent in uniform and white gloves. The skin is skilfully sliced with the merest sliver of flesh, and rolled inside a fine pancake and served with spring onions and **hoisin sauce** (see Hoisin Sauce later in this chapter).

Hung Xiu Baat Bou Ab (Braised Eight-Jewelled Duck)

In this dish the duck is first fried then slowly stewed with ginger and spring onion until very tender. The eight jewels accompanying the duck can be exotics like braised sea cucumber, abalone, black mushrooms, lotus nuts, bamboo shoots, dried scallops, prawns and Chinese greens.

Hed Yi Gei (Beggar's Chicken)

This is an elaborate dish exclusively made in restaurants. A whole chicken is partially deboned, stuffed with pork, vegetables, mushrooms, ginger and other seasonings, wrapped in Lotus leaves and wet clay or pastry and baked for several hours. The result is a fragrant chicken that can literally be carved with chopsticks. Of course there is a story behind this dish: legend has it that a beggar stole a chicken and was building a fire to cook the clucker when its rightful owner appeared. The quick-thinking beggar smothered the bird in clay and threw it in the fire. Once the coast was clear, he cracked open the clay mould and a taste sensation was born.

Ja Ji Gei (Crispy Skin Chicken)

With this dish, the chicken is poached. Maltose, salt and flour mixed with the poaching stock is poured over the chicken and the bird is hung in a draughty spot to dry. It is deep fried until the skin is crisp and brown. Once done it is sliced and served with fresh lemon and a roasted salt & pepper dip called **jiu yim** (prickly ash).

Jeung Cha Ab (Camphor Tea-Smoked Duck)

The first cousin to the legendary Peking Duck and is equal if not better. Three cooking techniques are necessary for the unique result: steaming, smoking, then deep frying. The smoky succulent pieces are served with hot, fluffy steamed buns.

Xiu Ngoh (Roast Goose)

A Hong Kong speciality found at many yum cha houses. The marinating and roasting technique is the same as for roast duck. The resulting meat is extremely tender and the skin very rich and crisp.

Jui Gei (Drunken Chicken)
So named because the poached chicken is marinated in poaching broth and rice wine. It is served chilled in small pieces, as an appetiser.

Ning Mung Gei (Lemon Chicken)
This dish has many variations. The classic recipe is crispy skin chicken served with fresh lemons, however, more westernised versions use bite-size fillets dusted with egg and flour, deep fried and served with lemon sauce made from simmering lemon juice, sugar and chicken stock.

Yim Guk Gei (Salt-Baked Chicken)
The signature dish of the Hakka people. A whole chicken is wrapped in cooking paper and 'buried' in a deep cooking pot or wok containing very hot (fried) rock salt. The chicken is baked in the heat of the salt, and the result is a golden, moist chicken with a unique salty-sweet taste and delicate fragrance. Historical records of the area of Dong Jiang in Guangdong reveal similar recipes for cooking chicken in salt.

Chui Jau Lou Sui Ngoh (Chui Chow Soyed Goose)
The goose is gently stewed in a rich sauce made principally of soy sauce, and served with a garlic and vinegar dip.

Xiu Ab (Roast Duck)
This dish starts with the bird being seasoned on the inside with spices, sewn up securely, basted with a honey-soy-vinegar mixture and hung to dry. It is then roasted until the skin is a glowing chestnut brown. Roast duck is served chopped or can be bought whole or in halves at specialist Cantonese restaurants and takeaways.

Hot birds, Yung Kee Restaurant, Wellington Street Central, Hong Kong Island

STAPLES

PEKING DUCK OPERA

Hong Kong being Cantonese, I did not think it the place for Peking Duck. Surely Beijing was the only place to sample the famous dish. And it was 20 years ago I had the opportunity to travel to Beijing and satisfy my quest for original Peking Duck. But disappointment ensued as Beijing's restaurants in those days were less tributes to old dynasties as homages to ancient grease. Nor did the names of the restaurants communicate the romance of Peking Duck. One restaurant, near a hospital, was called Kao Yan Dian, which translates as Sick Duck.

Perhaps I would never find out what Peking Duck should taste like. But Hong Kong, as always, gave me the answer. This city had the combination of relative prosperity, an indigenous population who felt that one lives to eat, and tourists who wanted the best. And over the years, the finest Chinese chefs had migrated to the then British colony to prepare the best. My friends and I made our Peking Duck pilgrimages virtually every Sunday. For every Sunday brought a different duck experience.

As dining on Peking Duck was a serious occurrence, a restaurant's atmosphere was as important as music is to opera. Peking Gardens was a spotless and shiny establishment, reminiscent of a Chopin piano piece. The Pine & Bamboo restaurant, by the side of the racetrack, was usually crammed with suddenly wealthy gambling families, noshing on their duck with the joy of a Rossini opera. Spring Deer was a clattering, hell raising, bawling eatery, a scrumptious family affair, a Charles Ives orchestral piece replete with duck, jellyfish, prawns and lost babies. And the misnamed American Restaurant, filled with British soldiers and their families, had the bonhomie of a Gilbert & Sullivan production. But no matter the atmosphere, when the Peking Duck appeared it had the presence, dignity and promise of Maria Callas.

Some would allow the kitchen to simply bring out the carved skin. We, though, would act like French revolutionaries and insist the victim be wheeled out on a cart to be carved in public. Some would be happy when the executioner hacked out chunks of skin and meat, the fat drizzling off the carcass. We, however, insisted the chef make a slight incision to the skin, then deftly peel it off. A waiter in the raucous Spring Deer revealed the secret of separating the skin so seamlessly: once the duck had been barbecued, a bicycle tyre needle was inserted in the body, and the skin was pumped.

Once we had the golden skin on our plates, once the floury breads appeared, once the dark sauces and cucumbers and spring onions arrived, we were in duck heaven. We saw others gently put a slice or two or three on their lightly floured pancakes. We cared little for that covering but piled the black-to-brown speckled skin pieces one atop. The accompanying hoisin sauce was sweet, thick and black. One spring onion would add a soprano crunch to the alto bite of the duck skin itself.

Succulent Peking Duck from the Spring Moon Restaurant, Hong Kong Island

STAPLES

Peking Duck, Shang Palace, Kowloon

The coda to our symphony might have been the duck meat. The chunks of white and dark were delicious enough, but also ordinary enough in comparison to the skin. One legend (of thousands) is that the emperor ate the skin, the nobles had the meat and the servants were satisfied with the carcass boiled up for soup. And we were indeed emperors.

Harry Rolnick lived in Asia for 20 years as author, editor and food critic. He now lives in New York.

Removing the skin, Spring Moon Restaurant, Hong Kong Island

Soup

Soup, beautiful soup, quoth Lewis Carroll. In Hong Kong they might just say "more soup". A balanced meal simply must have soup. Traditionally it was the beverage component of the meal, (Chinese soups are traditionally clear) and nowadays it shares that role with other liquids. It is also one of the chief means by which the Chinese maintain their health. Soup is the main vehicle for the delivery of medicinal and balance enhancing properties of foods. It gives you heat in winter, keeps you cool in summer, and if you have a little cold in the nose, well, Jewish mothers and Chinese mothers sing the same song of soup.

Yin Woh Geng (Bird's Nest Soup)

A prestigious soup served at banquets. Preparation is long and tedious with much soaking and cleaning. The soup must be a superior chicken broth, and the cleaned and soaked birds' nests are gently cooked with finely minced chicken and egg whites. Birds' nests are also served in a sweet syrup as a cold dessert. (For more on birds' nests see Shantou in the Culture of Hong Kong Cuisine chapter.)

Wen Ten Tong (Won Ton Soup)

Dumplings stuffed with pork and shrimp served in chicken broth. Sometimes noodles are added to make **won ton mien**.

Dung Gua Tong (Winter Melon Soup)

Made by simmering diced winter melon, chicken, shrimp, crab meat and shiitake mushrooms in a high-grade chicken broth. For a stunning visual effect it is sometimes served in a hollowed-out winter melon (see the recipe in the Hong Kong Banquet chapter).

Bin Lou (Cantonese Steamboat)

This is not really a soup, but a soupy system. Raw, fresh ingredients including chicken, pork, seafood and vegetables are placed around a vessel containing boiling broth. The idea is to dip the finely sliced ingredients into the broth and cook your dinner at the table. Wire utensils are provided so you can fish out ingredients when cooked.

Lai Tong (Chinese Cabbage Soup)

This is often the house soup served in eateries and restaurants and is offered free of charge to regular patrons. The soup is usually pork and a green vegetable such as Chinese cabbage (one of the most versatile vegetables in the Chinese culinary repertoire) or watercress simmered in a light broth. Chinese cabbage soup is not usually listed on the menu, but is available on request.

Daan Fa Tong (Egg Flower Soup)

Also called **egg drop soup**, this soup is very popular in Hong Kong because it is so quick and simple to make; ideal for busy homemakers. There is no one single recipe; and it is rarely made the same way twice. This is a concept, not a formula. Basically, you start with a light stock that may or may not contain solids. This you garnish with raw egg (chicken, duck, even goose if you can get them), which quickly cooks in the hot broth.

Ingredients

6 cups	stock
3 Tbs	cornstarch
100g (3½oz)	lean pork or chicken, finely shredded
2	Chinese black mushrooms, sliced and soaked in one cup of water (reserve the soaking liquid)
2	eggs, beaten (whole eggs or just the whites if you prefer)
1	egg white, beaten
1	spring onion, thinly sliced
1 Tbs	soy sauce
1 Tbs	dry sherry or rice wine
1 tsp	salt
¼ cup	bamboo shoots, chopped
	few drops sesame oil

Combine one tablespoon of the cornstarch with the pork, wine, sesame oil and egg white. Bring the stock to simmer and add the mushrooms, bamboo shoots, soy sauce and salt. Stir the remaining cornstarch into ½ cup of the mushroom-soaking liquid and add it to the stock, stirring until the stock thickens and clarifies. Add the pork mixture and continue cooking about one minute. Remove from heat and slowly pour in the eggs, stirring until they separate into threads. Garnish with the spring onion.

Serves 2

Winter melon soup, Hoover Restaurant, Hong Kong Island

Eggs

Eggs are eaten in innumerable ways in Hong Kong. All kinds of eggs. If a creature lays eggs, the Chinese will eat them. Chicken, duck, goose, fish, prawn, crab; Hong Kongers are over the moon for ova. One sort of egg treat that you may have heard of is the thousand year egg. Also called century egg, ancient egg, Ming Dynasty egg, its proper name is **pei daan** (preserved egg). Individual eggs are packed in a mixture of ash, lime and salt, then buried in shallow pits for about 100 days. The lime 'petrifies' the egg during this time causing it to harden like a three-minute egg, and turns it to a dark, blue-green colour. It tastes kind of cheesy and smells kind of fishy. And we mean that in a good way. They are sold individually and eaten plain for breakfast or a snack, or chopped and mixed with other eggs for an omelette.

Baskets of eggs, preserved and fresh, for sale at the Reclamation Street Market, Kowloon

Haam daan (salted eggs) are soaked in brine for about 40 days. This process causes the yolk to harden and turn orange. Unlike preserved eggs, these must be cooked. They might be broken into a dish of stir-fried tofu or fried rice, or hardboiled and chopped up into a bowl of juk. You can recognise salted eggs at the market because they are wrapped in what looks like cow manure, but it's just packed earth.

Sauces & Flavourings
Black Beans & Black-Bean Sauce

Fermented black beans are in fact a type of soybean. The sauce made with these beans is a favourite ingredient in many stir-fry dishes, including asparagus in black bean sauce (see the recipe later in this chapter).

Five-spice Powder

This fragrant, reddish brown powder is a blend of ground star anise, fennel or anise seed, clove, cinnamon and Sichuan peppercorns. It is used to flavour barbecued meats and stews.

Ginger

Ginger is an important spice for both its gustatory and medicinal properties. It is added to fish, seafood and organ meats. It not only adds to the flavour of food, it can also mask unwanted odours.

Hoisin Sauce

This sweet, piquant brown paste is made from soybeans, red beans, sugar, garlic, vinegar, chilli, sesame oil and flour. It's an essential with Peking Duck.

Oyster Sauce

This thick dark sauce is concocted from oysters, water, salt, soy sauce and cornstarch, and often contains some form of colouring. It is used mainly as a seasoning, giving dishes a smooth and rich flavour, and its bouquet makes it excellent for stir-fried meat and poultry, seafood and fried rice. Oyster sauce can also be used as a condiment for fried eggs, juk, chicken and roast pork.

Prickly Ash
This is a roasted salt & pepper dip that is served with chicken dishes.

Sesame Oil
The local type of sesame oil is a rich-flavoured, amber-coloured oil obtained from pressed and roasted sesame seeds. A dash or two is added to marinades or at the last moment of cooking to flavour certain dishes.

Soy Sauce
This is the quintessential Chinese condiment, cooking ingredient and *sine qua non*. It is made through a fermentation process involving soybeans and wheat flour or barley. There is a wide range of soy sauces available, all of which can be divided into light and dark soy. Light soy is used in things like soup when the cook wants a delicate flavour of soy but not the colour. It's also used as a table condiment. Dark soy contains caramel and is darker, richer and thicker. It's also used as a condiment, and when the cook desires a full soy flavour, as in marinades.

Star Anise
This is the dried pod of an exotic tree of the *Magnoliaceae* family, native to China. This bark-like spice has cloves that resemble an eight-pointed star. It is not related to aniseed, yet yields a strong liquorice flavour. Star anise is used to enhance soups and stews, and when chewed, sweetens the breath and aids digestion.

Traditional soy sauce factory, where soya beans are fermented, Tong Chun

Stock

Stock is critical in Chinese cookery as a flavouring agent and for bringing out the natural tastes of delicate foods. It is more important than soy sauce in stir-fry dishes and soups. There are three grades of stock: superior, secondary and third. Superior is the resulting liquid made when meat and bones have been simmered in water for hours. It will usually be made with chicken (pork is less common) including the bones, as well as ham bone pieces. The bones are important not only for their flavour, but their gelatine gives the stock body. Secondary stock is made from uncooked bones. Third stock uses bones left over after cooking. Menu items described as being made with superior stock should have a superior taste.

TAKING STOCK

Yi Bing Shou (1754-1815) was famous as a gourmet. When his cook died he advertised for a replacement, stipulating that the applicant who prepared the best vegetarian dish would get the job. One applicant, Chef Wong, knew what a difficult task that would be. So the day before the test he soaked his apron in a clear superior chicken stock, then hung it up to dry. The next day he soaked the apron again in the water he used to prepare the vegetarian dish. He got the job.

STAPLES

Tapioca Pearls

These teardrop-size pearls are made from the starch of the cassava root. They are used as a thickener in soups and sweet puddings.

XO Sauce

XO Sauce is a very popular condiment made from dried crushed scallop, chilli, garlic and oil. The term 'XO' is from the label on a bottle of Cognac and has come to mean 'superior' in Hong Kong vernacular. It is always served in a small round dish with two little red chilli peppers laid across each other. The peppers and the dish represent the letters X and O.

Fruit & Vegetables

One of your chief gustatory memories of Hong Kong will be of fruit. The aroma of fruit is afloat upon the air in every market, grocery and corner store. All the fruits of the world seem to be here all year long, from tropical treats such as guava, coconut and starfruit (and don't forget durian), to temperate fruits such as apples, pears and grapes. And there is just as great a variety of vegetables. Nowhere else in China is asparagus a table staple. Yet it comes in fresh by the plane load, along with fresh herbs, avocados, even such seemingly mundane items as carrots. Much of this produce comes from Europe, California, Australia, New Zealand, South America and beyond. At any given moment of any given day there are fleets of aircraft bearing down on Hong Kong, laden with produce. Without the Wright brothers, Hong Kong's table would be impoverished.

Plums for sale, Graham Street Market, Hong Kong Island

Fruit

Pomelo

Similar to a large grapefruit, pomelo (sometimes called pamplemousse) has a thick skin and pith, and yields a sweeter, less acidic fruit than ordinary grapefruit. Pomelo is often eaten with salt.

Custard Apple

A smaller, more civilised version of the durian, the custard apple is apple sized and has a bumpy green skin that blackens as it ripens. The black pips inside can hinder the enjoyment, but persevere for its sweet peach custard taste and texture.

Durian

This is the king of fruits, and the most praised, and the most damned. You either love it or hate it. You may well regret hacking into the armour-like skin of a durian, as the powerful aroma will linger long in your memory. But if you can stand the smell, you will enjoy the creamy dense flesh and its complex flavour reminiscent, to speak kindly, of avocado, peanut butter, old cheese and honey. This gigantic and very expensive fruit is in season from May through to August.

Guava

High in vitamins A and C, and in iron and calcium, the pink, fall-apart flesh of the guava is sheathed in a thick green avocado-shaped skin. Eat it raw or drink its juice.

Jackfruit

Jackfruit is a giant thorny fruit that contains chewy, perfumy yellow segments. It is a good source of vitamins A, B and C. Jackfruit tree wood is often used for carvings.

Longan

This tiny tasty fruit grows throughout South-East Asia. Its smooth, light brown skin covers a translucent white pulp, which in turn covers a large black seed. The thicker the pulp, the juicier and more fragrant the fruit.

Lychee

You'll see clusters of dark red, lumpy lychees throughout Hong Kong. Although commonly used as a sweet dish, lychees can also be used with chicken, duck and sweet & sour pork.

Mango

Mango lovers are spoiled for variety in Hong Kong. The sweetest are the large, round ones with a bright yellow skin, which are in season March through to June.

Mangosteen

Looking like a dull purple peach, the mangosteen seems pretty ho-hum. But within the thick smooth skin is the delectable white flesh that has a delicious sour-sweet flavour. In the balance of Yin & Yang, mangosteen complements durian.

Papaya

High in vitamins A and C, this large, gourd-shaped fruit has orange-red flesh, and a refreshingly sweet flavour. It is often taken with a squeeze of lime juice to bring out its subtleties.

Pineapple

One of the most popular ways to enjoy this fruit here is to sprinkle it with salt and chilli powder.

Rambutan

A fiery red and hairy skin gives rambutans the look of tiny suns. The interior tender white flesh has a cool sweet flavour. It is distantly related to the lychee and has a similar taste. Look for them during Hong Kong's rainy season (May to October).

Starfruit

This fruit has a smooth and shiny skin, the colour of which is a blend of yellow, orange and green. Cut into cross sections its star shape is revealed. It is intensely juicy and biting into one can cause droplets to fly.

Tamarind

Originally from tropical Africa, these brown seedpods resemble vanilla beans and contain a tart mushy flesh. Tamarind's sour taste makes it a useful flavouring agent.

Winter Melon

Although resembling honeydew melon, winter melons taste like zucchini. Used extensively in stir-fry dishes and soups (see Winter Melon Soup earlier in this chapter and the recipe in the Banquet chapter).

Vegetables
Asparagus

The asparagus here is just like the asparagus you know at home. But in Hong Kong it is an exotic import and a great favourite. It's one of those 'strange' foods that Hong Kong chefs love to embrace, and thereby shock their countrymen on the mainland.

Heg Jiu Jap Pa Lou Sen
(Asparagus in Black Bean Sauce)

Ingredients

1 tsp	light soy sauce
1 tsp	ginger, minced
2 Tbs	rice wine or dry sherry
1 tsp	sugar
500g (1lb)	beef, thinly sliced
2 Tbs	peanut oil
500g (1lb)	fresh asparagus, cut into 2cm pieces
2 Tbs	fermented black beans, chopped
4	spring onions, cut into 2cm pieces
½ cup	chicken stock
1 tsp	cornstarch
1 Tbs	water mixed with 2 tsp cornstarch

Combine soy sauce, ginger, rice wine and sugar in a small bowl. Add the beef and let it marinate for 20 minutes. Heat half the oil in a wok until it begins to smoke. Add the asparagus and stir fry for two minutes. Remove with a slotted spoon and set aside. Drain the oil from the wok, add the remaining oil and heat to smoking. Add the beef, black beans and spring onions. Stir fry for two minutes. Return asparagus to the pan and add the chicken stock. Cook for one minute, stirring. Add the cornstarch and water. Reduce heat and stir until the sauce thickens.
   Serves 2

Aubergine
Also known as Chinese eggplant; this long, thin purple variety used in Hong Kong has a sweet flavour with little bitterness.

Bamboo Shoots
Fresh, pickled or dried (the most delicious), bamboo shoots are a popular ingredient in Hong Kong. Fresh shoots, which have a savoury sweetness and crunch, are peeled and boiled for about 30 minutes before using. Dried shoots are soaked and boiled.

Bean Sprouts
Mung bean sprouts, the most widely available variety, are found everywhere in Hong Kong. They are prized for their crunchy texture, and are eaten raw, added to soups, or stir fried.

Bitter Melon
This hard gourd looks like a fat, knobby cucumber. It has a very crisp texture and a strong, bitter taste. Before cooking, the seeds and inner membrane are removed and the outer pod is sliced into small, crescent-shaped pieces and fried or added to soups. It can also be pickled, or hollowed out, or stuffed with minced pork and then braised.

Daikon
Also known as **oriental white radish**, daikon is a root that looks like a large white carrot. The flesh is crisp, juicy and mildly pungent and lends itself well to soups and stews. It's also enjoyed raw in salads or pickled.

Flowering Cabbage
This cabbage has yellow flowers, firm small stalks and crisp leaves, and is held in high regard by Hong Kong cooks.

A garnish of spring onion, often paired with ginger in Chinese cuisine

Jicama

A brown-skinned root vegetable tasting somewhat like a turnip. It must be peeled and may be eaten raw in salads or cooked.

Long Beans

The immature pods of dry black-eyed peas. Just like the name says, long beans can measure up to 60cm (2 feet) in length. Sometimes they are called **chopstick beans**.

Chinese Black Mushrooms

These mushrooms are expensive but popular for their distinctive fragrance, flavour and texture. They have thick caps, up to 5cm (2 inches) in diameter, and are light brown in colour with prominent white cracks on their surface.

Tree Ear Mushrooms

Also called **cloud ear** or **wood ear**, these mushrooms are named for their convoluted shape, reminiscent of a human ear. Their texture is somewhat jelly like and translucent, yet crisp. They are mainly used to add texture to stir-fry dishes, stuffings and vegetarian dishes.

Straw Mushrooms

These mushrooms have pretty little umbrella-shaped caps with a yellowish brown colour. They are also known as **paddy straw mushrooms** because they grow on straw and rice husks.

Dried mushrooms at the wholesale seafood market, Hong Kong Island

STAPLES

Jiu Si Fu Yu Tung Choi
(Water Spinach with Chilli & Tofu)

Ingredients

300g (10oz)	water spinach
1½ Tbs	peanut oil
½ cup	tofu, coarsely broken and moistened with water
1	red chilli pepper, stem and seeds removed, minced
2 tsp	garlic, minced
¼ tsp	sugar
¼ tsp	sesame oil

Wash the water spinach and trim the stems. Drain and dry with a paper towel. Heat one tablespoon of the peanut oil in a wok until it is fragrant but not smoking. Add the water spinach and stir fry until just tender. It will release a lot of water. Remove the water spinach from the wok and drain. Set aside. Heat the remaining oil and add the rest of the ingredients. Cook for one minute, then return the water spinach to the pan and stir until heated through. Serve immediately.

Serves 2

Mustard Greens

These look a bit like head lettuce in size and shape, but differ in that the leaves wrapping the heart are thick stalks. They have a sharp flavour, adding a clean taste when combined with other ingredients. When parboiled, the stalks become tender and succulent and the assertive flavour mellows.

Taro Root

This is an oval-shaped tuber with brown, hairy skin and encircling rings. The flesh may be white to creamy and is sometimes speckled purple. Cooks use taro the same way you would potato or sweet potato (it tastes a bit like potato). Steamed chunks of taro are also added to stews and sweet puddings.

Water Chestnut

This is in fact not a nut, but a tuber. Inside is a crunchy white kernel with a sweet flavour, which does indeed resemble a chestnut.

Water Spinach

Water spinach is unrelated to the true spinach but is used in much the same way. An aquatic plant, it grows equally well on wet or dry land. It has hollow stems and light green arrowhead-shaped leaves. Cooks use it for the contrast in its texture between crunchy stems and tender leaves, as well as its spinach-like taste. It is sold by the bunch at Chinese greengrocers, and finds its way into stir-fry dishes and soups, and can be added raw to salads.

すいか

drinks

What to whet your whistle with in Hong Kong? In order of commonality: tea, beer and wine. There is a universe of tea here for you to explore, so vast that you'll need help to navigate it. Then there's a whole sea of beer. Suds from the seven seas flowing foamily into the Fragrant Harbour. And every year wine grows in popularity. Not long ago it was a novelty; soon it will be a necessity. So have a crystal glass, have a pint, have a cuppa. Have them all. You're in Hong Kong. Consume conspicuously.

Alcoholic Drinks
Beer

What can we say of beer in Hong Kong? The picture keeps changing. Under British reign it was one of the great constants. Thousands of troops kept it so. And troops being troops, they are used to privations, to going without, to the steel and flinty couch of war and all that. They'll drink just about anything. We know this. Some of us were troops, once upon a barstool. And so Hong Kong, while known for wild excess in the pursuit of quality and luxury, was never known as a brewing capital, though it was awash in suds. Now with the Tommies gone the situation is both better and worse.

Hong Kong doesn't even make its own major brand beer any more. Both the San Miguel and Carlsberg breweries, long fixtures in the New Territories, have packed up and moved to China to take advantage of lower production costs and a growing market. Evidently, the quantity of beer consumed in Hong Kong has decreased. But the demand for variety and quality has zoomed up. Of course prices have also skyrocketed. Except during happy hour you can expect to pay western European or US prices for the pleasure of bellying up to the bar and ordering a San Miguel. But you can, if you like, order almost any major brand in Hong Kong. Maybe not in every bar, but what you want you can find. As long as your money holds out, so will the beer. Even Mexican beer is sold at the California, and Ned Kelly's promotes Czech Budvar. Japanese beers are for sale at ferry landings. You might get near beer at a 7-Eleven. And the microbrew craze has finally landed in the Fragrant Harbour.

As late as 1994 Hong Kong was woefully without that staple of trendy tippling: microbrew. But David Haines, a visionary psychologist/business-man/brewer discovered this niche and filled it. With business plan in hand, hope in heart (and thirst in mouth) he found local investors and soon had the wherewithal to lease space, purchase the right equipment and hire the hirelings for a proper brewery. As San Miguel and Carlsberg were packing up and shipping off to China, Haines' South China Brewing Company (SCBC) was being born. Haines began operations in 1994, and a year later had rolled out the first barrel of Crooked Island Ale, known by wags as CIA. A careful scientific analysis of the brew's taste and smell constituents, and serious judgement of its specific gravity was conducted by esteemed experts at Mad Dogs, a pub on D'Aguilar Street in Central. Their verdict was a resounding "One more round!" Soon thereafter more than 70 local establishments were carrying Crooked Island Ale.

SCBC is now also producing at least five private-label brews: including an Irish-style stout and a British-style bitters. Look for Haines wherever microbrews are sold.

Beer, beer and more beer, Hong Kong Island

Wine & Spirits

When we speak of wine in Hong Kong we have two avenues of approach: Chinese and western. Chinese 'wine' is a bit misleading. For the most part this is any alcoholic beverage made from rice or other grains such as millet or sorghum. Such wine is rarely, if ever, used as the liquid component of a meal, although it may very well be present on the dinner table. People will knock back shots of wine between courses and use it to make many a solemn toast. But Hong Kongers do not wash down their food with Chinese wine. They basically use it to warm the stomach to the task of digestion. And to cop a buzz.

Chinese wine does occupy an important place in the culture and life of China. It was long connected with learned Chinese men of letters, and was essential at imperial banquets. But it has been enjoyed by common folk as well. Perhaps the most famous Chinese wine is the sorghum-based Mao

Enjoying a Bruce Lee and a Fish Bowl cocktail, Embassy Bar, Mandarin Oriental Hotel, Macau

DRINKS

Tai. This is the stuff that The Great Helmsman, Chairman Mao, used to toast US President Nixon when he travelled to Beijing. And if president Nixon actually finished a glass of that stuff, he was far braver than we.

The story of grape wine, from Europe, California, Australia and New Zealand, is rather like that of beer. It was always available, even from the early days. Though what you could get was limited. Not that what you could get was bad. Well, some of it was bad. In the 20th century there were always fine French wines to be had. Vin ordinaire was plentiful, and cheap. But only since the 1980s has wine taken root in the everyday consciousness of Hong Kongers. Until then even the expats drank mostly beer, whisky and gin. And those are fine drinks. But no one lives on beer, whisky or gin alone.

So what happened? For one thing, health conscious Hong Kongers discovered the benefits of red wine in moderation. Numerous articles and books by doctors, scientists and food writers (who are revered in the region) have been educating their readers on this subject. People are interested in the fact that they can consume alcohol and reduce their risk of stroke and angina, and keep their cholesterol in check. Who wouldn't be pleased?

Wine has also become a mark of sophistication and a way to flaunt one's new wealth. And if you can't flaunt that, what can you flaunt? It's not merely fashionable, it's dead chic to be seen drinking a first-growth Bordeaux and commenting knowledgeably on it. The craze for Bordeaux got to be so bad that it created a drought in Hong Kong. There just wasn't enough to go around. And prices went through the roof. They were even high by Hong Kong standards! One of the silver linings of the Asian currency crisis of the late 1990s was that it forced consumers to think more intelligently about wine, and why they drink it.

These days are good days for wine in Hong Kong. Growers in Australia, California and Italy have planted new vines in order to satisfy the demand in Hong Kong. And an ever widening range of wines are available throughout the territory. Even 7-Eleven stores carry good French wines. However, one thing to be careful of when buying wine in Hong Kong is storage. Wine is often exposed to the tropical heat and kept upright, allowing the corks to dry and the humid air to get in. You'll find more oxidised wine here than anywhere. Go to reputable, air-conditioned shops where proper storage and shipment is understood. Just walk around. You'll see them. You might start at the corner of Queen's Rd and D'Aguilar St, Central.

Among Hong Kong's more wealthy drinkers, cognac is the liquor of choice. Hong Kong accounts for nearly 11% of the worldwide market for cognac, and has the world's highest per capita consumption. The way to drink cognac here is neat and quick; it is not considered a tipple to sip.

DRINKS

Non-Alcoholic Drinks
Tea

Were it not for tea, Hong Kong Island would perhaps be an island of fishermen, Kowloon would be pasture land, and Macau might have been a bigger place. But Hong Kong was created for the express purpose of carrying on the tea trade. Of course there were other items of exchange, luxury goods like silk and porcelain. But it was tea that was the commercial driving force. By the time of the first opium war it had gone from novelty, to luxury, to essential commodity. And the British were willing to fight for it.

It is believed that the first commercial consignment of tea to England arrived in 1664, in a package weighing one pound, two ounces. In 1738 the weight was 2600 tons. Between 1700 and 1750 the amount of tea imported into England increased 200 fold. This statistic does not take into account tea smuggled into the country. It is estimated that the illegal stuff was as much as triple the tea counted by the customs service. Smuggling tea was big business. As would be the method of paying for it.

The Chinese were not interested in exchanging goods. They would take only cash for their tea and silk, usually in the form of silver. This caused a terrible drain on the British economy and efforts to sell goods to the Middle Kingdom were in vain. "We possess all things in abundance", quoth the Emperor, "we have no use for your pitiful manufactures." But Britain's Indian opium soon found customers in the drug lords of Guangzhou. To cut a long story short, the Emperor kicked the barbarians out, and the barbarians shot their way back in. Britain finally had a secure place where they could never again be given the imperial order of the boot when China ceded the territory to them. And so Hong Kong, for the sake of a good cup of tea, was born.

TEA LEGENDS

There are any number of legends about the beginnings of tea, its properties and its consumption. Some legends credit simple folk with tea's discovery, others philosophers. Some say it was a medicine and others a digestive or even a sacrament. A little more winsome, but a legend that appeals to us tells of a pious monk who was meditating, but kept falling asleep. He was very serious, this monk, and admonished himself several times for having such lazy eyelids. Finally, in frustration, he took out a knife and cut his offending eyelids off! He threw them on the ground, where they took root and grew to be the first tea plant. Thus explaining why tea helps you stay awake.

Jabbok Tea Shop has reinvented tea culture by offering vintage teas, Kowloon

DRINKS

DRINKS

Tea History

Tea first appears in the extant written record in AD 350, not in a culinary or medical text, but in a dictionary updated by Chinese scholar Kuo P'o'. He defines it simply as "a beverage made from boiled leaves". We do not know if he ever actually tasted the stuff. Unlike such drinks as Coca Cola, tea did not simply appear on the market ready to consume. Its not only as "the cup that cheers" but as a cultural icon was long and slow. Tea's natural habitat is in mountainous areas, and it was probably used by mountain folk in various ways for centuries before Professor Kuo took up the pen. By the time it became known to lowland folk it was made like a soup, simmered in a cooking pot with water, ginger, orange or other flavourings. It was not yet cultivated, but gathered from the wild, and its use was chiefly medicinal rather than gustatory. Records show that it was commonly prescribed for digestive and nervous conditions, and even today we appreciate it for those qualities. Despite its then limited use, it had become a commodity of great value and was used for trade, even currency. By AD 600, tea was no longer merely medicine, and the wild could no longer supply the market. Farsighted farmers in Sichuan Province began to cultivate it, and soon others followed suit throughout the Middle Kingdom.

By AD 780 tea had matured into something of a cult, albeit among those who could afford to pay not only for the leaves, but for the complex paraphernalia it had come to require, and the leisure time in which to enjoy it. It was in this year that Lu Yu, who would become known as The Father of Tea, wrote the *Ch'a Ching* (*Tea Classic*). It was a three volume tome, and covered everything to do with tea from the proper techniques of growing plants to the brewing of the brew and its thoughtful enjoyment. It also detailed the formal tea ceremony with its requisite 27 pieces of equipment. The work was a must-have for the upper crust, and is a milestone in the development of Chinese culture.

CHOICE TEA CHOICE

When choosing which tea leaves to buy, take Lu Yu's advice. In his seminal book on tea, the *Ch'a Ching* (*Tea Classic*), he states that tea leaves should have:

Creases like the leathern boot of Tartar horseman, curl like the dewlap of a mighty bullock, unfold like a mist rising out of a ravine, gleam like a lake touched by a zephyr, and be wet and soft like fine earth newly swept by rain.

Large concrete tea pot stands at the entrance to Jabbok Tea House, New Territories

DRINKS

Tea culture, with its trade, crafts and traditions became very much like the wine culture of Europe. The harvest was not merely a task to perform, it was a ceremony that would bring favour from the deities. The oracles were consulted for a best day to begin, and the tea pickers sang songs as they worked, accompanied by drums, cymbals and flutes. In what we might call 'boutique plantations', the pickers were young girls who had to keep their fingernails long in order to pick the leaves without touching them with their skin. We hear legends of even greater efforts where the young nubile pickers picked in the nude! Sadly, these are only legends.

Once the precious leaves were brought to the processing sheds they were sorted and graded. The best leaves were often sent to the emperor in lieu of tax. In those days tea was a more perishable product and was not shipped as loose leaves. It was ground coarsely, then pressed and moulded into a brick. This greatly reduced how much of the tea would be exposed to the air, enabling it to keep for months, even years.

Pickers and peasants got the sweepings, and the finer stuff went to the equivalent of the wine snobs of our modern era. Tea houses and tea salons opened to accommodate these connoisseurs and separate them from a bit of their discretionary income. Tea meisters tried to out do each other in their complex ceremonies, and on their ability to identify a tea, and even the source of its water in a blind tasting. The making of tea services became an art unto itself.

And finally, as it became more plentiful, tea became the beverage of choice for everyone, rich and poor, Chinese and Europeans. It was a cash crop, an important commodity, medicine, beverage, something over which to struggle.

Hong Kong's tea culture suffered a great decline in the middle of the 20th century due to generational differences, the rise in popularity of soft drinks and the inoppertune interruption of supplies during China's Cultural Revolution. But in the last decade or two tea has made a resurgence. It has once again become a symbol of Hong Kong and its demand for quality goods no matter the price. Many tea shops, such as Jabbok, offer courses in tea and tea culture. It sells the finest teas in the world, as well as beautiful tea services (see the boxed text The Tea Mistress later in this chapter). Tea can also be enjoyed informally at street-side herbal tea stands and formally as part of high tea in many of Hong Kong's major hotels (see Non-Alcoholic Drinks in the Where to Eat & Drink chapter). Today, tea is the most widely consumed beverage in the world bar water.

Tea Types
Black tea, green tea, pouchong tea, oolong tea, the list goes on. So many different kinds of tea, there must be a multitude of species and varieties of the plant. Not so. All teas come from the same plant, *Camellia sinesis*. The difference is in the processing. True, as with wine, location, season and agricultural practices will result in teas of different taste, smell and colour. But they are all from the same leafy bush.

Probably the single-most important process in tea production is fermentation (or the lack thereof). This process determines the taste, smell and colour of a tea, as well as its shelf life. The longer the fermentation, the longer the tea can last. The leaves are crushed, rolled, or otherwise broken so as to allow the inner liquids contact with the air. The 'fermentation' that results is actually a process of enzymatic oxidation. And the extent of fermentation determines the type of tea produced. And then there are teas that are allowed no fermentation at all.

Next time you have your cup of aromatic green tea remember that this is the purest form of the leaf. It has not been subjected to fermentation. What you taste in this cup is the original flavour of the leaf. The leaves are still broken, but the fermentation process is arrested by pan roasting or through steaming. These teas maintain their green to slightly yellowish hue and mild aroma, although they are sometimes scented with jasmine.

For a rather exotic cup of the unaltered stuff look for white tea. Like the green stuff, it is not subjected to enzymatic oxidation. At harvest it is immediately dried at a high heat. Many discriminating palates find that this produces the purest tea taste of all.

When you have a cup of oolong tea you are drinking what is probably the best known (at least in the west) of the semi-fermented teas. These teas are allowed anywhere from 10-80% of the fermentation process. If you remember your oolong you'll recall a slight yellow to brown hue, a fragrant aroma, and a long lasting aftertaste. A common type of oolong is **Ti Kwan Yu** (see the boxed text Tea Treasure later in this chapter), which undergoes 50% fermentation. Champagne oolong tops out at 80%. In addition to oolong, semi-fermented teas include Pouchong. Its fermentation does not exceed 20%. The hue is still yellowish to brown, and it tends to have a more delicate flavour and mild bouquet.

Fully fermented tea is the stuff most of us grow up with – 100% fermented tea, known as black tea. Most Chinese prefer green or semi-fermented tea, but in the early days of the European tea trade green teas would not survive the long voyage to England without deteriorating. Black tea, on the other hand, can last almost indefinitely.

Post-fermented tea is made by letting the leaves fully ferment and dry, and then sprinkling them with water to allow them to ferment again. The most common example of this type of tea in Hong Kong is **Pu-erh**, which has a dark reddish colour and a strong, earthy taste. The standard English spelling of the name of this tea is useless as a pronunciation guide. But if you say "power" tea, most people will understand what you're getting at

DRINKS

FINGER TAPPING & FILLING TEAPOTS

When you see tea drinkers tapping the table with three fingers, do not think it is a superstitious gesture. It is a silent expression of gratitude to any member of the gathering who has refilled the finger tapper's cup. The gesture recreates a tale of Imperial obeisance, an evocative story of a Qing Dynasty emperor who would frequently visit his domain on incognito inspection visits. While in south China, he visited a teahouse with his companions. To preserve his anonymity he participated in the tea-pouring, so as not to reveal his special status. His shocked companions wanted to kowtow to him for the great honour he was doing them. Instead of letting them reveal his identity, the emperor told them to tap three fingers on the table. One finger represented their respectfully bowed head and the other two fingers represented their prostrate arms.

And if your teapot is running empty, let the waiter know by taking the lid off the pot. The story behind this custom tells of a diner who, while enjoying his meal, decided to keep his prize pigeon warm in the empty teapot. When the waiter refilled the pot with scolding tea, he boiled the bird in the process.

THE TEA MISTRESS – Faces of Gastronomy

Madam Eliza Liu is a queen, and she knows it. Her realm may be small, but it does not lack honour or dignity. The extent of her domain is the walls of the Jabbok Tea Shop (120 Argyle St, Mong Kok) and an interior province of the knowledge of the science and art of tea. She sits serenely behind a tea table, 'waking up' the vessels she will use by pouring hot water into and over them. Her movements are graceful, with the studied attention of a musician whose mastery is such that she need not think of how to work the bow or finger the strings.

"The weather at harvest time is very important", she says as she opens a box of black tea that has been ageing for 40 years. Its earthy aroma fills the room. "It should be a sunny day, yet early in the morning, so that the leaves may have time to dry and not moulder."

Eliza began her career by taking courses in agriculture. Then, as neophytes follow a holy man, she followed a tea master for seven years. She worked in all aspects and stages of tea production. She harvested, roasted, dried and blended. She studied. "My tea studies are also studies in Chinese culture, customs, legends and lore. Tea is reflective of the Chinese and their way of thinking and living."

International tea conferences invite Eliza to address them about her research, particularly as to the healthful benefits and uses of tea. She tells us that the simplest use for tea is as a deodoriser. "Take your used tea leaves and tie them in a porous cloth, then place them in your shoes overnight. They will not have an odour in the morning. You can also put the same in the refrigerator. More importantly, tea does help to reduce carcinogens in the body. And it is a tonic for the blood vessels. It is also good as a topical treatment for sunburn. But I would not go so far as to say that it is a medicine. However, when used wisely, ritually, and regularly, it does produce a state of mind that reduces stress and preserves youth."

And we are simply shocked when she tells us that she is 57 years old and a grandmother! We had guessed 35 at most. We ask for more tea. Wisely and ritually, please.

Making Tea

No matter what kind of tea you're making, you want to follow some fundamentals. No cup of tea is better than its leaves, and the final brew will taste as good as the water you use. Also, utensils must be thoroughly clean.

There is some debate as to the correct water temperature. Some say it must be at a rolling boil when poured over the tea. Some say you must boil it then let it cool a few minutes. Still others say that you should remove it from the heat as soon as it starts to 'dance', not letting it come to the full boil. We prefer the last, but argue with none.

In Hong Kong the preference is for brewing in cups. In most restaurants it will be poured from pots, but in a yum cha house, where tea is more highly regarded, it will usually be brewed one cup at a time. This will include a handle-less cup (normally of generous size), a saucer, a concave lid, a teacup for each person, a waste bowl and a large pot of hot water. Start by 'bringing the cup to life', which means scalding it with a splash of the water and letting it sit. Swirl and pour water into the waste bowl.

Add a healthy pinch of tea leaves per person to your now alive cup, cover and let steep a minute. When the aroma tells you it is ready to drink, pour the tea from the larger cup to the smaller. Do this while using the lid of the larger cup to strain the tea, the leaves of which will be floating on the top. Hold the cup in one hand and use the forefinger of that hand to push the lid slightly back, allowing the tea to flow when you tip the cup. This takes a bit of practice but nobody will mind if you spill some.

Once you have emptied your brewing cup, do not call for more tea. Add more water for a second infusion. Even a third is customary. Perhaps you are aghast at this advice, particularly if you are used to English teas. But Chinese teas are different, and most people say that the second infusion is the best.

DRINKS

TEA TREASURE

In the grounds of a dilapidated temple stood a statue of **Kwan Yu** (the Iron Goddess). The only caretaker of the temple was a simple farmer, who tried but could not maintain the temple's appearance. In appreciation of his efforts, Kwan Yu appeared before the farmer and told him of a cave where he would find a treasure. The farmer entered the cave but all he found was a tea plant sapling. Nevertheless the farmer let the plant grow, fermented its leaves then brewed a pot of tea. It was fragrant and fruity, like nothing he had ever tasted. The farmer shared cuttings with the rest of his village and the once-poor region began to prosper.

Coffee

Coffee has been discovered in recent years. And that is a blessing for coffee lovers because Hong Kong was indifferent to it for a long time. Even the better restaurants and hotels poured poor stuff, and instant was the norm, stirred into a cup of tepid water and softened with non-dairy coffee creamer. But these are new days, and the range of coffee now available is quite rich. Locals also enjoy **dong gafei** (chilled coffee), which also comes in cans.

Fleecy

This is Hong Kong's version of the fruit smoothie. It's a sweet, cold drink that contains some sort of lumpy mixture, usually red or green mung beans, and sometimes pineapple or other fruits, and black grass jelly. Milk or ice cream is usually part of the the mixture, but not always.

Soy Drinks & Soft Drinks

When it comes to quick, cool refreshments, Hong Kong is king. A kaleidoscopic array of fizzy drinks, soy drinks and juices can be found at any convenience store or supermarket. You can quench your thirst with everything from lemonade to green tea-flavoured soy drink. Restaurants will have cola and juice at the very least.

home cooking
& traditions

You will find no extravagances in the home kitchen, there just isn't enough room for flaming woks and racks for drying geese. What you will find, however, is a simple and soulful side of Hong Kong, marked by humble yet hearty dishes. Unless of course you are invited for a home-cooked meal, in which case modest meals are replaced with excess to impress.

A kitchen is a kitchen is a kitchen ..., Hong Kong Island

Home and restaurant cooking are quite different in Hong Kong. A restaurant kitchen is often a huge space with plenty of room for giant woks and walk-in refrigerators; for towers of steamer baskets and cutting boards the size of surf boards. Not so the home. Hong Kong is the epitome of high density living, and the typical kitchen only has room for a two-burner cooker that looks like a big camp stove. There will be no convection oven, but many apartments will have a small microwave oven. This is rarely used for cookery, though, just for heating things up. Every kitchen will have an electric rice cooker (see Rice in the Staples & Specialities chapter). There is virtually no bench space for prep work, so the cook will perform that on the dinner table.

Not a temple but the tranquil interior of a private home

HOME COOKING

Utensils

The essential, and quintessential, cooking vessel is the wok, which has many advantages over a skillet – it distributes heat more evenly, requires less oil, and food tossed during frying is more likely to land back in the wok and not on the cook. There are many types of woks available, including ones made of aluminium, copper and stainless steel. Most restaurant chefs insist on a traditional cast-iron wok. They come in a variety of sizes, and restaurants may use woks that are several feet wide. When they get that big they are referred to as the 'knights' shields'. A 35cm (14 inch) wok is about standard for home use. Maintenance of the wok is very easy. After use, the cook simply rinses it with plain water and wipes it dry. It should never be washed in detergent, and if any scrubbing is necessary it should be done with a bamboo brush so the surface isn't scratched.

The standard cutting board in a Hong Kong kitchen is a thick, circular piece of wood about 25cm (ten inches) wide. This is used for all cutting, chopping, mincing and trimming. Obviously there will be no sides of beef carved in a home kitchen.

A restaurant will have some speciality knives such as those used especially for garnishing, but a home kitchen does not require them. The Chinese cleaver is generally the only knife needed here. Most cleaver blades are made of carbon steel, are about 10cm (4 inches) in height and 25cm (10 inches) wide, and have a wooden handle. The multipurpose cleaver is used for slicing, shredding, chopping and mincing.

Leave it to cleaver, late-night dinner preparations

Frying strainers are used to hold foods while they are deep fried, and to collect noodles from the boil. The best frying strainers are made from wire mesh with long bamboo handles that won't conduct much heat so you don't need pot holders or gloves.

Mr Lo Ho-Kee making his legendary wire mesh utensils, Ladder Street, Central

Wide-blade spatulas are used for scooping up food that has been stir fried. The long handle helps keep the cook's hands from the heat.

Instead of using tongs, Hong Kong cooks often use long wooden chopsticks for moving fried food from the hot oil or steamed food from the steamers. The wood conducts little heat, but they are not used in deep frying as they can actually get cooked themselves.

The steamers used in Hong Kong kitchens are made of bamboo and are designed to fit inside the wok. They can be used one at a time or stacked one on top of another, and they sit just above the boiling water inside the wok. The cook replaces the water as it evaporates. (See also the boxed text Old Doesn't Mesh with the New in the Shopping & Markets chapter.)

HOME COOKING

THE ART OF HOSPITALITY

While in the throes of chasing photo opportunities and checking destinations off our to-see list, my friends and I had sadly neglected the great food on offer in Hong Kong. Every morning we ate rock buns from the bakery a few doors down from our hotel in Tsim Sha Tsui, then nothing until we were bent over with hunger six hours later. Needing something immediate, we turned to McDonald's. The Golden Arches were easy, clean, fast and provided a respite from the summer humidity. However, every time we ate there I felt increasingly guilty that I wasn't experiencing more of the cuisine from the culture that my family came from.

I am fourth generation Chinese American and the dinner table is the main place where we've stayed connected to our past. I hoped that while I was in Hong Kong I'd get to taste dim sum like my great grandmother would make for us when she came to visit. A bowl of Hong Kong **cao min** (chow mein; fried egg noodles with a topping of meat, seafood or vegetables) or **juk** (rice porridge) would surely remind me of my grandmother's cooking and how the whole family, aunts, uncles and grandkids would get together regularly to catch up with everyone.

It was easy to forget about food when we were rushing from the bird market to Victoria Park, over to Lantau Island, out to Stanley, and more. So when Sean, my travelling companion, told me we were invited to the home of Cho Li, a local woman he'd met the week before on the train, I was thrilled.

We took the MTR subway from Tsim Sha Tsui to the New Territories where Cho Li lived. On our way up, Sean told me that he met Cho Li while she was chatting with three Germans, and that they would be at the dinner as well.

At our stop, there was a cluster of massive high-rise apartments. The identical buildings were only differentiated by the numbers on the walls. Cho Li lived with her roommate in a two-bedroom apartment. We took the elevator up to her apartment only to find the three Germans had already arrived.

I was amazed at how small the apartment was. The living room was about the same size as the kitchen and the card-come-dinner table took up nearly all the available space. There were a few decorations including some stuffed animals, which made me think a young girl lived there, even though Cho Li was a 30-year-old architect.

Cho Li sat us at the table and brought out three large bottles of Beck's beer that dwarfed her frame. The Germans were a bit confused, but appreciative of her nod to their homeland. As soon as the beers were on the table, Cho Li disappeared into the shuttered kitchen. We chatted amongst ourselves, drank the beer, and looked out the small window on to myriad equally small windows looking straight back at us. It was a panorama of sameness and smallness.

We heard cutting, crackling and sizzling noises from the kitchen, and when Cho Li returned she brought out a Sichuan tofu dish in a spicy brown sauce. She encouraged us to try it, and then without joining us, flitted back into the kitchen like a nervous bird. The dish was delicious. Once we finished it, and not until, she brought out a plate of spicy green beans. They were fresh and crisp, and came with a sauce that added flavour, but didn't leave them soaked or soggy.

I thought it peculiar that Cho Li wasn't eating with us. But then I thought of my grandmother and remembered that she was always the one to get up and go to the kitchen if anyone needed anything, or to serve another helping.

As if Cho Li were watching us from behind the kitchen shutters, she appeared with the next course the minute we were finished with the last. She brought out a tray of what looked like brown rubber bands. We had no idea of what it was. It was definitely from an animal, but what exactly we didn't know. Sean asked Cho Li and we thought she said that it was chicken intestines. This was also the first dish we didn't like, but because Cho Li seemed to be listening to us eat from the kitchen, we held it together and made various 'yummy' sounds.

A few more dishes came out with Cho Li dropping them at the table and retreating as if she'd just given us a hand grenade. I wanted her to join us, but it was obvious that there was a line between being a guest and being a host.

HOME COOKING

Then, as we were near full, she came out with a whole fish decorated with orange slices and lightly bathed in sauce.

"I don't think this is very good. It came out wrong", she said as she set the platter on the table and disappeared back into the kitchen. This reminded us all of a similar scene in the *Joy Luck Club* and Sean suggested that it was the main dish and that she was probably very proud of it. We knew to compliment her, but there was nothing to fake. It exceeded all the other dishes in presentation and taste. When she cautiously returned from the kitchen (for the first time not carrying a new dish of food) and stood near the table looking like a guilty child awaiting punishment, we said it was wonderful. She lit up, her spine straightened, her eyes beamed and she said with a huge smile, "I am very happy".

I knew how she felt. I love feeding people, and for the first time, I wondered if I got this from my grandmother. She always served our food without expectations or waiting glances of approval, but my grandfather taught us to say "ho-me cook", a gesture of thanks and to let the cook know the food was good. I thought about saying it now, trying out my Cantonese in Hong Kong, but she left again and the moment was gone.

After we were finished, Cho Li cleared the plates and moved the table so we'd have more room. She joined us for a glass of beer, but we didn't see her eat any of the food she'd prepared for us. It had been like a performance, and one she'd done masterfully.

Later, Sean told me Cho Li had said that in China, the way a woman cooks is valued more than her looks. That night in the New Territories, Cho Li had given us her beauty, and an artful dinner.

Jennifer Leo is an editor at Travelers' Tales in San Francisco

Home Cooking

So now with such a workshop what can a cook produce? Generally home cooking concentrates on less expensive ingredients: tofu, vegetables, preserved vegetables (a speciality in Hakka kitchens), cheap seafood such as squid and salted fish, and beef. Unlike a restaurant meal, where the focus is on individual dishes produced by the chef's mastery, a meal at home has rice as its focus, and the other dishes play a secondary role. People may eat two, even three bowls of rice for a meal at home, but in a restaurant one is the

Traditional clay pot simmering on the stove

norm, and they might merely pick at it. So home dishes tend to be those that aid the digestion of large amounts of carbohydrate. Salted plums are popular, pickles, dried shrimp, and savoury sauces and condiments like oyster and hoisin sauce.

Home cooks are more inclined to improvise with whatever is available that day at the market. One of the most versatile ingredients, lending itself to much improvisation, is eggs. A basic recipe is to beat eggs with water and then steam the mixture for what is called **jing sui daan** (literally, water egg; a kind of omelette). To this the cook can add virtually anything: flaked crab meat, chopped ham, steamed vegetables; water egg makes a canvas for whatever might be on the cook's palette.

Beef is a popular ingredient in the home kitchen. It doesn't have the status of pork, the premier meat, and is considered homely fare. Any and all parts of the animal go into the wok. Everything but the moo. Fish is also common home fare, though not the steamed whole fish that you see in restaurants. More often the cook will buy a piece of fish and deep fry it or use it in a soup. And the home is where you'll find a great variety of soups, far more than you'll find in restaurants. Soups are considered to be one of the chief means of maintaining good health through a balanced diet (see the Food as Medicine chapter). They are usually cooked with medicinal herbs and other health-inducing ingredients. Lotus roots, which are available at the market most days, are thought to be good for mild anaemia. Many kinds of mushrooms are both tasty and a good tonic. And ginger is always good for you in some way. Soups are often double boiled, that is in a pot on top of a double boiler. In this way the soup is not exposed to direct heat, but to the suffused and steady heat of steam.

Catching up on the latest

Hospitality

Meals at home are generally simple, convivial and undemanding. Families in Hong Kong are like families anywhere at dinner, hungry and unconcerned about ceremony. But just let them bring home a guest or two, or more. The Hong Kong host will turn the place upside down, do the labour of an army, and then go without eating just to see that the honoured guests are well fed and satisfied. And just to make you feel at home, many will tune the TV to an English-language station. No one will watch it, but it will be left on for the duration of your visit. At high volume.

HOME COOKING

celebrating
with food

The Chinese live for the feast, and will grasp at any excuse for it. Hong Kong's festival circuit bespeaks diversity with a calendar chock-full of celebrations that mark the passage of the seasons. Life is full of births, deaths, triumphs and marriages, all replete with their special foods and a riot of feasting.

It all begins with the Lunar New Year, initiating a season of feasting. On the first day there is a banquet, on the second day lunch. There is a 'birthday for all' on the seventh and a 'new 15th' on, you guessed it, the 15th. And any other time during the first two months is appropriate for holding a spring banquet in order to entertain associates, visitors or relatives who are visiting Hong Kong for the holidays. New crops are prized at this time, to reaffirm the newness of the year: the new tea, the new vegetables, spring onions and spring rolls.

In the fifth lunar month the Dragon Boat Festival is held, and the famous boats are raced. This ancient custom nearly died out after the Chinese Revolution, and it was Hong Kong that kept it alive. And kept alive the tradition of eating glutinous rice dumplings, made of sticky rice that is wrapped in bamboo leaves and steamed. In the seventh month the Hungry Ghosts are fed, in the eighth month the Moon Festival is observed with moon cakes. And interspersed throughout the year are the seemingly endless celebrations of life and death, marked with solemnity and cheer at the table.

Festivities
Lunar New Year

You can feel when Lunar New Year is about to turn. There is great anticipation in the air. There is a sense of impending renewal, physically, spiritually and morally. People are cleaning house in order to get rid of the old year's dust and detritus. People are paying their debts, financial and those of honour and morality. They are mending fences, putting away old quarrels. For New Year is a chance for new beginnings, new opportunities. On the 24th day of the 12th lunar month the Kitchen God leaves the hearth and reports to heaven on the uprightness of the family. Before leaving he is given a meal of sweets and wine, laid upon his altar. No sense in sending him off angry. On the last day of the year people make inscriptions of red 'lucky paper' and post them on doors and lintels, on the masts of junks, in elevator cars. Next day, the feast!

On New Year's Day, everyone speaks in terms and phrases suggesting auspicious things. No one must utter unpleasant words, and bad thoughts are not permitted expression. And no profanity. Even salty sailors watch their language. The concept of 'right speech' continues to the kitchen and table where every dish has been given a name suggesting health, honour and riches. A spiced shoulder of pork is called Mist of Harmony, a soup is called Broth of Prosperity. Jade of Ink, Gold of Darkness is a combination of sea cucumber, squid and seaweed; Silvery Threads of Longevity describes thin strands of rice vermicelli.

Hard-boiled eggs (one for each member of the family) symbolise happy reunion, and any kind of noodle carries the connotation of long life. The longer the noodle the longer the life. Dishes made with chicken wings imply the possibility 'to soar one thousand miles' and pigs' trotters suggest that you may 'tread the azure clouds of good fortune'. Served whole with head and tail, dishes of chicken and fish recommend 'a favourable start and finish'. And when the meal is over, parents give their children small red envelopes that contain 'lucky money'. Then all look ahead to eating their way through the year.

Jing Yu (Steamed Whole Fish)

Ingredients

1 whole	grouper fish, 1-1½kg (2-3lb)
2 Tbs	peanut oil
6	spring onions, sliced
½ cup	soy sauce
1 Tbs	sugar
2 Tbs	ginger, finely chopped

Clean and gut the fish, then steam it for 15 minutes. While the fish is steaming, heat the oil in a wok. Once the fish is done, add the spring onions, soy sauce, sugar and ginger to the oil and cook for 1 minute. Pour this sauce over the fish and serve.
    Serves 4

Cheung Chau Bun Festival
Cheung Chau Island's Bun Festival is held around the sixth day of the fourth month, but precise dates are decided by village elders about three weeks before it starts. This is a Taoist festival and there are three or four days of religious observances. At Pak Tai Temple, a massive bamboo scaffold is erected and festooned with edible buns. These buns symbolise good luck, and are handed out to those present. Lucky for them.

Birthday of Lord Buddha
On the eighth day of the fourth month, Buddha's statue is taken from monasteries and temples and bathed in a concoction of water scented with sandalwood, ambergris (a waxy substance secreted from the intestine of sperm whales and often found floating in the sea), garu wood, turmeric and aloes (a drug used for clearing the bowels, made from the fleshy, spiny-toothed leaves of the aloe plant). The mixture is drunk by the faithful, who believe it has great curative powers.

Hungry Ghosts

Not every feast is for the living. In Chinese tradition the people in the spirit world are generally alive and well. And the good ones are looking after you. But there is one class of ghost that you don't want to upset. They are the murder victims and the suicides, people who died in childhood or those who died without having children. They have no one to tend their graves, no one to make sacrifices for them and lay tasty treats upon their altars. They are not happy. And they will take it out on you. On the 14th day of the seventh month the gates of hell are thrown open and the Hungry Ghosts are allowed out into the world of the living. And you're going to have to buy them off.

Never refer to them as spooks or monsters. They'll get you for that. Always call them **hau xiong di** (good brethren). On the day that they swirl around the earth, people will make many offerings to appease the troubled souls. They will buy clothes for them, perhaps jewellery, even cars. And stacks of money. All of these offerings are made out of lightweight paper, for when they are burned the ghosts will receive them.

But most importantly the people will feed the 'good brethren'. They will place sweet offerings such as cakes and fruit for them at grave sites, on altars, even on the decks of boats or in parks. But never in the home. Just as you wouldn't admit a group of beggars into your home, pity them though you might, you don't want any Hungry Ghost sneaking into a closet and staying behind. It's either trick or treat when the Hungry Ghosts are visiting. Of course once the ghosts have consumed the essence of the sweets and other offerings, the living have their turn at them.

SYMBOLS OF CELEBRATION

Gourd	magical containers	**Crab**	repels bad magic
Frog	wealth and protection	**Fish**	prosperity
Peach	immortality	**Duck**	marital harmony
Turtle	permanence	**Pomegranate**	abundance and fertility

The moon plays an important part in Chinese mythology as the dwelling place of the gods. Consequently it is an object of aesthetic admiration and delight. The 15th day of the eighth lunar month marks the Moon Festival, when people will 'take the moon' just as they might 'take the view' of a landscape. The moon festival is an especially female occasion, as the moon is essentially female (Yin).

Interior of Man Mo temple with burning incense cones suspended from the ceiling by worshippers, Hollywood Road, Sheung Wan, Hong Kong Island

MOON FESTIVAL

The legend of the Moon Festival describes Chang Er, a young woman who worked in the palace of immortals in heaven until she was banished to earth for breaking a valuable jar. Her husband on earth was a tyrannical man, who demanded a special elixir so as to prolong his life. Not wishing her husband longevity, Chang Er swallowed the elixir. Her hubby was outraged and chased her out of a high window. Instead of falling, Chang Er floated to the safety of the moon. In the middle of the eighth lunar month (during the festival), it is said that Chang Er can be seen, as this is when the moon is brightest.

There are no parades or races or large temple rites associated with this festival. It is largely a family affair, and a pleasant but quiet one.

Boxes ready for the Moon Festival

Traditionally family groups would take a table outside and set it with dishes of round foods: such fruits as apples, oranges, peaches, and pomegranates, which symbolise fertility. And then there are the famous moon cakes. These are made of a flaky pastry filled with sweet taro and egg yolks, and sometimes lotus seeds or coconut are added. They are always small, no more than 10cm (four inches) wide, and they are extremely heavy. One cake is meant to serve an entire family or about four people.

It is believed that moon cakes were used to end the Mongol-controlled Yuan Dynasty (AD 1271-1368). Chinese rebels sent them as gifts to their supporters. The Mongolian rulers thought moon cakes were being distributed as symbols of happy and prosperous times. However, inside each moon cake was a message telling the recipients the date when the rebellion would begin: the 15th day of the eighth lunar month.

In Hong Kong only the super rich have the ability to take a table outside and lay it with all the traditional treats. So most people will have a quiet dinner at home, or else they might take their children to a nearby park or rest area (Hong Kong has many), set a blanket on the ground, bring out their moon cakes, and just eat and admire the moon. The Moon Festival is a very contemplative moment in a very busy city.

CELEBRATING

MOON CAKES

Moon cakes are synonymous with the Autumn Moon Festival. Eaten and exchanged as gifts these little round balls of goodwill symbolise the roundness of the moon. Their distinctive chrysanthemum pattern and embossed Chinese characters are created by pressing freshly-made dough into purpose-built moulds. The dough rarely changes but fillings do. Myriad variations include: red azuki bean paste, date paste or lotus seed paste. Eager festival attendees must try moon cakes filled with duck egg yolks.

Weddings

New Year is the single-most important feast of the year; Hungry Ghosts the most fun; and the Moon Festival the most charming. But weddings are by far the most joyous and the most frequent. If you are invited to one you should move heaven and earth in order to attend. And it is not difficult to get invited. They are huge affairs, as the larger they are the more face is gained by the families hosting them. If you have one friend in Hong Kong you could be invited to their cousin's sister's friend's associate's wedding.

Traditionally the wedding invitations were sent by the bride's family. These invitations were accompanied by a gift of 'wedding cakes', prepared by the bride's family. But these wedding cakes aren't the multi-tiered, white-frosted constructions that we think of when we think of wedding cakes. Chinese wedding cakes are like moon cakes: small, sweet and heavy. Like a sweet bun. Nowadays in busy Hong Kong the invitation comes to you in its traditional red envelope, and also tucked in are gift certificates for wedding cakes at a local bakery. Possibly the largest issuer of these certificates is the famous Kee Wah Bakery with outlets all over the city. They even have them as far away as California. And amazingly you can even redeem the certificates there!

The actual wedding ceremony is a private affair often carried out in the home. The official ceremony involves simply traipsing down to the Marriage Registry and signing a paper. But the banquet is the big show.

Silvia and Alberto's wedding banquet: 45 tables, 18 courses and one very busy kitchen, Beverly Hotel, Central Macau

CELEBRATING

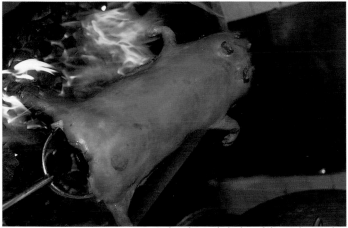

Pork sizzling in the kitchens of Shang Palace, Kowloon

Gastronomically speaking, things begin the day before when the bride, dressed in her nuptial finery, calls on the groom's family. There she serves tea to all the relatives who are older than the groom, in order of seniority. This order determines the amounts of 'lucky money' each of them will give her.

The day, or more likely evening, of the feast will be a noisy one held in a restaurant or hotel and may be attended by hundreds of people. Ostensibly the hosts are the groom's family, as they are the ones gaining a daughter. What with the number of people and the rich foods planned for the dinner, this could break the bank. But the Chinese are nothing if not practical. You are expected to bring a gift of cash or a cashier's check in the obligatory red envelope. How much you bring depends on your relationship to your friend's cousin's sister's associate. At the least it should be enough to cover the cost of your dinner.

Your table will be set with cognac or scotch and plenty of soft drinks. And the poor bride and groom will probably get nothing to eat or drink the whole night as they have to greet everybody and pose for innumerable photos. Listen for a cheer and some applause when the first course is served. It should be whole roast pig. No matter what colour the bride's gown, the presence of a whole roast pig is a public proclamation of the bride's virginity. After this reassuring culinary gesture of feminine virtue, course will follow course of fine fare. The serving of dessert signals that the party is about to end. Enjoy your sweet, say your goodbyes, and go.

CELEBRATING

Offerings

With food, the Chinese communicate with ancestors, gods and ghosts.
In placing offerings upon the altars
and graves, the spirits consume the
essence of the food, after which it
may be shared by mortals. Of course
in a hierarchical culture there will be
a hierarchy of offerings, from the
humble and simple to the extrava-
gant and delicious.

Votive fare in the kitchen of a Kowloon eatery

The simplest offering is three sticks of incense, but to this most people
will add tea and or fruit. The most common fruit offering you will see in
Hong Kong is the orange. It is because of this votive use that Hong Kong
consumes more oranges per capita than anywhere else in the world.

Next in the offering hierarchy is the addition of wine or an expensive tea.
The decision of what is offered might be based on the offerer's generosity or,
if leaving an offering to an ancestor, based on what the departed liked. You
might see a bowl of noodles, a can of Coke, or even a burning cigarette.

Simple meat dishes indicate a very important offering. It might be
important for the occasion or for the offerer or for the departed one, or all
three. The offering usually consists of dishes of the three sacrificial meats:
pork, fish and chicken, with pork as the centrepiece.

To truly impress the ancestors, gods and ghosts, the pious mortal will
bring to the altar an entire roast pig with all the trimmings. Vegetarian
sacrifices are made similarly with pigs and other animals made from dough,
gluten or tofu.

food as medicine

The Chinese believe that food, medicine and health are all part of the same continuum. This is derived from the Chinese philosophy of Yin and Yang, which applies as much to human health as it does to the cosmos. When all in the universe is in its proper balance, harmony reigns. But in a condition of imbalance, we risk ill health, misfortune, violence and destruction. Lesson: Seek balance!

Jabbok Tea House, New Territories

What determines human life is the mind, which is master of the body. If the body is at ease and in harmony with its environment, the mind will be able to deal with all changes in life. Thus it is important to keep the body in good repair and maintenance, the essence of which is to keep to the golden mean, that is, not to be deficient in nutrition and not to indulge in excesses. Use the five tastes to temper the five vital organs. If these are at peace, the vital fluid in us will flow smoothly, then our mind will find its equilibrium and the whole person will be in a state of wellbeing.

Hu Shihui, Imperial Dietician AD 1315-30

Acupuncture is a well-known way of restoring balance. Food is another. A practitioner of traditional Chinese medicine will take a patient's pulse in several locations to determine what the imbalance is, then advise the patient to avoid certain foods, or take others, or both. Only if this approach fails will the doctor prescribe medicine. And how does the learned sawbones determine which foods will restore function?

In the Chinese world all things fit to be eaten have certain qualities, or lack them, and will affect the body accordingly. To refer to these qualities as 'medicinal' in the classic western sense is somewhat misleading. Nor should they be confused with the herbal remedies found in traditional Chinese medicine. They don't kill germs or alter the central nervous system. They simply help to restore the body to its natural healthy state. These qualities are: hot and cold; warming and cooling; damp and dry; supplementary; and neutral.

Preserved salted lime in soda water at Tung's Kitchen, Tsim Sha Tsui, Kowloon

Not surprisingly, chilli and other spicy foods are considered hot, while beef, carrots, ginger and other 'dense' foods are warming. While white sugar is cooling, brown sugar is warming. Vinegars are warming, but red more so than white. Warming foods are said to generate heat in the body, thus stimulating the metabolism. That can be a good thing if you live in a cold climate, or have poor circulation or loss of energy. On the downside, too much warming can result in a sore throat, infection or ulcers. Next time you feel tired or chilled, have a dish of ginger beef, or something dressed with wine vinegar. But not if you're prone to ulcers.

If you have an imbalance on the cold side, too much heat in the body, you'll want to take bitter foods, such as leafy greens, and sour fruits like citrus or pineapple. Salty foods and certain shellfish such as crab are also considered cooling. These are obviously good foods for hot weather. And they are said to help rectify excessive weight loss due to lack of appetite.

Water retention, skin complaints and aching joints indicate excessive dampness in the body. Constipation, coughing and persistent thirst indicates dryness. For the former, enjoy a bowl of lychees. For the latter, mangoes are sovereign.

Supplementary foods are thought to remedy certain deficiencies in the body. They are usually high quality protein foods such as shark's fin and bird's nest. Neutral foods are such carbohydrates as rice, bread and beans.

Now to further complicate the matter, methods of preparation and cooking can alter, enhance or reverse the qualities of a given food. Ginger is warm. But ginger ice cream is cool. A cool cucumber gets warm if you

Bird's Nest Company herbalist store, Wellington Street, Hong Kong Island

cook it, but not if you steam it. Even the coolest crab gets hot if you deep fry it. Certain vegetables are never fried, but always cooked in soup. Some are only fried. Some go with anything. Some are only right with beef.

Organ meats are thought to have strengthening effects on the corresponding organs of the diner's body. Eat liver if you have cirrhosis. Offal for strong bowels. A woman would not generally benefit from deer penis soup (see The Bold Palate chapter), but certain conditions of lost energy could induce her to the table for a bit of buck's broth.

It all sounds hopelessly confusing, doesn't it? But Chinese people grow up with it. Their parents talk to them about food so that they will

Herbalists preparing herbs for traditional Chinese medicine, Hong Kong Island

grow up big and strong and healthy. During shopping, cooking or dining a Chinese mother will drill her children in food lore. She'll pepper them with two-word aphorisms of cuisine just like it were arithmetic: What's five times five? "Twenty-five!" Ginger? "Expels wind!" Soybeans? "Cold and dry!"

Recognising and utilising food's properties is a fundamental of Chinese cookery. A meal should have a balance of all the healthful properties in order to be healthful. This is one reason a Chinese meal often has so many courses. It is difficult, though not impossible, to incorporate all medicinal characteristics into a single dish. So remember that mung beans are warm, but when they sprout they turn cold. And when you cook the sprouts, they stay that way. Your tummy needs to have some warmth in order to properly digest, so when you cook them you might want to add some warming ginger for balance. And remember the advice of the Imperial Dietician:

> Saltiness makes the blood circulate faster, and is bad for people with blood disorders; sweet food is bad for muscles; sour food is bad for veins; drinking tea on an empty stomach is bad for health; after eating hot food and perspiring, avoid draughts; after a full meal, do not wash your hair, avoid sex like an arrow, wine like an enemy; people with heart disease should avoid saltiness and eat more small beans and dog meat.

It should be noted that the Chinese philosophy of food as medicine is not based on western science. However, the Chinese have been using food as medicine for a long time. Simple trial and error over a span of three millennia will produce many things that work well. We may not be able to tell why they work, but the Chinese will swear by them. And maybe that's one reason they do tend to be so healthy and recover quickly from illness when they get sick. A good dose of belief in the cure is often as powerful as the medicine itself.

Yin Yang soup (chicken and vegetable) at Tung's Kitchen, Tsim Sha Tsui, Kowloon

When in Hong Kong you can partake of the healthful or 'medicinal' foods in several ways. Many foods are indeed prescribed by practitioners of traditional Chinese medicine: figs, garlic, ginger, lily bulbs and buds, various seeds and a wide variety of mushrooms. You can buy them in musty old shops, and you can learn what they are and what they're good for, if you speak Chinese. Or you can visit a modern medicinal herb shop. There is a chain in Hong Kong called Eu Yan Sang. One of its branches is at 152 Queen's Rd, Central. It's spiffy, modern, clean and bright. From across the street you might mistake it for a an office supply store. All of its goods are clearly labelled in both Chinese and English and include directions for use and what to use them for. Not only can you get the individual ingredients, you can get pre-mixed and dry-packed concoctions ready to take home and cook, such as a package of **run fei tang** (good for cough due to excessive bodily dryness, or smoking and drinking). Take it home and put it in a pot with meat and water to make a healthful and restorative soup.

Ching Bo Leung Soup

Soup is the most common way to take Chinese medicine and, according to the Cantonese, is an essential element in all balanced meals. But like the poltices and potions in ancient poetry, fables and fairytales, some soup recipes list enough obscure ingredients (musty leaves and pungent roots) to fill a forest floor. This soup is eaten as a general tonic and can be made savoury by adding meat to the recipe. Alternatively, a sweet version is possible if the meat is omitted and sugar added. But beware. . .should you decide to prepare it we suggest a quick visit to your local Chinese herbalist for the correct ingredients rather than foraging in the backyard!

Ingredients
15g (½oz) pearl barley
30g (1oz) polygonatum (a medicinal herb, also known as Solomon's Seal)
30g (1oz) lotus nuts (olive-sized seeds of the lotus plant)
30g (1oz) fox nuts
15g (½oz) Chinese yam
30g lily bulbs
10g (⅓oz) dried longan
As much pork or sugar as you may desire

Combine all ingredients in a stockpot and cover with enough water to triple the volume. Bring to the boil, reduce heat and simmer for two hours. Bon sante.

All over Hong Kong you will see small shops selling 'medicinal turtle pudding'. You'll recognise these shops from their displayed turtle pictures and by the piles of turtle shells being steamed to extract their goodness. People believe that turtle has the power to flush toxins from the body. Even to expel cancers. You can also sample turtle in an ordinary restaurant. It's likely the chef will include pieces of the shell in the recipe, as that's where so much of its goodness lies. Turtle dishes, however, are expensive. Most people get their dose of detox from the medicinal pudding.

Green tortoise jelly from the Number One Herbal Teashop, Hong Kong Island

There are restaurants in Hong Kong, not many but a few, that claim to cure what ails you with their food. Upon entry you will be met by a waiter and a diagnostician. Before the former seats you, the latter will take your pulse in several places then claim that you have too much Yin or not enough Yang, or maybe too much of both. Depends on his mood. He will relay your grave condition to the waiter who will make helpful suggestions for ordering what will put you right again. Curiously, we have never known anybody to enter one of these establishments in completely good health. Lucky for them they wandered in.

Tony Chan, owner and chef with staff at Tung's Kitchen, Tsim Sha Tsui, Kowloon

There are, however, reputable restaurants where the chef is indeed very knowledgeable about the medicinal qualities of foods and skilful at their preparation. Perhaps the best known is Tung's Kitchen (32 Lock Rd, Tsim Sha Tsui). Chef Tung appears frequently on local television as a proponent of good cooking, good eating and good health. He or his staff will be able to tell you what the healthful properties are in a given dish on his menu; how a given dish is crafted to help restore or maintain, especially maintain, a given balance in your body. But he will not 'diagnose' you, and he will not claim that his soup will cure your bursitis, or that his goose will fend off the cholic or that anything in his kitchen will supercharge your libido.

Lizard soup with chicken and cloud fungus, Tung's Kitchen, Tsim Sha Tsui, Kowloon

END NOTES – Lilian Li

She is radiant with good health, her pink cheeks aglow, and when she smiles she brightens the room. When she approaches you with the tool of her trade you know that you will soon be one step closer to her healthful condition. That tool is a thin, flexible, clear plastic tube that she will gently, adroitly insert into your anus. Lilian is a colon hydrotherapist. One of a growing number of posterior practitioners in this city of conspicuous consumption.

"Hong Kong people are so busy these days", she says. "Too busy to be careful about their health, both physical and mental. Too busy to care about how they eat. They just gobble it up and call for more. They don't chew their food long enough. And I see the result."

"You actually see it?"

"After I fill the colon I normally leave the room. But sometimes the colon is so blocked that the client calls for me to help them. I massage them until they break loose.

Lilian says that you should chew every mouthful 14 times before swallowing. She explains that saliva contains digestive enzymes, and that if they are not allowed to do their work, she will do hers. She holds forth her tube as she speaks, and suddenly it doesn't look quite so thin. Or flexible.

"Are you compacted?" she asks.

"Oh no. No, not at all. No problems here. I'm a perfect asshole."

"Hmm. Yes. Well, good colon health is important to good overall health. Chinese people used to know that. But here in Hong Kong everything is busy and fast and excessive. You wouldn't believe what I've seen come out of people. I see even soft foods like fruits and vegetables. People swallow them almost whole. I've seen tape worms. And fish bones. People shouldn't swallow fish bones."

Lilian practices what she preaches. Of course she chews her food 14 times before swallowing, but she also enjoys a good flushing out. Hers is a sort of colon-hydrotherapist-heal-thyself ethic.

"Some people are in it just for the money. My goal is to help people and to stay healthy myself. A malfunctioning colon can result in many ills: low blood pressure, poor circulation, impotence and general unhappiness. There is also a transcendental aspect. The colon resides in one of the energy centres of the body. If you have a poorly functioning colon, you will feel a loss of **chi** (the Chinese concept of energy)."

Lilian demonstrates her technique on a training device: an inflatable client. Not a whole inflatable client. Just the business end. She first runs warm water through a pair of filters. She applies a generous amount of water-based lubricant to the end of her tool, then gently guides it into the client to a depth of about two inches. The water flows.

"A dry colon is a lazy colon. I restore its natural balance so that it functions well. Are you sure you're not compacted? You look pale."

MSG & The Chinese Restaurant Syndrome

Most people never suffer from it. Others can't seem to avoid the 'Chinese Restaurant Syndrome' (and we don't mean that feeling of being hungry an hour later). The food additive, monosodium glutamate, is said to cause headaches, dizziness, blurred vision, a tingling face and/or a tight chest. Why such a fuss over a simple seaweed extract?

A form of kelp called **kombu** (literally, sea tangle), has been used as a flavour-enhancing ingredient in Japanese cookery for centuries. But in 1908 Japanese scientist Kikunae Ikeda was able to extract MSG as an isolate of kombu. In 1909 Ikeda and a partner started the first company to market MSG called Ajinomoto, literally 'the essence of taste'. Ajinomoto is now synonymous with MSG throughout Asia, and the company remains the world's largest producer. It even has a factory in Iowa.

MSG can be sold in liquid form, but the granulated form is what we find in grocery stores. How it works to enhance the taste of food is not fully understood. Food scientists believe that it stimulates the taste buds, though it has no distinct taste of its own. Many people in Asia believe that it simply represents a fifth taste, in addition to salty, sweet, sour and bitter. It's called **umami**, from the Japanese word for 'tastiness'.

MSG is perfectly safe, according to the industry's Glutamate Association. Stories of adverse reactions to the flavour enhancer have been labelled as 'superstition' by some researchers. Still, many individuals claim to suffer skin rashes, breathing problems and an irregular heartbeat. Some critics have gone so far as to suggest a link to Alzheimer's and Lou Gehrig's disease. In his book *In Bad Taste: The MSG Syndrome*, Dr George Schwartz (a toxicologist) claimed to have recorded incidents of brain damage, heart attacks and even deaths linked to MSG. He wrote that MSG is "the DDT of the 1990s". Schwartz theorised that MSG's toxic effect is derived from rapid absorption as an artificially isolated free glutamate. Whereas in normal conditions, the naturally occurring glutamates in proteins are linked to other amino acids by peptides and can be broken down slowly in the digestive process. Lab tests have shown MSG to act as an excitatory neurotransmitter, which can cause damage to nerve cells in the brain.

Many common ingredients contain MSG in varying amounts: hydrolysed vegetable protein, hydrolysed animal protein, autolysed yeast extract, vegetable protein, textured soy protein, sodium caseinate and calcium caseinate. These ingredients can be found in such things as broth, bouillon, stock, seasonings, natural flavourings, tomato paste, texturised protein, whey protein and dried yeast. And while the United States Food and Drug Administration still lists MSG as "generally recognised as safe", it must be listed on the ingredient label of any food containing it.

So what to do if you believe you suffer from Chinese Restaurant Syndrome? Avoid Chinese restaurants? Or you could tell the waiter that you want no MSG. He'll tell the cook, but the cook might be using a stock that, unbeknownst to him, contains MSG. So if you do find yourself with a touch of the syndrome you can at least treat the symptoms: antacid for heartburn and aspirin for headache. See a doctor if you have a more serious reaction.

the
bold palate

Three men, an American, an Indian and a Chinese, were standing on a hill. A spacecraft landed in front of them and out came an alien. It was like nothing any of them had ever imagined. The American demanded of the alien, "take me to your leader!" The Indian, pious Hindu that he was, threw himself down upon the ground and worshipped the alien as a god. All the while the Chinese gentleman searched his memory for an appropriate recipe.

Preserved eggs, some cracked open, revealing their yolks: Sheung Wan

Shakespeare said that all the world is a stage. A Chinese writer might counter that all the world is a dinner. If it contains calories and will nourish the body the Chinese will eat it. They will eat anything with legs except the furniture; anything that swims except a submarine; and anything that flies except an aeroplane (the contents thereof possibly notwithstanding). 'Anything that turns its back to Heaven' is the dietary credo of China. And nowhere is this embraced with more gusto than in Hong Kong.

Hong Kongers pride themselves on their guts (take that any way you like, it's all applicable). To the chefs and diners of Hong Kong, all things edible have attributes that can benefit the body and mind. For example, many things are eaten not for taste but for texture. For texture is just as important as taste or aroma in the balance of a satisfying meal. All the senses must be stimulated. Hence it is not unusual to serve jellyfish alongside roast pork. The pork is delicious and aromatic, tasty and succulent. The jellyfish, when cooked, has an almost crunchy quality that, juxtaposed to the tenderness of roast pork, is highly prized for the balance it provides. Bear's paws, eaten mainly for their gelatinous texture, have long been a delicacy. They were so prized by the Chinese philosopher Mencius that he waxed poetic about them and equated them to virtue.

> Fish I love; bear's paw I love;
> If I cannot have both
> I'll forgo fish for bear's paw.
>
> Life I love; righteousness I love;
> If I cannot have both
> I'll forgo life for righteousness.

A given organ of a given animal might be especially warming or cooling, dry or moistening, or have some other power. When paired with something else, this organ could be especially efficacious in restoring bodily harmony, thus helping to cure an illness.

Cantonese Restaurant Advertisement

The autumn winds have risen
The snakes are in good health
It's time to nourish your body

Foods work together to nourish the body. Nothing is complete by itself. Everything is a part of the greater whole. The effort to sustain the body is, in great part, a balancing act. Always keep this in mind when contemplating the 'dark' side of Chinese gastronomy. For even the light of Yin must be balanced by the dark of Yang, lest there be an imbalance of life forces and illness or misfortune ensue. So do not look at worms as bait, look at them as lunch. Rats? A resource. Snakes are sustenance, and so are slugs; gonads are good, worms are wizard, brains are smart, and organs of generation (yes, yes, eat a penis) will 'restore function'. And let us not leave out the gustatory and healthful enjoyment of gametes. Before you rush off to your medical dictionary we will confirm that by gametes we are talking about eggs and sperm. Not exactly a vegan diet, is it? But it is a tasty one, and healthy. And if you follow the Chinese regimen, your Yin will always be in harmony with your Yang (for more bold palate eating see the Macau chapter).

Sit down at a **dai pai dong** (food stall) and order a nice bowl of hot & sour soup. You've probably had this dish at home before, and found it very appetising. Remember those chunks of tofu afloat in that delicious peppery broth? Look closely into your street stall version of the same soup. See the chunks? They're dark brown, rather than white, aren't they? That's because they're not tofu. They are chunks of congealed blood. You'll see congealed blood for sale at the food market on Graham St. It's sold in pudding-like cubes, shimmering and bouncy. When the blood is cooked it turns brown. Do not be afraid. It tastes a bit like liver and contains virtually all the nutrients you need to stay healthy. It's almost the perfect food. The Maasai of Kenya live almost exclusively on blood and milk. The Chinese would never go about excluding things, though. Their attitude is one of inclusion. Think about that when you next order hot & sour soup.

When we of the west think of snakes we think of dangerous creatures; creepy, crawly, maybe slimy monsters that bite and betray; agents of the Devil. Many Chinese Taoists also connect snakes to the supernatural. They believe them to be messengers to the gods. There are temples where pit vipers are kept sedated during the day by a heady incense. The worshipers chant their prayers to the creatures, believing that at night they crawl down into the earth where gods dwell and deliver the suppliants' pleas. But when

Hong Kongers think of snakes they think of warming soups that fend off the autumnal chill, give strength to the heart and heat to the blood. Such soups are often made with chicken stock, slivers of chicken meat, tree ear mushrooms, bamboo shoots and shreds of fish bladder. And not much snake. A little goes a long way when it comes to serpents. The meat is white, has little taste, and breaks up into small flakes resembling fish. Mrs Ng of the Ser Wong Fun restaurant (30 Cochrane St, Central) will sell you a steaming bowl when it's in season. Or you can buy your own viper to take home at the snake store called Shia Wong Hip (170 Apliu St, Sham Shui Po, Kowloon). The staff will kill it for you – that's probably best for both you and the snake.

Baby Mouse Wine

This wine is made by preserving still-suckling baby mice in rice wine. Taken as a tonic, its healthful properties are believed to include the rejuvenation of the body's vital organs.

Hong Kongers like to finish a meal with a sweet, and that sweet is often chilled **tong sui** (sweet soup). It's the standard dessert fare in a Hakka restaurant. It's also popular as a snack. People here consume sweet soup as we might consume ice cream. The **hasma** soup served at Heng Fa Low (49-57 Lee Garden Rd, Causeway Bay) is a good example. It's made with tapioca pearls and bits of this and that, and it comes either hot or cold, but it's always sweet. And it's fortified with the sperm of a Chinese tree frog. One always thinks of tadpoles when one thinks of baby frogs, doesn't one? Don't look for them in your soup, though. They're too small. To call it frog sperm soup would be something of a misnomer, as the little beasties are hermaphroditic. When their reproductive apparatus is harvested for culinary purposes you can get both gametes. Long life to you, fearless diner!

If you've travelled in tropical Asia before you've likely encountered – or fled from – the infamous durian. It is a melon-size fruit with an outer armour of spikes, and a smell that will knock your socks off. The odour of durian has been charitably described as reminiscent of pig shit, turpentine, onions and dirty gym socks whirled in a blender. And you're going to smell it all over Hong Kong. Don't worry. You'll only catch little whiffs and sug-

Snake handler with King Cobra (Ophiophagus hannah), Kowloon

gestions of its presence because no one will open the fruit in public. There are even notices on public conveyances not to do so, but this is probably a throwback to the British who, in the minds of many Chinese, don't like the smell of anything but bangers and beer. Many Hong Kongers love durian and fondly refer to it as the 'king of fruits'.

But there is one item of diet that even the most ardent fans of the durian will take steps to avoid, literally. The fermented treat **chiau deo fu** (stinky tofu) can be hard to find, though easy to smell. This stuff begins innocuously enough as that bland but wholesome food: **deo fu** (tofu), but some clever people inoculate it with yeast and let in ferment for a day or so. The result smells and tastes like a very very ripe limburger cheese. It is then deep fried and served on a stick with a dollop of chilli sauce. You'll find a shop selling it at 41 Dundas St, Mong Kok – just follow your nose. When you get there, watch as foreigners pass by. Sooner or later one of them will stop and check their shoe to see if they have stepped in anything. But the shop is doing a brisk business and it needs the revenue. Due to complaints from the nearby residents and shop keepers it is regularly fined as a public olfactory nuisance!

ANIMAL CRACKERS

When the British ruled Hong Kong they could often be tiresome in their ways regarding gastronomy. An afternoon in a Peng Chau bar with globe-trotting journalist Alan Yu brought this into sharp focus for us.

"They could only look at a dog as a pet or faithful companion," he explained. "A cat belonged in your lap not on your plate, and quite simply, you wouldn't even think about feasting on primates. Of course if you were an animal rights type of person that was all for the better."

"But these things still went on, didn't they?" we asked. "You just had to search for them, right?"

"And you didn't have to search far," he laughed. "I remember when a television production company came here to do an exposé on the treachery of consuming rare and exotic species. They were animal activists themselves. And they thought their locally hired crew were as well. Imagine their chagrin when they took off to find a vegetarian restaurant for lunch. For on returning, they found that their crew had, with the assistance of a local restaurateur, killed and eaten the animals they had just been filming."

As told to Richard Sterling by Hong Kong-based journalist Alan Yu

THE BOLD PALATE

shopping
& markets

Shopping in Hong Kong is, to say the least, a modern experience. Family grocery stores have moved to outlying islands or have been converted into boutiques. There are chain stores, shopping malls and supermarkets everywhere, and they carry anything you should wish to buy, from five-spice powder to live fish. But dig a little and you can experience the real heart of Hong Kong shopping.

There are still pockets of the old Hong Kong to be found. Peeking out from behind the gleaming towers of international commerce and commotion you'll see the odd glimmer of greenery and grocery. You can still visit wet markets, so called because they continually hose down the floor to wash away the detritus spilling from the fishmongers and fruit stalls. However, the government, ever vigilant against things deemed unhygienic, has shut down many wet markets or converted them into sterile and soulless places of shiny aluminium and white tiles, where foodstuffs are merely bought and paid for rather than lingered over, discussed, bargained for and delighted in. But don't worry. Follow us. The Sheung Wan complex building at the corner of Morrison and Connaught streets, Sheung Wan, reserves its first three floors for a traditional market. Food stalls on the 3rd floor. You can also wander through the street market at the eastern end of Wan Chai Rd, Wan Chai. But our favourite is the outdoor market on Graham St, Central.

Take a stroll down Stanley St walking westward any fine morning. When you see a cluster of **dai pai dong** (food stalls) up ahead you'll know you're almost at Graham St. Turn left and you'll see a ribbon of greenery and humanity running up the hill, offering all that could ever be desired by the Chinese cook. Well, maybe not birds' nests or monkeys' brains, but anything an average householder could desire on an average day.

So start your ascent into the cacophony and bustle and press of goods, people and appetites. Fishmongers sing their goods and prices down through the street. Herb sellers rely on the aromas of their goods to lure business. A bouquet of mint, coriander and garlic beckons. Across the street colourful spices laid out on trays like painters' palettes compete for your attention. How many artists will choose their colours here today? Fish are laid out on beds of shaved ice. Ducks and geese are hanging from entry ways, their golden and brazen skins glinting in the light.

"You buy!" urges the seller. "No!" cries another. "You buy here!"

Up the hill where the market branches out onto Cage St, the butchers are hanging their offerings on hooks and poles; curtains of meat, freshly slaughtered. If you're here early these curtains are dripping blood. If you're here late, well, they may be drawing flies. Best to come early. In the midst of all this hanging flesh are a cluster of restaurants, which offer a calm refuge within this bustling market street. Stop in for tea and a snack.

We visit Graham St with our friend Alan Lu. As with most Hong Kong shoppers, every ingredient Alan buys is carefully chosen for beauty as much as anything else. He probes and prods every item individually, subjecting it to the test of fragrance and ripeness, and giving demerits for blemishes. Alan thinks nothing of searching long and hard for the perfect papaya, the crispiest bean sprouts, the greenest water spinach.

Serious fruit selection at Graham Street Market, Central

This is not some dreary chore. Alan knows the owner of each stall, for he has been coming here for years. The shopkeeper asks Alan about his father. Alan commends the merchant for the superior goods available today. Yet he doesn't hesitate to ask why some goods are hidden while others are on prominent display. "These are good people here at this market", Alan tells us. "But even they can be sold poor goods by unscrupulous dealers. Be sure to inspect everything you buy. It was my mother who taught me to shop. She is even stricter than I. She will scold a merchant who offers her anything less than perfect. They fear her."

He leads us over to a butcher. The larger chunks of meat are draped in front of the stall, with entrails and organs just behind. Alan sniffs, then smiles. "Still warm. Just killed."

Heading back down Graham St we stop at a fishmonger. A woman is yelling out the fish varieties she has for sale. She has a few live ones in a tank and dozens laid out on ice. Alan eyes the tank suspiciously. "Some

people have used the polluted water of the harbour to fill their fish tanks", he explains. He can't decide if this tank is good or bad, so he buys from the ice bed. "Always look at the eyes. If they are not bright and clear, the fish is no good. Press the flesh with your fingertip. It should rebound. And then smell it. If it smells fishy, it is no good."

"But shouldn't fish smell like fish?" we inquire. Alan looks disturbed, and mutters something in Cantonese. We continue down the hill, Alan buying small amounts of this and that, chatting with the merchants, catching up on gossip, talking horse racing – the city's passion. When we reach the bottom of the hill at Stanley St we realise that we, ourselves, have purchased nothing. But here's the herb seller we passed on the way up. She smiles from behind her fragrant display of leaves and buds. We buy a bouquet of mint. We have no idea what we will do with it. We don't care. Goods and money exchange hands. We nod and smile, both happy with the transaction. Then we catch up with Alan, satisfied that we have been to market.

Graham Street market, Central

SEASONAL SPECIALITIES

Hong Kong's seasonal offerings are a large part of its character. In Spring everyone is silly for seafood such as abalone (consult your banker first) and shark's fin. Grouper is caught in the Pacific and brought live in tanks to Hong Kong so you can have it fresh. The lobsters are running and they are meaty and tasty and on display in the restaurant's tanks.

Summer is the time for greens, but not the kind of greens that immediately spring to mind. Here it is melons. Fresh juicy melons are said to have a cooling effect on the body, even when cooked, and so help you to cope with the summer heat. Winter melon (even in summer), fuzzy melon, luffa and watermelon are all prepared in myriad ways. A common touch is to serve winter melon soup in the hollowed-out melon (see the recipe Winter Melon Soup in the Hong Kong Banquet chapter). Other melons are cooked with a variety of mushrooms, tofu and other vegetables or fruits.

Autumn is the season for crabs, especially the freshwater hairy-legged crabs that the Shanghainese chefs prepare so well. But there are also green crabs, giant crabs, soft-shell crabs and tiger crabs. Females are preferred by many, as they carry their delicious roe.

Bound hairy crabs for sale, Hong Kong Island

And winter is the time for those warming dishes such as hotpots or steamboats (see North China in the Culture of Hong Kong Cuisine chapter). Winter is also the time for vegetables such as kale and kohlrabi, and chestnuts, lotus roots and chrysanthemum greens. And for those with a bold palate, you can always find a warming bowl of snake soup (see The Bold Palate chapter).

Things to Take Home

For decades Hong Kong was a shopper's paradise. Anything and everything was on sale and the bargains were incomparable. Well it is still possible to get anything and everything, but the bargains are now very comparable. In fact, they are comparable to Tokyo, New York, Berlin, London and anywhere else in the affluent world. Hong Kong is all grown up; big, strong and rich. You might get a wok at home for less than in Hong Kong. Remember, virtually nothing you buy in the shops is made in Hong Kong, shops like Mr Lo's notwithstanding (see the boxed text). It's all imported and you have to pay the freight. There is little or no import tax, but shop space rental is staggeringly high.

So what to look for if not bargains? Look for those things you can't find at home. You'll notice that all the finer restaurants seem to compete with each other for the most beautiful, and unusual, chopstick rests. We rarely see these at home and when in Hong Kong buy them as gifts from house and kitchenware dealers. Cookware and crockery can be cumbersome, but small bamboo steamers such as those used in yum cha houses are light, chopsticks are small, and teacups fit well in the corners of your suitcase. Such things may be available in your home country, but there is an almost infinite variety available in Hong Kong.

Bamboo steamers

As for edibles, be sure to bring home some XO sauce. Every top restaurant has its own recipe and sells jars of it. Tasty and widely available brands include those produced by Lee Kum Kee and Amoy (see XO Sauce in the Staples & Specialities chapter). Packaged herbal soup mixes are available at places like the Eu Yan Sang, and these make for tasty and healthful souvenirs (see the Food as Medicine chapter). And while your there, get a deer's penis. Only twenty bucks.

OLD DOESN'T MESH WITH THE NEW – Mr Lo Ho-Kee

Mr Lo Ho-Kee has the finger dexterity of a master weaver, and the calluses and bandages of a farm worker. The 74 year old makes the wire mesh kitchen utensils that are essential tools of the Chinese cook. With spools of steel wire he makes sieves, spatulas, wok covers, steamer baskets, even bird cages and a few items for which we have no names. All these things he has been making for decades in his small, nameless shop in Ladder St, Central (close to Circular Pathway). His customers are mainly restaurant workers, but demanding home cooks also come to him, often for something custom made.

His goods are of such high quality, and so durable that he may be putting himself out of business for want of repeat customers. "I have three daughters who own a restaurant in Australia", he explains. "I made all the mesh tools for them when they opened about 10 years ago. They're still using them." The only replacement work he does is to cover loss or pilferage. New business comes from newly opened Chinese restaurants. What with the current trend in western and concept restaurants, business has been slow these days. "I've been exporting some", he says. "Chinese restaurants opening overseas have heard of me. They send me enough orders to keep me in business. But I've known better times."

He commenced his career in 1944 as an apprentice to a mesh master. Then later he set up his own shop. It may be a surprise to many foreigners, but his is an age-old craft and is held in high esteem by other artisans and customers alike. But his craft, like that of the blacksmith, has for the most part been superseded by the factory. Yet there are still enough people who cherish the skill, the dedication and the love that goes into the making of an exceptionally beautiful utensil. There are those who will acquire a finely wrought piece even if they never use it; just to admire it, hold it in their own hands and feel the mastery. If you are such a person, then take a stroll down Ladder St, shake the gnarled and bandaged hand of Mr Lo, and admire his wares while you still can.

Mr Lo Ho-Kee

Hong Kong Picnics

There's a great deal of green space to be found in Hong Kong. This may seem to fly in the face of it's well-known image, but it's the truth. In the New Territories and on the outlying islands you will see local people taking in the natural surroundings, the relative calm and the relatively clean air. They usually visit these areas in family groups, as they are a gregarious people who seldom go in for solitary pursuits. And although they carry their water bottles, their thermoses of tea, and perhaps a few pieces of fruit, you couldn't really call them picnickers. Wherever you see them they already have a restaurant in mind and are working up an appetite. Another thing working against a picnic culture here is the fact that Hong Kongers love to be waited on. And who is going to wait on you at a picnic? And then there are the picnic foods, to which Chinese cuisine does not lend itself. It's easy for the western alfresco diner to pick up a nice crusty loaf of bread and some cheese. But where are you going to buy a pot of cooked rice to take away? Stir-fried, deep-fried or even steamed dishes need to be eaten immediately, not packed the night before and eaten cold (last night's leftovers notwithstanding). But don't let this dissuade you. You'll have all the good picnic spots to yourself. And since Hong Kong is restaurateur to the world, you'll have plenty of food to choose from for an alfresco feast by the Fragrant Harbour.

Breakfast on the go, Kowloon

An obvious choice for a picnic is Lamma Island. Now the residents of Lamma made us swear by all that is holy not to mention their island in this book. So keep mum! Take the ferry from Hong Kong Island to the village of Yung Shue Wan. In the main street, the only street to speak of, you will find many grocers and other purveyors of provender selling all manner of food fit for a picnic. All of them carry wine, cheese, fresh fruit, biscuits, soft drinks and water. One of them sells readymade sandwiches, another sells all manner of deli goods, including Parma ham and baguettes. Load up then set out on the trail to Sok Kwu Wan on the other side of the island (in warm weather be sure to wear a hat and sunscreen, and carry water). The paths are well marked. But you're only going half way. For at the halfway point, at the summit of the hill, you will find a small pagoda offering friendly shade, and a stunning view of the South China Sea to whet your appetite. The hillsides are verdant and cloaked in wildflowers. The air is calm and quiet. You can enjoy your repast at leisure then hike back to Yung Shue Wan, or continue on to Sok Kwu Won. There you can have a cold one or two then take the ferry to Aberdeen for dinner.

There are even places in the city to enjoy a little outdoor lunch. In Kowloon there is the beautiful Kowloon Park at Nathan and Haiphong roads. It's a 10-minute walk north of the Star Ferry Terminal. The park is startlingly calm compared to the frenzy that can develop during a busy day in Tsim Sha Tsui. Like any good city park, it offers respite from the smoke, noise and traffic. So buy your goodies at the shops along Haiphong Rd, or even at (sit tight) the local 7-Eleven. You can get dim sum snacks and French wine in a Hong Kong 7-Eleven. Don't knock it until you try it.

And then there is Hong Kong Island. We doubt that anyone ever set aside a place just for picnics here. Probably never even thought of it. But there are little interstices in the deep bends of the wicked city's guts that make for admirable picnicking. Hop on the Mid-Levels escalator and ride up to Staunton Street. Hop off, walk back down Shelley St to Tsun Wing lane. Turn left and at the far end of the lane you'll find the most charming sitting area in the Mid-Levels. A perfect escape from noise and pollution, surrounded by one of the territory's oldest neighbourhoods, and yet just a walk away from shops, ferries, bars and restaurants. It's a little hideaway and hardly anybody knows about it.

where to
eat & drink

How many kinds of restaurants are there in Hong Kong? How much time do you have? How big is your appetite? What is your gastronomic interest? Getting the idea? Hong Kong is entrepot to the world. And so it is restaurateur to the world.

Consider this: an Australian opened a chain of Italian restaurants (The Spaghetti House) that claims to be the home of American pizza. At Ned Kelly's (another Aussie concern) two Korean businessmen entertain their Japanese clients over hamburgers and French fries, while listening to American jazz played by a Filipino band. And in SoHo, German wine is being poured alongside Russian caviar before a meal of Peking duck in a restaurant that calls itself a bistro. So what can you get? Well, what do you want? You can have anything. Okay, one caveat: this would not be an honest book if we did not tell you that Hong Kong's Mexican community comprises about three persons. If you want Mexican, better you should get yourself invited home to dinner with one of the three, or book a flight to Monterey. But that aside, you can find all kinds of Chinese, Thai or Tibetan, Indian or Italian, Nepali or Neapolitan; you'll even find what's called 'New British' wherein food is not colourless, vegetables are not boiled into submission, herbs are not used strictly as ornamental plants, and cream, sugar and Marmite are banned.

Red market tea house, Macau

Hotel Restaurants

Many of the best and oldest restaurants in Hong Kong are in the major hotels. And in our recommending them we are departing from our own gastronomic advice. We normally advise readers to avoid hotel restaurants. They tend to have a 'captive audience' and need not be among the best in order to survive. Theirs is not the Darwinian world in which most restaurants thrive or face extinction. This is not to say that every hotel restaurant in Hong Kong is good. Nor is it to say that a hotel that justifiably prides itself on one of its restaurants has any reason to boast of its others. But for as long as Hong Kong has had hotels, fine eateries have been lodged within many of them. This is in part due to the fact that real estate is so gawdawful expensive and always has been. Restaurants operate on profit margins so thin that even popular and successful establishments can go out of business overnight. And they do. But hotels, with their long-term leases, can weather the storms that often blow through the balance books.

Hotels in Hong Kong have always been social and cultural centres, the places where social intercourse takes place, where celebrities can see and be seen, and where important events occur. The surrender of Hong Kong to the Japanese was solemnised in the lobby of The Peninsula Hotel. Diplomatic receptions are held in the Ritz-Carlton. Famous musicians perform in the Kowloon Shangri-La. And great dining takes place in these and other hotels. Local residents, perhaps even more than tourists, dine in them (the best testimony of all). A popular weekend getaway, in a city that does not really have any getaways, is a stay in one of the major hotels, with, of course, meals included.

Another advantage to hotel dining is that all the service is rendered in the western style, and in English. The table settings are familiar, the waiter asks if you'd like a cocktail, the menu is readable, and the crystal and silver are finely polished. It's all just like home, except that the food is better. If you've never been to Asia before, this is a good way to ease yourself in. And it's a fine way to get yourself pampered.

Here we provide you with a starting point, or a point of departure. From there you can settle in, or strike out on your own gastronomic voyages of discovery. In high tourist season you should make reservations.

Gaddi's in The Peninsula is the oldest French restaurant in Hong Kong (open since 1953) and the best, Frenchwise. All the more remarkable when you consider that the chef de cuisine is English (we make no apologies for that observation). The decor is pure posh without being prissy, the service is old-world attentive, the wines are superb and the food is so un-English that you'll swoon. You'll also swoon when you get the bill, but, hey, when you die you'll regret your economies more than your extravagances.

THE CONSERVATOR – Faces of Gastronomy

Up to 200 rolls and baguettes per day, 150 slices of focaccia, flour from France, three kinds of Normandy butter (as well as cream), flour from Italy for the pasta. Marc Toutain, executive chef of Avenue Restaurant in the Holiday Inn faces this ingredient list every working day. You can also throw in vegetables, hams, sausages, wine, oil, fresh herbs, everything that it takes to operate a European restaurant. And it's all flown in from the Rungis Market in Paris, Marc's home town. But put meat and vegetables and all that aside, for today Marc is talking bread.

"It's the great comfort food of the west. It's what defines us gastronomically. Can you imagine a Chinese person giving up rice? Of course not. It's the food of their childhood, and one can never give that up. The first thing I do every day, the first thing I think about is my bread, and how I am going to make it succeed."

That is a tough challenge in Hong Kong, because the climate here is simply not bread friendly. It's hot and it's humid. Staggeringly so at times. The crustiest baguette, or the hardest roll can be reduced in a mere 30 minutes to a steamed bun. "So I never let it go outside the climate control of the hotel. I bake it in the bakery downstairs. I count it, I store it, I move it and I make sure it doesn't come up the service elevator where it might be exposed to the outside air. A western meal is simply incomplete without bread, and I won't let that happen in this restaurant. There are any number of European, American, even South American chefs here in Hong Kong. But most of them lack the means to make a good honest bread."

Marc's eyes shine when he speaks about his bread. But we have found that most chefs in Hong Kong, regardless of their tradition, are passionate about their work. They are artists, artisans and designers. Marc sums it up nicely. "It's like any job, whether it's making dinner or making shoes: you need the skill, you need the right materials and tools, and you need the dedication."

Freshly baked bread at the Avenue Restaurant

Toscana in the Ritz-Carlton is where you'll find the best Tuscan cuisine outside Tuscany. This is the domain of Chef Umberto Bombana, who is a local celebrity. He attributes the Chinese affinity for Italian fare to a few cardinal tastes: for pasta; for flavour balance; for beautiful presentation; and for sheer panache. Bravo!

Tang Court in the Great Eagle is popular with mainland Chinese, perhaps due to Chef Kwong's implacable insistence on maintaining **wok chi** (see Hong Kong Flavours in the Culture of Hong Kong Cuisine chapter).

Shang Palace in the Kowloon Shangri-La has to have the most beautiful kitchen in all of Hong Kong. It is a happy place. And that makes for happy cooks. And happy cooks make for happy diners. And while it is an extremely traditional Cantonese joint, Chef Ip Chi Cheung has the Hong Kong verve. Among other bold manoeuvres, he will combine Iranian caviar with Chinese thousand year eggs. Need we say more?

The kitchens of the Shang Palace, Kowloon

Shang Palace, Kowloon

Concept Restaurants

There have always been western-style restaurants in Hong Kong, but they were always very traditional. Concept restaurants are, more than anything, reflections of the personalities of their owners. The concept may reflect where the owners come from, or it may reflect where they would like to have come from. It may be a place, a time or an era, an idea or a desire. They tend to be owned by North Americans, or people who have spent a lot of time in the US, Canada or Australia. Hence, English is the lingua franca. Some concept restaurants are simple and fun, some are dead chic, others are cosy and comforting. It is wise to make reservations, especially on weekends.

IndoChine Restaurant in Lan Kwai Fong, Hong Kong Island

California Cafe is the original concept restaurant and gastronomic cornerstone of Lan Kwai Fong. What is the style? Dude, the name says it all.

Al's Diner is the home of American retro. The 1950s are alive and well in Hong Kong.

Café Au Lac offers sophisticated Indochinese cuisine in a sedate atmosphere.

Va Bene is darkly stylish and very Italian. The cool kids hang here.

Cubana offers Hong Kong diners a taste of Cuba, but with virtually no Cubans in Hong Kong nobody really knows if this joint is authentic. Nevertheless it is popular.

The Bayou is a joyful piece of Louisiana on the coast of China.

Neon Restaurants

Identified by huge neon signs, neon restaurants are usually very spacious with high ceilings, and they are brightly lit and well ventilated. And it's a joyous cacophony within. This is where Chinese people go most often when they go out to eat. The menus are very extensive, and most are Cantonese. A prime example of a neon restaurant is the Treasure Inn Seafood Restaurant (3rd floor Grand Centre, 8 Humphreys Avenue, Tsim Sha Tsui). As with so many others, the neon sign is not attached to the building in which the restaurant is located. It's across the street. And the restaurant is not on the ground floor, nor is any part of it visible from the street. But look around. Seek and ye shall find a small notice directing you to the 3rd or 4th floor, or you may see the building directory and so find your way. These places have been in operation for years, and they have a steady stream of regular customers who learned how to find their way here in childhood days when their parents brought them twice a week.

Most neon restaurants have at least one English speaker on duty at any given time. Quite often it's the head waiter, so you'll generally get pretty good, though utilitarian, service. The obsequious waiter, the sniffing sommelier, the pompous captain and the pimply busboy are not the tradition in a Chinese restaurant. Here the staff's job is to take your order, serve your food and drink and get out of your way. They won't tell you their names and say that they are glad to be serving you tonight. They will not brandish an instrument that looks like an Aztec's club and ask you if you'd like any freshly ground pepper. They will keep you in the corner of their eye and come when they are summoned. They anticipate that you will want your drinks recharged or, if you are a larger party, that you will find you need to order more food. And when you leave they will not smile like a flight attendant and say, "please come again".

So enjoy. Rarely will you need reservations, except at the most popular venues. They usually have plenty of room. And if a given restaurant is full, there will be another nearby. You will find neon restaurants everywhere in Hong Kong, but their greatest concentration is in Tsim Sha Tsui where there's enough neon to rival Las Vegas. On the outlying islands their

Locals say the restaurant belongs to Jackie Chan, Fisherman's Wharf, Hong Kong Island

WHAT'S IN A NAME?

Some things just don't translate well. Curses, for example, can come out sounding weak when rendered into English. A curse like "You dead ghost" just doesn't pack much punch for the Anglophone. Romance is another: "I love you with all my liver" says the Chinese swain to his lady fair.

So it is no wonder that the names of Chinese restaurants translated into English can be, shall we say, mirthful. Names of restaurants are meant to convey the spirit of the place, or to have auspicious connotations. And in Chinese they do exactly that. Thus, you will encounter the Good Seafood Restaurant. And if that isn't good enough for you then you can go to the Very Good Seafood Restaurant. Or to the Quite Good Restaurant. Or if you need even better you can go to Taste Better Curry. And if nothing but the best will do for you, then nothing will do but The Best Restaurant.

You'll never be lonely at the Good Companion, Kowloon

Are you health conscious? Then dine at the Healthy Mess. Don't find the food tasty there? Then try Delicious House. If you're feeling lucky then the Jackpot Familiar Cuisine is the one for you, if not the Lucky Seafood. You'll never be lonely at the Good Companion. You'll feel good at Happy Fast Food, and twice as good at Double Happiness. Your fortunes will rise at the Rich Seafood Restaurant. And your sweet tooth will always be satisfied at Honey Honey Dessert House. Aww, had too much of a good thing? Tummy upset? Then visit the Get-Healthy-Land Pharmacy.

So our wish for you in Hong Kong is that you be good, be quite good, be the best, get rich, get healthy, and uh, bon appetit!

Neon's everywhere, Hong Kong Island

counterparts are the outdoor seafood restaurants. They are basically neon restaurants that have swapped their neon signs for terraces facing the water. And the grandest neon restaurants in all Hong Kong are the floating restaurants on the south side of Hong Kong Island. They are just like the neon restaurants of Tsim Sha Tsui, except that they float. If you are prone to seasickness, do not worry, as these things are very stable. Their greatest danger is fire, as they are constructed of wood and they have many fires going in their kitchens all the time. And when they do burst into flames they put the neon to shame.

Fook Ying Hot Pot restaurant in Central, Hong Kong Island

Working-Class Restaurants

Dining in Hong Kong can get expensive. It can also be intimidating with such a wide variety of choice, and strange and unfamiliar venues and customs. And did we mention that it could get expensive? Furthermore, we are of the opinion that to make a successful culinary journey we have to perform some of it 'close to the ground'. We need to rub shoulders with ordinary folk, break bread with the common man, see how the other half lives, eat like them and with them. And so we patronise everyday low cost Chinese restaurants. A perfect example is Cammy restaurant (on Portland Street between Nelson and Shantung, Mong Kok), not to be confused with the nearby up-scale Cammy Club. This kind of restaurant is the soul of Chinese gastronomy: unpretentious, a bit earthy, a place of exuberance and life affirming noise. At any time of day or night the neighbourhood residents and local workers will come to the Cammy. They are filling up the plain wooden tables and booths, chatting, arguing, cussin' and discussin'. And of course smoking, flicking their cigarette ashes on the floor as often as not. They call for the simple dishes that such a place can serve. Noodle soup, fried rice, vegetable dishes. There might be a roast duck somewhere in the kitchen. Perhaps they are not eating. Perhaps they are only drinking iced coffee or hot tea.

Locals enjoying an afternoon with friends and Chinese tea, Hong Kong Island

The floor wants sweeping, the wall paper is peeling and the ceiling decaying, and the air-con is wheezing and belching mist as the cooled air condenses in the thick humidity. Maybe it's dripping onto your table. But this is a restaurant in the truest meaning of the word. It comes from the Latin verb meaning 'to restore', and this is where people come to be restored, in body and in spirit. The food is wholesome and plentiful. And all the hubbub, bustle and kitchen clatter serves to restore the spirit, to make one feel part of this greater whole.

Take a seat under a wall lamp resembling a gas street light (perhaps it was a gas street light and the proprietor got a good deal on it). Maybe there is a reduced English-language menu. Maybe not. Don't worry. If none of the staff speak English a poll will be taken of the patrons and the one deemed best able to communicate with you will be nominated. Your order taken. Just point to something on a nearby table, and the words 'beer' and 'yum cha' will always be understood. The cook may look tired or be at the end of a 12-hour shift. But a smile or a nod always gets the same in return. This is likely to be a family operation, with father in the kitchen, sisters and aunties serving and mother at the cash register.

Soon great heaps of rice are brought proudly to your table. Your neighbours are chewing on squid on a stick, slurping noodles or gnawing on ribs. Sister keeps you well supplied with tea (poor stuff but plentiful). And mercifully there are very few mobile phones.

In Hong Kong's maelstrom of activity, in its winds of change and commerce, and storms of traffic, there is refuge in the working-class restaurant. Here, for a rather small sum, you will be restored. No need for reservations. They wouldn't take them anyway.

Noodle & Congee Shops

Hong Kong would grind to a screeching halt if it woke up one day and found no **juk** (congee; rice porridge) and no noodles. These eateries are found virtually everywhere that humans can be suffered to walk upon the ground. It's Chinese fast food, comfort food and peasant fare all rolled into one. It's chicken soup, Vegemite, peanut butter, jug wine, tacos and a dry martini. It's all those consumables that you just can't live without.

Noodle and congee shops are almost always on the ground level, close to where life is taking place. We are not aware of any noodle shop on the top floor of a major hotel. They are most common in Kowloon, but you'll find them anywhere there is foot traffic. Often these shops are one and the same (although you wouldn't want to mix your juk and your noodles). They are generally small concerns with large windows that allow you to see just what is going on within. And it's hard to mistake the sight of noodles and juk (see the boxed text Congee Cravings in the Staples & Specialities chapter).

Roasteries

Chinese restaurants specialising in roasted or barbecued meats are common in Hong Kong. You'll know them when you see them; they have all their wares hanging in the window. Menu and sign translations typically say 'roasted meat restaurant'. However, unlike a western steakhouse these are not places in which to indulge in mountainous portions of animal flesh, even if the meat is what attracts people. Indeed a typical meal at a Chinese roastery would be an extremely balanced one. A common lunch here might be a simple noodle soup garnished with a few slices of roast duck. A dinner might be comprised of vegetables, rice, soup and an ample portion of roast pork.

Roasting, especially the roasting of fowl, is a highly specialised skill in Chinese cuisine, especially since it requires an oven, something most people lack. The Hakka people make do admirably with a pile of salt on a hot surface; others with a measure of mud and a wood fire (see Salt-Baked Chicken in the Staples & Specialities chapter). But the golden-skin goose, burnished duck and the crackling-skin pig all require the dry heat produced in ovens.

Roast goose and duck restaurant, Mong Kok, Kowloon

WHERE TO EAT & DRINK

Care for a night-time feast of fowl? Mong Kok, Kowloon

Of all the roasted meats available in Hong Kong the most popular is goose. Locals call it flying goose, not because it is a bird of flight per se, but because it is so tasty and aromatic (and the Hong Kong version so superior) that airline crews buy it to take home. The roast goose restaurants of Hong Kong are beloved by the people although, curiously, they are not as numerous as duck or pork roasteries. You will find them here and there, such as on Hau Fook St just off Carnarvon St in Tsim Sha Tsui. But the greatest concentration is in the Sham Tseng district on Castle Peak Rd, about 30 minutes out of town in the New Territories. The Chan Kee restaurant (48 Castle Peak Rd) is the best known. A place like Chan Kee is like a neon restaurant in many ways: large, airy, well lit, full of families or groups of business associates. It's cavernous, cacophonous, full of chatting and laughing, it's boisterous and roisterous. A TV is playing, though no one seems to be watching it. It's just for the noise (get used to it, the Chinese like noise). The ceiling is done in colours we cannot name and do not believe are found in nature. The whole effect seems to scream Early Las Vegas. But behind this familiar scene you'll find the birds being readied for the kitchen – marinating, hung up to dry and roasting in cylindrical ovens that look like little rocket ships. If you have a Chinese speaker with you, ask one of these prep cooks to show you how to tell the difference between a roasted duck and a roasted goose.

Yum Cha Houses

In the long view of Chinese culinary history, dim sum is a newcomer. A mere 1000 years old. Still, in this brief time the Chinese have managed to develop around 2,000 varieties of these morning and lunchtime treats. The larger yum cha houses will offer up to 100 items on any given day. You'll be able to have dim sum every day of your stay in Hong Kong and not eat the same thing twice.

Eating in a yum cha house can be quite an experience. Firstly, you must gird yourself for the courteous combat required to wrest a vacated chair from all competitors. Unless you have come early, you must wait, though generally not for long. When you see a patron rise, make your move. He who hesitates is lost. You'll likely be sitting at a table full of strangers, but hey, so are they. No need to make conversation. Just read your newspaper as they are.

In a traditional yum cha house there is no menu. Instead, ladies (they are always ladies) carry trays or push little trolleys laden with all the goodies. The drill is to summon them if they haven't already seen you. Arriving at your table they will begin to sing. No, they are not serenading you, good looking though you may be. They are singing out their wares, just as the fishwives do in the market. If you've got the tune but can't manage the words, it is perfectly acceptable to reach over and lift the lids of her little steamer baskets and see what looks good. In a more modern place you will be given a menu and a pencil, tick off what you think you might like and hand it back. Don't be shy, all the dishes are small and you are meant to have a wide selection, so it won't matter if you don't like something. There is no succession of courses. There is no 'this only goes with that'.

Your table will soon be piled high with steamer baskets and other containers, teapots, crumbs and spills. Keep the emptied baskets and plates on your section of the round table: they are the 'counters' your table waiter will use to calculate your bill if you are in a place with no menu. And they will be used to settle disputes in a place with menus.

In our opinion the best time for dim sum is 10-11am. If you come earlier or later, the noise, the rush for vacant seats, the chatter and clatter of waitresses pushing their trolleys, and the overall bustle can make the whole thing look like the New York stock exchange. On the other hand, maybe that's your cup of yum cha.

Restaurant Dim Sum (63 Shing Woo Rd, Happy Valley) is a good example of a modern yum cha house, and Luk Yu (24 Stanley St, Central) is the oldest one in town. Dim sum selections range widely and for a snapshot of popular Dim Sum see the boxed text Yum Cha & Dim Sum in the Culture chapter.

Steamed bun with BBQ pork, Fook Ying Hot Pot seafood restaurant, Queen's Road West

Dai Pai Dong

The dai pai dong is usually a mobile concern that can flee the cops when they try to shut it down for being unlicensed. And they are an institution fast going the way of high tea and fish & chips, becoming a culinary fossil, albeit one of great sentimental value. Few Hong Kongers over the age of 20 are without those sensory memories of pushcarts, mobile kiosks, or people with a tray of snacks all serving 'alfresco Chinois'. They were visible at all hours, but especially after dark. They congregated in such numbers down by the waterfronts that the festive scene of dining, socialising, hawking of wares, juggling, magic or fortune telling was known as a poor man's night-club. School children could stop for a sweet or a savoury treat from their local dai pai dong. It was their equivalent of the ice-cream man. Workers went to them for lunch, and tourists and sailors bought gustatory memories from them.

The term dai pai dong literally means 'big licence food stall, and refers to the large sheet of paper on which their licence was printed. Sadly, in the 1980s the government stopped issuing these big licenses. The dai pai dong were considered to be unhygienic by council bureaucrats. A calumny in our *not* so humble opinion! We have consumed kilos of comestibles, pounds of provender and floods of drink at dai pai dong, and we have never suffered so much as a rumble in the tummy. But despite our advice, the government will do as it will. Those licences still in existence are permitted to remain in business until the second generation. That is, the current licence holders can pass it on to their children, should they wish to make use of it. But when they expire, so does the big licence.

The best place to find dai pai dong these days is at the Temple St night market. Most of them sell seafood of one kind or another. Clams and snails are common. But the local speciality these days on Temple St is oyster omelette, made with fresh oysters, spring onion and coriander. Among the other popular things for sale on Temple St are pornographic VCDs. It seems that no oyster omelette seller is out of sight of a VCD seller. Hmmm. We don't know if there is, in the Chinese mind, a connection between the two. And we prefer not to ponder this. It might spoil the mood.

You will still see the odd dai pai dong on the outlying islands. Watch for those selling **deo fu fao** (a custard-like tofu dressed with a sweet syrup), which is very refreshing on a hot day. There is also a restaurant chain called, appropriately enough, Dai Pai Dong. You will see it all over Hong Kong. It strives to keep alive many of the recipes that old dai pai dongers sold for years: pig's trotters, mud crab, spareribs, as well as pastries and snacks. However, in the air-conditioned and ultra-hygienic confines of the duly licensed restaurant, it is impossible to recapture the experience. Other

WHERE TO EAT & DRINK

dai pai dong operators, seeing the writing on the wall and wanting to retain their independence, have moved operations indoors, often to a space above a fresh-food market. Very wise. A blessed example is Tung Po Seafood (2nd floor, 99 Java Rd, North Point). And then there is our favourite among the permanently affixed, Heng Tat (429 Lockhart Rd, Wan Chai; open 24 hours). Order **laat jiu hai** (chilli crab) and weep for those who'll never taste it.

SoHo is a good place to stakeout and watch for some small, lonely dai pai dong at night. And these are the most poignant examples. Unlicensed solitary individuals, standing behind a little cart, bearing food offerings perhaps made by his or her own mother or father. One eye open for customers, the other for the cops. On a good night, enough business to run another night. You can't get rich this way. And why be in Hong Kong if there's no chance of getting rich? Simple. Ask any one of these operators. Independence. The ability to be the captain of your own ship, even if that ship is small. No such thing as fate. Just you and your will. And that, reader, is quintessential Hong Kong, right in your mouth.

Street vendor on Rua da Felicidade, Macau

Speakeasies

There are numerous unlicensed restaurants in Hong Kong and not all are dai pai dong. Many are proper sit-down places and are among the best in town. Just ask the government officials who are dining there. They tend not to invest much in decor, after all, such finery could end up in a police auction. But the food is magic. They are owned and operated by people who are in the business for the love of it. Often times the restaurateur is by day a broker, or a manufacturer of garments, or even a police officer. But by night they are the Scarlet Pimpernels of Clandestine Cuisine, bringing you their illicit best.

You have to know somebody to get into a speakeasy. You have to know somebody just to find one. But all serious gastronomes know a few. When you are invited you will be told to rendezvous at a secret location at a certain point in time. Do not be early. Do not be late. One of the cardinal rules of both espionage and illegal provender is punctuality. At the appointed hour people will emerge as one from the shadows, from behind bushes, from around corners, and converge upon a suddenly opened door. Now rush in, quickly, for the door must close before the cops cruise by.

A speakeasy, Hong Kong Island

Soy Sauce Western

These eateries serve western-style food for the Chinese palate. Consider a meal of spaghetti with brown gravy, mashed potatoes eaten with chopsticks, breaded and fried pork chops, Swiss chicken cooked in soy sauce. Yum! One of the best examples of this is Tai Ping Koon restaurant (6 Pak Sha Rd, Causeway Bay). It was founded in 1860 by Mr Chui LoKo, who originally worked as a chef for a western trading company in Guangzhou, and his specialities were western dishes. Later Mr Chui opened his own restaurant in Tai Ping Sha, Guangzhou, and he named it after the place. It was the first restaurant in Guangzhou specialising in western cuisine. Three of his signature dishes, roast pigeon, smoked promfret and Portuguese-style baked chicken, were celebrated among aficianados in south Guangdong Province and are standards on the menu even today, a century and a half later.

He later moved to Hong Kong, where where he opened two more branches. At the time of writing, the current chef's recommendations included roasted young pigeon, boiled corned tongue and Russian borscht soup (by definition, borscht is both Russian and a soup). Although traditional borscht is made from beetroot, at Tai Ping Koon it is a rich vegetable beef soup – the best grandmotherly sort. During British rule, Russian borscht soup was not an unusual menu item in many restaurants, and they all hewed to the Tai Ping Koon 'interpretation'. Tai Ping Koon's influence reaches far, and offers the curious Chinese diner a tentative exploration of western cuisine, but with select Chinese ingredients providing a comfort factor.

Waiting for broth, noodles with vegetables, meatballs & frankfurts

Vegetarian

There's good news and bad news for our vegetarian friends (you're probably used to that by now). If you're the sort whose dietary code is simply 'nothing with ears', then you've just landed in food heaven. There is no better place in the world to eat those earless treasures called fish. And if chicken floats your boat, get ready to set sail. And of course every Chinese menu will feature a whole section dedicated to nothing but the pleasures of greenery, verdure and roughage, roots and tubers, fungi and fruit. Many will also feature egg dishes and pastries. There is a vast universe of tofu dishes. And don't forget noodles and rice. Even western-style restaurants will offer at least one or two tasty dishes for the transient herbivore. They'll always have some kind of salad. There will be fried potatoes, vegetable soups, bread and all those things that you know to look for when you're dining out at home.

Now if you adhere to the stricter code of 'nothing with a face' you've got a bit of a problem. All those herbivorous dishes listed above will very likely have been prepared with one of the most important flavouring agents of the Chinese kitchen: chicken stock. They might also contain fish sauce or oyster sauce. And if they don't, they will probably contain MSG. To further muddy your meatless waters, if you are keeping Kosher, be advised that Chinese superior chicken stock is enriched with ham bone. And sea cucumber is not really a cucumber. It's an animal. It barely qualifies as a member of the animal kingdom, but it is flesh.

Out of Buddhist piety many Hong Kong people will go vegetarian on the first and 15th day of the lunar month. But many will still consume dishes made with chicken stock, which seems to be regarded as liquid vegetable substance. Eschewing anything fit for food gets little sympathy among Hong Kongers. They believe that all things edible have certain benefits, and that the body needs some of all of them (see the Food as Medicine chapter).

But there is hope of rewarding dining for our vegetarian friends. There are about 100 dedicated vegetarian restaurants in the territory. These sanctuaries are usually neon restaurants and their neon notices boldly announce Vegetarian Restaurant, so you can't miss 'em. They are for the most part Cantonese and strictly vegetarian, as they are owned and operated by strict Buddhists.

All Hong Kong Chinese understand Buddhist ways of eating. If you are a Buddhist (or would like to try it out for as long as it takes to eat your dinner) and tell the waiter as much, you'll most probably be accommodated. But you've got to speak up. If the waiter doesn't understand English, and you speak no Cantonese, press your hands together prayerfully and look

WHERE TO EAT & DRINK

Gau Choi Fa, (flowering Chinese chives), particularly good braised with tofu, also used as a general substitute for green onions, Graham Street market, Central

heavenward to indicate your Buddhist belly. We know people who do this. And it is guaranteed to work, sometimes.

Naturally you will tire of eating Cantonese vegetarian everyday (even Cantonese vegetarians tire of it), so look for alternatives. Vegetarian congee is easily had in noodle and congee shops. Yum cha houses serve a number of no meat treats; mostly sweets, but also such delightful things as **chung yau beng** (onion cakes) and **fu pei guen** (crispy tofu roll). Indian and Nepali restaurants are plentiful, and they all offer vegetarian dishes. Look for some up-market ones in SoHo, and some cheap ones in Chungking Mansions. For a salad fix there is a continuing growth in California-style restaurants, the original being California in the Lan Kwai Fong district. The Napa restaurant in the Kowloon Shangri-La Hotel features a salad bar along with its stunning view of the harbour. Fresh fruits of innumerable kinds are available in all markets all the time. You can even get a vegetarian pizza.

Lastly, you can contact the Vegetarian Society of Hong Kong (PO Box 91001, Tsim Sha Tsui). It organises a free vegetarian lunch every Saturday at the Kung Tak Lam Shanghai restaurant (45 Carnarvon Rd Tsim Sha Tsui). Also make sure you check out the Hong Kong Vegan Society's Web site at www.ivu.org/hkvegan for a comprehensive listing of the city's vegan and vegetarian restaurants.

Children

Virtually all Chinese restaurants are child friendly. It is the norm rather than the exception for families to dine out together, whether it be a casual Wednesday dinner, a Sunday afternoon seafood feast or a dim sum breakfast any day of the week. There are no special menus for kids, they eat what the adults eat for the most part. Small children can be wide-eyed curious about foreigners, but they are invariably well behaved and often very charming. If you and the kids share enough smiles it is perfectly okay for you to go and say hello. Just don't approach them looking hungry. Likewise if you're travelling with children, they may well become the centre of attention. The one type of Chinese establishment where kids might be out of place would be in a karaoke restaurant. Even though it serves food, it still has a nightclub-type atmosphere. Besides, exposing children to the tortures of karaoke would be cruel.

Hotel restaurants also cater to kids, often in a big way. Both business travellers and tourists alike are bringing their children in increasing numbers and the better places are reaching out to them. The Peninsula, Hyatt Regency, Island Shangri-La, and Mandarin Oriental in Macau all operate cooking classes for kids. It might be one hour of cookie baking or it might be a half-day program of Chinese or French cookery that lets the parents off the hook for a while.

Young patron goes in for a refill at Fook Ying Hot Pot restaurant, Hong Kong Island

Neighbourhoods

Hong Kong is a city state. It has no regional variations like France or India. There is no highland versus lowland style, no difference in the crops grown between north and south – there is no highland, lowland, north or south. Whatever you may desire you are within 30 minutes of it. It would seem then, on the surface, that it wouldn't matter where you dine. A steamed fish is a steamed fish, and a pizza is a pizza. But Hong Kong is more complex than that. Hong Kong is a city of neighbourhoods. Behind the massive walls of office towers the human scale is restored. The monotony of tall buildings is relieved by a delicious variety of neighbourhoods. Some of them stretch for blocks along such paths as The Golden Mile of Nathan Rd. Some are comprised of a small cluster of warehouses and old office buildings. Others are narrow bands of human habitation snaking their way up a hillside. And all are distinct and different. Even those lying cheek by jowl with one another clearly demarcate their limits by the smell, the feel, the topography and of course the dining. You can eat the same fish cooked in the same way in a different neighbourhood every night for a week and never have the same experience twice.

Lan Kwai Fong

Like Hong Kong itself, Lan Kwai Fong is an invention. Canadians Alan Zeman and Richard Feldman, and American Karin Jaffe, came in the mid 1980s to what was then a grubby collection of crumbling old colonial buildings and cobbled streets and saw the vein of gold shining in the ore. It was not then without its charms or attractions. It's name means 'place of orchids' and even now is home to many flower sellers. But Lan Kwai Fong was a dowdy neighbourhood in need of a makeover, so Zeman and Jaffe opened California and the rejuvenation of a neighbourhood began (see Concept Restaurants earlier in this chapter). Now dozens of restaurants, bars, night clubs and coffee houses occupy the area and have transformed it into something almost approaching a foreign country.

If you know San Francisco, Lan Kwai Fong at night will remind you somewhat of Little Italy at the cusp of Chinatown. Its narrow sloping streets bristle with Italian restaurants, and yet there is always a teasing odour of joss sticks afloat upon the air. English constantly echoes off the red-brick pavement and masonry walls. The music pouring out of the numerous clubs and bars, such as Yelt's Inn or Al's Diner, is jazz, rock and western pop. The buildings on D'Aguilar St bear very little Chinese signage; the Marlboro Man is more in evidence. English is the language of international commerce, and it is an international crowd thronging the streets and lanes, turning them into a system of pedestrian malls, much to the vexation of taxi drivers trying to deliver their hungry charges. In the early evening they are

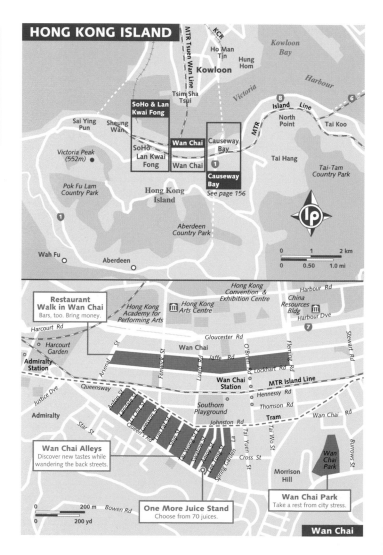

HONG KONG ISLAND

Kowloon Bay

KCR

Ho Man Tin

Hung Hom

Kowloon

MTR Tsuen Wan Line

Tsim Sha Tsui

Harbour

Victoria

SoHo & Lan Kwai Fong

Island Line

North Point

Tai Koo

8

6

Sai Ying Pun

Sheung Wan

MTR

Victoria Peak (552m)

SoHo Lan Kwai Fong

Wan Chai

Wan Chai

Causeway Bay

Tai Hang

Tai-Tam Country Park

Pok Fu Lam Country Park

Hong Kong Island

Causeway Bay

See page 156

1

Aberdeen Country Park

0   1   2 km

0   0.50   1.0 mi

Wah Fu

Aberdeen

Restaurant Walk in Wan Chai
Bars, too. Bring money.

Hong Kong Convention & Exhibition Centre

Hong Kong Academy for Performing Arts

Hong Kong Arts Centre

Harbour Rd

China Resources Bldg

Harbour Dve

7

Harcourt Rd

Gloucester Rd

Wan Chai

Stewart Rd

Harcourt Garden

Arsenal St

Tonnochy St

Fleming St

Admiralty Station

Wan Chai

Jaffe Rd

O'Brien Rd

Lockhart Rd

Queensway

Wan Chai Station

MTR Island Line

Hennessy Rd

Justice Dve

Admiralty

Star St

Anton St

Southorn Playground

Thomson Rd

Tram

Wan Chai Rd

Queen's Rd

Crescent St

Spring Garden La

Johnston Rd

Tai Yuen St

Tai Wo St

Wan Chai Alleys
Discover new tastes while wandering the back streets.

Cross St

Morrison Hill

Wan Chai Park

Burrows St

0   200 m

0   200 yd

Bowen Rd

One More Juice Stand
Choose from 70 juices.

Wan Chai Park
Take a rest from city stress.

Wan Chai

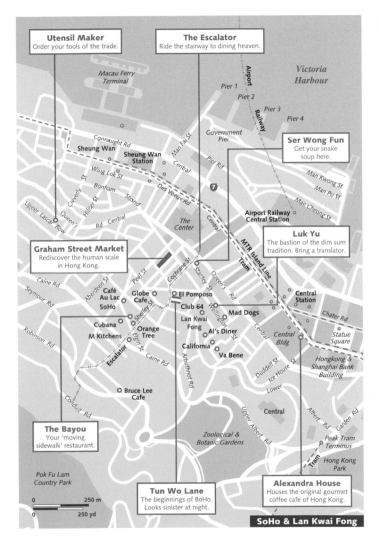

Utensil Maker
Order your tools of the trade.

The Escalator
Ride the stairway to dining heaven.

Macau Ferry
Terminal

Victoria
Harbour

Pier 1

Pier 2

Pier 3

Pier 4

Airport Railway

Connaught Rd

Sheung Wan

Sheung Wan
Station

Man Fat St

Government
Pier

Central

Pier Rd

Ser Wong Fun
Get your snake
soup here.

Man Kwong St

Man Po St

Wing Lok St

Bonham

Des Voeux Rd

Strand

Mac Cheong St

Upper Lascar Row

Crawley

Hillier St

Queen's

Rd Central

The
Center

Central

Airport Railway
Central Station

Luk Yu
The bastion of the dim sum
tradition. Bring a translator.

Graham Street Market
Rediscover the human scale
in Hong Kong.

Caine Rd

Peel St

Cochrane St

Stanley St

Queen's Rd

MTR Island Line

Tram

Central
Station

Chater Rd

Seymour Rd

Aberdeen St

Globe
Cafe

El Pomposo

Wellington

Central

Statue
Square

Café
Au Lac
SoHo

Shelley St

Club 64

Mad Dogs

Central
Bldg

Robinson Rd

Cubana

Orange
Tree

Lan Kwai
Fong

Al's Diner

Hongkong &
Shanghai Bank
Building

M Kitchens

Elgin St

California

Va Bene

Duddell St

Ice House St

Escalator

Caine Rd

Arbuthnot Rd

Lower

Conduit Rd

Bruce Lee
Cafe

Central

Albert Rd

Garden Rd

The Bayou
Your 'moving
sidewalk' restaurant.

Zoological &
Botanic Gardens

Upper Albert Rd

Peak Tram
Terminus

Pok Fu Lam
Country Park

Tram

Hong Kong
Park

0   250 m

0   250 yd

Tun Wo Lane
The beginnings of BoHo.
Looks sinister at night.

Alexandra House
Houses the original gourmet
coffee cafe of Hong Kong.

SoHo & Lan Kwai Fong

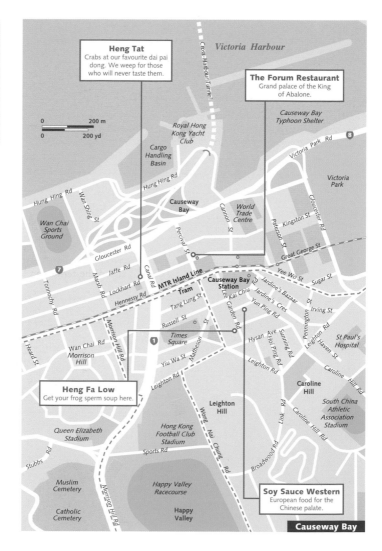

Heng Tat
Crabs at our favourite dai pai dong. We weep for those who will never taste them.

The Forum Restaurant
Grand palace of the King of Abalone.

Victoria Harbour

Causeway Bay Typhoon Shelter

Cross-Harbour Tunnel

Royal Hong Kong Yacht Club

Cargo Handling Basin

Hung Hing Rd

Victoria Park Rd

Victoria Park

Causeway Bay

World Trade Centre

Cannon St

Paterson St

Kingston St

Gloucester Rd

Hung Hing Rd

Wan Shing St

Wan Chai Sports Ground

Gloucester Rd

Percival St

Great George St

Yee Wo St

Sugar St

Jaffe Rd

Canal Rd

MTR Island Line

Causeway Bay Station

Jardine's Bazaar

Irving St

Tonnochy Rd

Marsh Rd

Lockhart Rd

Hennessy Rd

Tram

Tang Lung St

Lee Kai Chiu Rd

Jardine's Cres

Yun Ping Rd

Pennington St

Leighton Rd

St Paul's Hospital

Russell St

Lee Garden Rd

Hysan Ave

Hoi Ping Rd

Sunning Rd

Leighton Haven St

Heard St

Wan Chai Rd

Morrison Hill

Times Square

Matheson St

Yiu Wa St

Leighton Rd

Leighton Rd

Caroline Hill Rd

Morrison Hill Rd

Leighton Hill

Caroline Hill

South China Athletic Association Stadium

Caroline Hill Rd

Link Rd

Heng Fa Low
Get your frog sperm soup here.

Queen Elizabeth Stadium

Stubbs Rd

Hong Kong Football Club Stadium

Sports Rd

Wong Nai Chung Rd

Broadwood Rd

Muslim Cemetery

Morrison Hill Rd

Happy Valley Racecourse

Catholic Cemetery

Happy Valley

Soy Sauce Western
European food for the Chinese palate.

Causeway Bay

0   200 m
0   200 yd

7

8

1

just getting off work, leaving their high-pressure jobs at banks and broker-ages and looking for a place to let off steam. And here they find it. Good-looking people who come to drink, dance and dine; see and be seen. Especially at Va Bene or Tutto Meglio, favourites of the very smart set.

The smells continue to mingle: coffee, most likely espresso, rich and dark; garlic, lots of it; and now Thai fish sauce and chilli; balsamic vinegar; yeasty bread; and foamy beer and old whisky. And the smell of money. Be advised, this is no beggar's holiday. Come here with full pocket and purse. And pose for the TV crews that come here to shoot scenes of well dressed people on the rise: yuppies and their Chinese counterparts, chippies.

Up the hill on Wing Wah Lane a more casual crowd is gathering at the famous Club 64, named for the date of the Tiananmen massacre (June 4). This club was once a gathering place for political dissidents, and the beer was the cheapest in town. The politically aware patrons fretted that the new government would shut down their beloved watering hole, but no moves were ever made on it. Rather, it became a victim of its own success. It became trendy. And when a place becomes trendy in Hong Kong the rent goes up. And when the rent goes up so does the freight. The manage-ment tried gamely to contain costs, but eventually, and with profound regret, self criticism and apologies to all, had to increase prices. So the malcontents have moved on. And the new patrons sit on the terrace and watch the parade, that is, until the rent goes up again.

Down the hill in the California the crowd is now so thick that it spills onto the street, and the air-conditioning is running extravagantly at full blast, its cold air swirling out and cooling even portions of the streets. Conspicuous consumption even of air. But what would Hong Kong be without conspicuous consumption? And in order to sustain it (or is it just because they like to do it?) traders are still making deals. They are standing in the darkened lane, beer or wine in hand, men with collars open and women with hair down, striking bargains. It never stops. Can this really be China? No. Here in Lan Kwai Fong it is Hong Kong, the way Hong Kong was invented to be: a focus of people, appetites and commerce. The drug and flesh trades have been driven underground. The tea trade is long gone to China proper. But still commerce goes madly on.

Later in the evening, couples begin to arrive. Young women dressed to kill; young men whose eyes have turned from dollars to sex. Both looking for a good meal before trying to satisfy a more primal appetite. There are no families with children and few people over 40. They dine on the foods of the world in restaurants designed by inspired designers of restaurants, by inventors. The patrons' tastes are informed by the place, and they are enriched in mind and experience. They are all participants in the ongoing invention of Hong Kong.

SoHo

SoHo stands for South of Hollywood Rd. There was no SoHo before 1992. There was a Hollywood Rd on the island, and there was an area of residences to the south of it. It was populated by professionals and traders, and no doubt the area had its charms. But it was all up hill. So steep that even walking down hill was hard. Consequently everyone drove, and the traffic was unbearable. So in 1992 the city constructed the longest outdoor escalator in the world. Beginning at Des Voeux Rd down near the ferry landings, it snakes its way 800m up the slopes of Victoria Peak to Conduit Rd. And it is covered by an awning so it is usable in all but the worst weathers. In the morning, until 10am, it goes down. For the rest of the day and through the night it goes up.

The escalator, like any great trade route, has attracted crowds of merchants, and some of Hong Kong's best restaurants have appeared alongside it. It's a long, sloping corridor of cuisine. Hungry? Step onto the conveyor and be conveyed to satisfaction.

SoHo is one of the most sedate, calm and relaxing neighbourhoods in the territory. It is almost serene, that is, by Hong Kong standards. If Wan Chai is a rave, and Lan Kwai Fong is a party, then SoHo is a bubbly conversation with dinner included. The little restaurants, and most of them are little, that cling to the hill alongside the escalator were not purpose built. Many are converted houses and are often little works of art. One might be hushed and velvet draped, another might be bright with banter, another might be alive with the sounds of a flamenco guitarist. And there are also wine bars around, for civilised and contemplative imbibing.

This neighbourhood is old, for Hong Kong. Many back alleyways beckon with hints of red lights in their depths. There must be secrets there. And echoes of the wickedness of the old port city. Clusters of old apartment buildings are draped with overflowing windowboxes. Altars are built into cornerstones, and from them incense smoke rises into the heavy tropical air. Each little restaurant in this old Chinese neighbourhood is a portal to another place, another time, another culture. The escalator is your magic carpet to all of them.

Mount the escalator at Queen's Rd where it intersects with Cochrane St. As it rises up from the maelstrom of Central you first pass Ser Wong Fun, the snake soup restaurant (see The Bold Palate chapter). Somehow it seems fitting that next door is the Fetish Fashion Shop (playrooms available). You flow over Lyndhurst Terrace and pass by Restaurant Blue and Cafe Siam. Now you are delivered to a place over the Brezel Haus, Kathmandu and Globe Cafe. From here you must walk a few yards on the elevated walkway to where the escalator starts again. One flight up and you see The Bayou restaurant on your right and you are in the heart of SoHo.

You are moving up Shelley St, between Staunton and Elgin streets. The two latter streets host the greatest number of restaurants. They are Spanish and Argentine, Nepali and French, Russian, Portuguese and, good heavens, Chinese! This is the most ethnically diverse restaurant territory in the whole city. But keep climbing,

Club 1911 bar in SoHo, Hong Kong Island

past M Kitchens with its admirable wine list, past the Orange Tree with its exquisite Dutch cuisine (we know you rarely hear a term like 'exquisite Dutch cuisine' but we think you will agree). When you reach Robinson Rd, dismount. Down the street you will find the Bruce Lee Cafe. Check it out then amble back down the hill, peeking into all the charming little joints you passed on the way up. See which one's aroma most piques your interest.

Wherever you dine in SoHo, try to spend a lazy hour in the bar of The Bayou. Sit at the very outer edge of the bar, order something tall and long lasting, listen to the music, and watch the unfolding scene of Hong Kong life being lifted up, and walking down. There are young expats laughing as they explore the neighbourhood bars, there's a turbaned Sikh delivering a pizza, there's an ol Chinese woman in traditional dress labouring down the precipicious hill with a burden on her back, and there are local residents gliding up the hill in their suits. So much of Hong Kong life passing before you to the music. It's better than MTV.

At the time of writing SoHo seemed to be giving birth to what people call BoHo (Below Hollywood Rd). This is just to the north between Lyndhurst and Hollywood, currently concentrated mainly on Tun Wo Lane. If people go to Soho to escape Lan Kwai Fong, then some people surely go to BoHo to escape SoHo. While most of Hong Kong lives in noise and loves it, there is always a gang of grouchy malcontents who prize a bit of quiet. When SoHo doesn't give them a sufficiency, they betake themselves to BoHo. And remember that quiet is a relative term.

In BoHo you will find the Spanish restaurant, El Pomposo, on Tun Wo Lane. There are several other establishments on Tun Wo, but find the bar at number 2, called Petticoat Lane. It's the original BoHo establishment. Tucked into the end of the narrow lane, shrouded in shadow and dim light, it gives a deliciously sinister feel. A perfect place to meet a spy before dinner.

Kowloon

There may be no regions in Hong Kong, but there is a great cultural divide. On the map, this divide measures less than a mile, yet in human terms it can be measured in lifetimes. There are people who have lived their whole lives in Hong Kong yet never crossed the harbour. Many other people cross the harbour every day for work or personal business. Perhaps they are going from Kowloon to a wedding on

The star ferry, a 'must-try' mode of transport

the island. Or from the island to the airport. A truck driver might cross the harbour several times every day via one of the trans-harbour tunnels, but if he resides in Kowloon then that is where he lives. A woman might work in an office in Kowloon and take the ferry there every day. But if her flat is on the island then so are her family, friends, and social life. It is astonishing to consider, but seven minutes on a boat separates two populations as surely as seven hours in an aeroplane. Not only is this true of native and expat populations, but even of many if not most tourists. They tend to stay where their hotel is. They take the obligatory ride on the ferry, but then scurry 'home' to 'their' side of the harbour.

So what is the difference? Put simply, Kowloon is more Chinese. The island is the original Hong Kong, the first and central foreign community. This is where you will find the greatest concentration of expats and more westernised Chinese. English, both spoken and signage are more common here. In Kowloon you are only 1km closer to China proper but you are to her bosom culturally and gastronomically. Up the Kowloon peninsula through Tsim Sha Tsui, through Yau Ma Tei and through Mong Kok the neon restaurants positively clog the landscape. No one will have to convince you that the Chinese people live to eat.

Don't look for concept restaurants here. You'll find a few British pubs, the odd steak house and some franchise restaurants. On Knutsford Terrace there's a small cluster of Italian and Spanish restaurants. But all of these are all but lost in a sea of neon restaurants, roasteries, congee and noodle shops, working-class restaurants, and pastry shops. In short, the whole of Chinese gastronomy. A good exercise is to simply place yourself in the middle of it all, on Carnarvon Rd, then walk in any direction. You'll find that you can eat your way through all of China, and never leave Kowloon.

The neon signs of Mong Kok, Kowloon

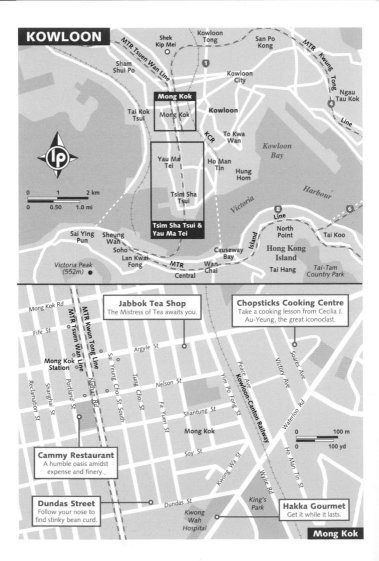

KOWLOON

MTR Tsuen Wan Line
Shek Kip Mei
Kowloon Tong
San Po Kong
MTR Kwung Tong
Sham Shui Po
Kowloon City
Ngau Tau Kok
Line
Tai Kok Tsui
Mong Kok
Kowloon
To Kwa Wan
Kowloon Bay
KCR
Yau Ma Tei
Ho Man Tin
Hung Hom
Harbour
Tsim Sha Tsui
Victoria
8 Line
6
Tsim Sha Tsui & Yau Ma Tei
Sai Ying Pun
Sheung Wan
North Point
Tai Koo
Soho
Lan Kwai Fong
MTR
Causeway Bay
Island
Hong Kong Island
Victoria Peak (552m)
Wan Chai
Tai Hang
Tai-Tam Country Park
Central

0   1   2 km
0   0.50   1.0 mi

Jabbok Tea Shop
The Mistress of Tea awaits you.

Chopsticks Cooking Centre
Take a cooking lesson from Cecilia J. Au-Yeung, the great iconoclast.

Mong Kok Rd
MTR Kwun Tong Line
Fife St
MTR Tsuen Wan Line
Argyle St
Peace Ave
Soares Ave
Victory Ave
Mong Kok Station
Sai Yeung Choi St South
Tung Choi St
Nelson St
Yim Po Fong St
Kowloon-Canton Railway
Waterloo Rd
Reclamation St
Shanghai St
Portland St
Nathan Rd
Fa Yuen St
Shantung St
Mong Kok
Soy St
Kwong Wa St
Wylie Rd
Ho Man Tin St

0   100 m
0   100 yd

Cammy Restaurant
A humble oasis amidst expense and finery.

Dundas Street
Follow your nose to find stinky bean curd.

Dundas St
Kwong Wah Hospital
King's Park

Hakka Gourmet
Get it while it lasts.

Mong Kok

WHERE TO EAT & DRINK

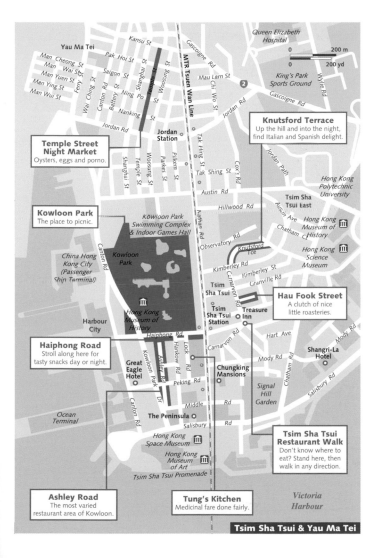

Queen Elizabeth Hospital

0 ———— 200 m
0 ———— 200 yd

King's Park Sports Ground

Yau Ma Tei

Kansu St
Pak Hoi St
Man Cheong St
Man Wai St
Saigon St
Man Yuen St
Man Ying St
Ning Po St
Man Wui St
Nanking St
Jordan Rd

Wai Ching Rd
Canton Rd
Battery St
Ferry St
Shanghai St
Temple St
Woosung St
Parkes St

Gascoigne Rd

MTR Tsuen Wan Line

Mau Larn St
Chi Wo St
Jordan Rd

Wylie Rd
Gascoigne Rd

Knutsford Terrace
Up the hill and into the night,
find Italian and Spanish delight.

**Temple Street
Night Market**
Oysters, eggs and porno.

Jordan
Station

Tak Hing St
Pilkem St
Tak Shing St
Cox's St
Austin Rd
Hillwood Rd

Jordan Path

Hong Kong
Polytechnic
University

Tsim Sha
Tsui East

Austin Ave
Chatham Rd

Hong Kong
Museum
of History

Kowloon Park
The place to picnic.

Kowloon Park
Swimming Complex
& Indoor Games Hall

Nathan Rd

Observatory Rd
Knutsford
Tce

Hong Kong
Science
Museum

China Hong
Kong City
(Passenger
Ship Terminal)

Kowloon
Park

Canton Rd

Kimberley Rd
Kimberley St
Granville Rd

Carnarvon Rd

Tsim
Sha Tsui

Hong Kong
Museum
of History

Tsim
Sha Tsui
Station

Treasure
Inn

Hau Fook Street
A clutch of nice
little roasteries.

Harbour
City

Haiphong Rd

Hart Ave

Mody Rd

Haiphong Road
Stroll along here for
tasty snacks day or night.

Kowloon Park Dr

Lock Rd
Hankow Rd
Ashley Rd
Peking Rd

Carnarvon Rd

Mody Rd
Chatham Rd

Shangri-La
Hotel

Salisbury Rd

Great
Eagle
Hotel

**Chungking
Mansions**

Signal
Hill
Garden

Ocean
Terminal

Canton Rd

Middle Rd

The Peninsula

Hong Kong
Space Museum

Salisbury Rd

**Tsim Sha Tsui
Restaurant Walk**
Don't know where to
eat? Stand here, then
walk in any direction.

Hong Kong
Museum
of Art

Tsim Sha Tsui Promenade

Victoria
Harbour

Ashley Road
The most varied
restaurant area of Kowloon.

Tung's Kitchen
Medicinal fare done fairly.

Tsim Sha Tsui & Yau Ma Tei

FAT CHANCE? – Faces of Gastronomy

They used to call him Chicken Wing Chan, but that was long ago, when he operated a small hawker stand by the ferry pier, selling – what else? – chicken to commuters.

Tiring of the routine one day, Chicken Wing Chan and his wife decided to get serious about their food, make a respectable living, stop dodging government hygiene inspectors, and open a restaurant.

And thus was born – wait a minute – and thus was born – what? The couple opened a restaurant, Chicken Wing Chan positioned himself behind his enormous wok. He started cooking, but he and his wife forgot one thing. They never named their restaurant, and today it doesn't appear they ever will. After 17 years, they really don't need a name. It is simply known by Chan's nickname, and that has changed.

When he opened his eatery on Hong Kong's tiny outlying island of Peng Chau, he and his wife abandoned their chicken wings, expanding into a variety of offerings. Since the old nickname no longer applied, the locals seized the initiative and affectionately selected a new one.

Reflecting that Chan's short stature was underscored by his equally wide stature, local wags dubbed him Fat Chan, a moniker that remains to this day. While his years behind a blazing wok in a tiny and increasingly popular kitchen have reduced much of Fat's girth, it has done nothing to relieve his height.

Fat Chan's opens every evening at 6pm in what is loosely referred to as the town square. On an island as unassuming, tiny, quiet and devoted to village life as Peng Chau, the town square is something of an anomaly.

First, however, you have to get to Peng Chau, and that is easy. Go to the Star Ferry Pier on the Hong Kong Island side. Jutting into Victoria Harbour like a finger pointing across to Kowloon, is spit of land, at the end of which are the outlying islands ferry piers. A five-minute walk will deliver you to Pier 7. The Peng Chau boats leave every 45 minutes, and offer a delightful half-hour ride.

Gently meandering streets wind through the village, past temples, shops and a raucous commercial street. The only vehicles on the small island are bicycles, although Mr Lee at the top of the hill does operate two motor carts to transport building materials.

The town square is just beyond the eastern end of the village. The only other business is a derelict drink shop, operated by chubby Mrs Lu and her half-blind husband with the wool hat. Her shelves offer a selection of vintage and indiscriminate sauce bottles caked with dust.

An abandoned movie theatre that has not operated in more than a decade towers over Fat Chan's, and the restaurant itself is no more than a ground-floor apartment with a roll-up steel door as a facade.

Dining is strictly al fresco, which is to say that the interior fits only three small tables and a refrigerator filled with beer. You will seek in vain for napkins on the sauce and utensil wagon. It's the rolls of toilet paper in the pink plastic holders you want. Oh, and don't bother looking for utensils: There are none. It's chopsticks or your own knife and fork. Fat does supply a spoon.

Fat has never had a menu, as such, although the hastily scribbled chalkboards announce his fresh purchases from the local market that afternoon. He's been feeding Peng Chau so long now that everyone knows the main items.

Sit outside at one of the larger tables, order a bottle of beer, and prepare for a memorable meal.

You will be served either by Fat's wife, dubbed simply Mrs Fat, or their delightful daughter, Adie. Occasionally, Fat's son will appear. Adie's English is excellent and, in exchange for your patience and good humour, will help you select the evening's top dishes. Three items, however, come highly regarded as infallible choices: the **cang jap gei** (orange chicken), the **ju pai gued** (spareribs) and the **wu tao yu** (river fish).

The first dish was created by Fat himself. It is found nowhere else in the world. Starting with chicken fillets, Fat carefully opens each, layering in a thinly sliced wedge of ham. As the fillets turn brown in the wok, Mrs Fat concocts a thick tangy sauce from fresh oranges and orange juice.

A platter is rimmed with orange slices, the browned chicken piled in the middle and the sauce generously poured over the top. A sprig of parsley and splinters of red pepper add an exhilarating dash of colour.

The pork ribs are chopped into bite-size pieces, flash fried with impeccable timing and served on a steaming tray. They are fresh, hot, firm, irresistibly tasty and, if you like a spark on your tongue, set off perfectly by a dash of chilli sauce. The challenge is to see if you can eat them only with chopsticks. Failing that, your fingers will have to suffice. By the way, simply drop the bones onto the ground beneath your table. It is standard practice.

The fish is Fat's masterpiece. The freshly caught animal is split and served whole, smothered in a rich salty brew of soy sauce, spring onions and a variety of judiciously combined spices. Again cooked with impeccable timing, the soft white flesh virtually melts in the mouth. Spoon the sauce into your rice. Watch for bones.

The fish-eating challenge is classically Chinese: Out of respect for the traditions of this little island fishing community, you are not allowed to turn over your fish to get at the bottom half after you have finished the top half. It is simply bad luck, and if you must flip the fish, do it quickly and quietly before anyone notices.

And then, as you drain the last of your beer, comes the bill, scribbled by Mrs Fat. If you can get a receipt, you will have accomplished something few have ever managed.

Tad Stoner is an American journalist and long-time resident of Hong Kong

Places to Drink
Alcoholic Drinks

For most of its history Hong Kong was infamous as the most bibulous port of call in the Far East. In the early days there seemed little else in the way of entertainment, so people drank themselves stupid. For a time rum was cheaper than tea. In later days, as it teemed with soldiers and sailors, the Fragrant Harbour was awash in floods of beer and rivers of gin and there were innumerable places, high class, low class and no class, in which to enjoy them, in moderation or otherwise. Especially otherwise. Oh, so very otherwise. But that was in other days. And as to Suzie Wong and her sisters? Only the faintest echo of their voices can now be heard.

These are new days in modern China. It's a much more sober and civilian society. The only soldiers in evidence are a token handful of lads from the mainland's PLA, who are confined to their barracks. Not by statute, but by economics. The poor chaps are paid a mainlander's wage, which is so little that they haven't got the price of a beer in the new Hong Kong. And you won't either if you're not careful! Pub crawling in this city can be ruinously expensive. But read closely of this book and you'll be able to slake your thirst and avoid destitution.

Virtually all bars in the city observe the ancient and honourable custom of Happy Hour. It commonly runs anywhere from about 4pm to about 9pm. In a few places in Wan Chai it's over by 7pm. At Ned Kelly's in Kowloon it starts at 11am (Go Ned!), but in general, sometime in the late afternoon the prices of drinks are reduced by as much as half. A painful little twist to this is the practice in far too many bars of offering not exactly half price, but 'two for one', and that might apply only to beer. And your companion has to have two too. No sharing. So if all you want is a quick pint on the way to elsewhere, this does you no good at all. And they didn't mention it was two for one until you ordered. The rats!

Some of the more reputable watering holes post their Happy Hour and Unhappy Hour prices side by side near the bar. Others might print it out as a flyer for you to take with you. Still others, and these are to be praised, hang large and detailed price lists outside so that you can make your financial decisions before you even enter their domain.

In looking for affordable elbow bending, remember that the farther you get from Central the lower the rents and, generally, the lower the price of a drink. What's the farthest you can get from Central? The outlying islands. And that is exactly where many people go for a weekend afternoon in some breezy seaside pub with it's whole front open to the view of the ocean. After a week of Hong Kong's intensity, noise, crowding and high cost, a few pints on a lazy island is bliss. Prices are about half (all the time), and you don't have to buy two. The cost of ferry passage is negligible, it's a fairly short, pleasant and relaxing ride, and you can begin your festivities while in transit. Yes, you can drink on the boat! All the ferry landings have kiosks and vending machines that will sell you your favourite beer in bottle or can (at a good price). You can have one while you wait for the ferry. You can have another while you're on the ferry in it's air-conditioned comfort. And since all the boats have toilets, go ahead and have another. Some of them have open decks at the stern to accommodate smokers. Stand upwind from them and enjoy the breeze, the sea, the passing scene and a nice cold beer.

Also far from central are Stanley, on the south coast of Hong Kong Island, and Sai Kung in the New Territories. Here you'll find remnants of the bygone British pub culture of Hong Kong. Stanley was formerly an important army post and the pubs were as integral to life there as they would be in an English village. It's now rather touristy, popular with both foreigners and local day trippers, but it's a beautiful ride over the hill. In Sai Kung it would seem that nobody has heard about the handover in 1997. There is a substantial expat community here and British-style pubs replete with pub grub are plentiful. So plentiful in fact that at the time of writing they were engaged in a price war! Regulars could hardly keep up (keep down?) with the falling prices. Some were wondering if they should wait an hour before drinking on the theory that it would be even cheaper then.

There is one other type of venue in which to drink (relatively) cheaply. This is not in any other guidebook so don't spread it around. And we surely don't want the owners of these places to catch on and raise prices. Chinese restaurants. Yes. The drinks are cheaper than in any bar. You don't even have to buy food. And if it's outdoors on a hot day, they'll bring you your beer in an ice bucket, so you can linger over it. Cheers!

Bar La Dolce Vita, Hong Kong Island

The Peninsula Hotel

Felix Restaurant in The Peninsula Hotel

Okay, so let's go up market now. If you're really in the mood to spend some cash, and you want skilfully mixed cocktails rather than noggins of gin and pints of beer, you'll find some of the best wet spots in some of the major hotels. One of the grandest, most audacious, the Hong King Kongiest in our opinion, is the Felix bar on top of The Peninsula hotel. The decor is wildly ultra-modern, the service is Johnnie-on-the-spot, the mixologist a master. But it is the majestic view, gentlemen (sorry ladies), the view. Oh yes, the view from the dance floor is stunning. From the tables in the adjacent restaurant it is panoramic. From a stool at the long zinc bar you could gaze at it for hours. But from the vantage point we have in mind you can only take it in for, what in the Middle Ages was known as, 'a pissing while'. That is, the time it takes to pass water. For this whiz of a view is from the urinals. The entire north wall of the men's room is glass, and the urinals are only waist high. Boys, we kid you not, this is the most inspiring pee you'll ever take. You'll feel like the great Rain God himself. You'll wish for a third kidney. After such an experience many lads have been known to rush from the men's room straight to the bar and order double shots and pints of lager in order to re-charge their bladders and have another go. And some guys find enjoyment in more than just the view and aesthetics.

Gents only   *Ladies please*

For though it's high enough that people on the ground look like ants, the wagging wags consider it the most glorious act of exhibitionism in the world. Only flashing the earth from the surface of the moon could top it.

Now for the ladies. You have not been entirely left out. The powder room is on the opposite side, with an equally generous view, from the wash basins. We are told that the architect considered situating the toilets so that they faced the window, but other voices counselled otherwise. So you must take care of your business without scenic gratification and behind closed doors. Some ladies were peeved at this inequity. And so a wise and generous policy has been promulgated. When there are no men in the men's room, the attendant will admit any lady who wishes and allow her to 'stand to' as a man. For a pissing while.

Felix in The Peninsula Hotel

JOHNNIE CHUNG – Faces of Gastronomy

Johnnie Chung is the chief bartender at The Peninsula. At the time of writing he has been employed for 59 years. He is the second generation of his family to work for The Pen; before him his father was Captain of The Lobby. Johnnie started as a messenger carrier, but a few years later he wangled a job in what was then the Lobby Bar. These days he works the early shift, mixing drinks for the restaurants and for room service from 7am to 4pm. Any drink you have between those hours will have been made by Johnnie. He is certainly the most beloved, and probably the most famous, barman in Hong Kong. And it was he who made and served the first screwdriver in what was then the crown colony.

"It was 1958. I was working the afternoon shift here in what was then called The Piano Bar. A man came in. I remember he was well dressed and handsome. The ladies would have sighed for him, had there been any here that day. But it was only him and me. He sat down, right here where you're sitting. 'Please give me a screwdriver', he said. He was very polite. I didn't understand why he would make such a request, but I tried to oblige him and called the house engineering department to ask them to bring the gentleman a screwdriver. He said, 'no. It's a drink'."

Johnnie still smiles warmly as he tells the story of how the handsome gentleman taught him how to make a screwdriver. Johnnie made several for him over the next few weeks. And the drink caught on with locals. The man's name was Clark Gable. He was in Hong Kong shooting a movie and was staying at The Pen. "I confess I didn't know who he was at the time", Johnnie says, "but since then I must have seen all of his movies. And I have been making an average of two screwdrivers a day since 1958. Which is over 30,000 screwdrivers". And we think he's got it right by now.

Service with a smile, Johnny Chung

As previously stated, hotel cocktail lounges are among the best places to go for serious mixology. The bartenders are well trained, exacting, efficient and friendly. You will rarely get from them the glass of uncaring ignorance that you might be served in the lesser bars. There is little worse than a badly rendered Rusty Nail, or a sloppily measured Margarita. Shots poured short are a sin. And a Rob with too much Roy is a disappointment. There are times when the only remedy for city stresses is in deftly blended gin and vermouth. A properly made martini can do more for care than a whole troupe of Jungian therapists. But the properly made martini is a rare thing, for though it is a simple thing it is unforgiving of mistakes or negligence. Wherever we find one we feel justified in letting you know. The muses of mixology at the Bostonian Bar & Restaurant in the Great Eagle Hotel will shake your martini till it hurts. Those in the lobby bar are equally skilled, and there you will sip to the music of a grand piano played every afternoon. And at the main bar in the Holiday Inn you can choose from 18, count 'em: 18, martini recipes! It took us hours, er, uh, days, to try them all.

As for independent bars, when you're feeling flush and there's a hole burning in your pocket, betake your thirsty self to Wan Chai. This is where you'll find the meat market bars. And here is where many young financiers and entrepreneurs come after a hard day of making piles of money. You'll find the prices as high as the energy and the music volume. And be warned, gentlemen, if there is so much as a scintilla of erotica in evidence at a given establish-

Temple Street night market, Kowloon

ment the prices can triple. They aren't trying to hook soldiers and sailors these days; they're after big fish. And that's what you look like. In Lan Kwai Fong there is a more genteel atmosphere than in raucous Wan Chai. It's still expensive tippling, but no rip-offs or scams, wet T-shirt contests or frat boy highjinks.

SoHo is laid back, and has only a few bars. But here is where you can find a couple of wine bars. Just stand at the corner of Staunton and Shelley and look around. In Kowloon the bar scene has almost disappeared. Most of what remains is in Mong Kok. And that's where to go for the territory's last whiffs of scandal and debauchery. Bring lots of money.

Non-Alcoholic Drinks

Not in the mood for alcohol? Need a soft drink or a cuppa? A recent and refreshing trend is the streetside juice bar. You'll see them dotting the landscape wherever pedestrian traffic is heavy enough to support them. In addition to fruit juices they offer vegetable juices as well. Indeed their most popular offering is freshly squeezed carrot juice. You can't miss these places. Just keep your eyes open for shiny stainless steel tubs of great, fat, juicy carrots.

Herbal tea stands are similarly numerous and similarly situated. You can spot them easily by the tall brass urns in which they brew their several herbal infusions. You can have it in china bowls if you want to linger locally and return the vessel. And if you want it to take away they usually have several plastic cups of the stuff drawn and waiting for you, lined up on the counter, so quickly does the product move. Not exactly fast food, but fast drink.

Number One Herbal Tea Shop, Hong Kong Island

Working hard in the Delifrance, a cafe-style fast food joint on Hong Kong Island

Coffee has been discovered in recent years. And that is a blessing for addicts and/or aficionados because Hong Kong was indifferent to the bean scene for a long time. Even the better restaurants and hotels poured poor stuff, and the norm was instant, stirred into a cup of tepid water and softened with non-dairy creamer. But these are new days. The Pacific Coffee Company has outlets here, as does Starbucks. The Cable Car Cafe's two branches maintain that recognizable San Francisco atmosphere and the smell of good coffee. And speciality shops, even some groceries, sell beans from around the world. Nowadays most restaurants pour a brew that you would not spit out in disgust.

The very first gourmet coffee concern in Hong Kong was Cafe Central in the lobby of Alexandra House on Chater Rd, Central. The beans are imported from that famous coffee centre, Seattle! It serves about 700 cups per day, and if you like it cold you can have a granita latte. Perhaps one of the best places in Hong Kong to enjoy your cup o' java is on the Star Ferry. Buy it to go at any of the landings just as you board. Be sure to ride the upper deck. Ensconce yourself near the railing. Lift the lid on your cup. Breath in the aroma, and drink in the view. It's the best seven coffee minutes you'll ever know.

Many people seem to think that Hong Kong is thick with 'tea houses'. They're not exactly sure what a tea house looks like or what goes on in it other than the brewing of tea. Perhaps intrigue or skulduggery. Maybe games of Chinese checkers. But we are often asked about these oft imagined places. The closest thing you'll find is a yum cha house, or a dai pai dong. Perhaps they existed in times gone by, but now people are busy busy busy. So one of the most popular tea venues is a Taiwanese chain called Saint's Alp Teahouse. These are all over the place, especially in Kowloon (find one of them at 94 Argyle St, Mong Kok) serving all kinds of frothy and sweet tea beverages, including **yuen yen** (a blend of coffee and tea). It also offers pastries and other snacks. Sit down in one and you are given a laminated sheet bearing photos of all the selections, and a sheet of paper with the menu printed on it. Use a pen or pencil to tick off what you want and hand it to the waiter.

High tea in the library, Island Shangri-La, Hong Kong Island

The tea houses of yore are gone, but the old British custom of serving high tea in the afternoon lives on. Many hotels offer this, and the most famous is in the lobby of the venerable Peninsula. This is the echo of empire. English-style teas are served to you accompanied by scones and finger sandwiches, cakes and candies, and above you in the alcove a string quartet plays Mozart. And almost all the patrons are local Chinese. By contrast, the Island Shangri-La's Library offers Asian teas and snacks. And the patrons are expats and western tourists! In either case, go early, or you will be standing in line waiting for seats.

understanding
the menu

If you remain in hotel and concept restaurants you will never know confusion in Hong Kong. Ah, but what is travel, and life for that matter, without a good dose of confusion? Where's the satisfaction in certainty? None, by Jingo! So sally forth into prandial pandemonium! But let's give you some advice on how to navigate the often murky menu milieu of the SAR of the PRC.

Chinese Proverb

Good fortune of the mouth is no mean thing.

In hotel and concept restaurants, the menu has been composed and designed with you, the foreigner, specifically the Anglophone, in mind. The menu might be big, thick, ponderous and bound in velvet and printed in florid script or embossed with gold letters; it might be a single sheet of paper spewed out by an ink-jet printer and changed daily; it might be hand lettered, photocopied and gravy stained. But it will be in English, as well as Chinese, and it will be comprehensible, familiar and user friendly.

Beyond that, the first thing to bear in mind is that since the departure of the British there has been a great reduction in the use of the English language – written, spoken and menued. When 30,000 of Her Majesty's troops and untold transient American sailors stalked the steamy streets in search of treats, the Queen's English was *de rigueur*. Now it's mainly Cantonese and, increasingly, Mandarin. You'll pass by restaurants with their menus boldly displayed in the windows, or sitting primly on a lectern outside the door, open for your perusal. And if you can say "perusal" in Chinese, you'll probably be able to read that menu. But if you can't, read on (see also the Eat Your Words section at the back of this book).

Restaurants displaying the symbol of the Hong Kong Tourist Association will always (well, okay, not always, but mostly) have at least one English speaker on duty when you arrive with rumbling tummy and no Chinese. That's the easy way out. And sometimes we need the easy way out. At bolder times, look for outward signs: you'll often see a painting, or even a neon representation, of the eatery's speciality: crab, goose, duck etc (the etc is especially good). Most restaurants will have their name rendered in English and that will often make things clear: Foo Lum Roasted Goose Restaurant, Super Star Seafood Restaurant, La Pampa Argentinean Steakhouse. You get the idea.

Roasteries proudly display their wares in the front windows, so there's no mistaking what's for dinner. In noodle shops you'll see steam-billowing cauldrons, piles of noodles, and bowls of meat, fish, fowl and other goodies to add life to the soupy blandness. Bundles of **yauh ja gwai** (fried baguettes) are the giveaway that you're at a **juk** (congee; rice porridge) seller's concern. And when you are lucky to see a true **dai pai dong** (food stall) there's no need for language of any kind. His wares are displayed and all you need to do is point. Indeed, in any of the above places you can depend on the digital approach. The cooks and waiters are used to it, ready for it, even expect it. So point to what looks good on display. Or if you see a fellow diner tucking into something tasty, point to that. The pointee will not be peeved.

View of Hong Kong Island from the Regent Hotel, Kowloon

MENU

Many neon restaurants photograph their most popular dishes and post the pictures on or near the door or in the front windows. If you see something you like, enter, beckon the waiter outside, point, then take a seat and wait to be served. Never worry that language will bar you from gustatory fulfilment in Hong Kong. Restaurateurs are in business for profit, and they will not let it be lost to a lack in language. A path to understanding will always be found.

In many restaurants you'll see a notice for the house's set lunch. It's usually about a four-course affair: soup, a meat dish, a vegetable dish and rice, or it might be a rice plate (a stir-fried dish or a few smaller servings on a bed of rice). All you have to do is sit down and say, "set lunch". There are certain English words and phrases that have crept into the Hong Kong lexicon and you will hear them everywhere, though the speakers might not even be aware that they are indeed English. The most common are: hello, Mummy, Daddy, set lunch, okay and bye-bye. So who needs Cantonese? A set lunch is one of the better culinary deals to be had in Hong Kong.

The buffet board of a Lan Kwai Fong Restaurant, Hong Kong Island

So now let's say that you have boldly swaggered into some place with a name like Delicious Sea Cucumber Pork Chop-Hot Pot House, or perhaps Tasty Offal Shop, and you are handed a menu printed in English. Note that it is probably smaller than the Chinese-language menu. This is because it has been greatly reduced to a few standard items thought to be popular among outer barbarians. The house assumes that you, the **gwailo** (foreigner), do not like many of the things that the Chinese like. This is no doubt true of many a gwailo. But not of you! If your waiter speaks English, wave this book at him and say that you want to know the house specialities (sometimes called chef's or daily recommendation). Make it clear that you have not come for eviscerated victuals, that you demand the genuine article, and will have none of his chop suey or fried rice. This is especially important in those restaurants that specialise in spicier fare, such as Sichuan cuisine. The staff will assume (they do so much assuming) that you do not like a fire in your mouth, that chillies frighten you and bold flavours upset your nerves. They assume (there they go again) that you are a gastronomic lightweight. Accept no substitutes! If you cannot communicate this linguistically, give them the finger: point. Point to something at a nearby table and order it.

Now, let's say that you are in a fine Cantonese eatery of high repute and bilingual staff. Your menu is in both Chinese and English, and it is huge, a tome, a compendium of Chinese culinaria! This is normal, and self-respecting restaurants take pride in it. Don't be alarmed or intimidated. Many of the items will not be available. They are dependent on season, market availability and cost, even time of day or skills of the chefs on duty. Your waiter will know.

Most Chinese menus follow the same structure. The pricier items lead, and it's here that you'll find the shark's fin dishes, the bird's nest soup, and the rare and expensive mushrooms. You will also find the best seafood, which will be swimming in the tank at the front of the restaurant. If you order fresh fish or shellfish you will be asked to walk over to the tank and make your selection. The waiter can give you a reasonable estimate of its weight before the kitchen puts it on the scales. Usually fowl follows the expensive eats on the mega menu: you'll find chicken a Cantonese staple, goose a Chui Chow (Shantou) speciality, and duck common everywhere. Roasted meats come next, the most common being pork. Beef dishes often follow. In northern-style restaurants you may see venison in the winter. Lamb is rare. Fried dishes should appear about now, then the usual soup suspects, which for the most part are very light with clear broth, as the soup was traditionally the beverage content of a meal. Then look for vegetable dishes (and for you vegetarians, remember that they are most likely prepared with chicken stock and might even include pork), followed by rice

and noodles. Desserts end the menu, and this is always the shortest section. Sometimes it might be nothing but fresh fruit or some not-too-sweet pastry. Often it will include sweet soups such as green bean with jelly, or **hasma** (see The Bold Palate chapter).

So now you've read the menu and made sense of it. What to order, and in what order? If you are dining alone (for which the gregarious Chinese people will pity you), consider a simple meal of noodles or juk or some other rice dish with maybe a soup, rather than, say, meat with two vegetable dishes, rice and dessert. Or you might order just a vegetable dish with a small bowl of rice. Servings are huge as they are designed for family dinners with four to a family. The general rule is to order one dish per person plus one more for the table. If you are alone and order a four-course dinner you will be wasting an awful lot of food unless you have some place to take your leftovers.

So let's say you are in a party of three or four. First, ask your waiter about the seasonal or daily specials. Armed with this intelligence, strive for balance and harmony in accordance with the Chinese way of living and dining. Try to incorporate all the five flavours of sweet, sour, bitter, salt and hot. Balance your textures: get something dry and get something in a sauce, such as roast pork and stir fried what-have-you; something deep fried like crab and something steamed like fish. Have something cold and something hot. Contrast your colours. Bright pink shrimp look lovely alongside verdant greens. Be sure to have soup or you'll have no proper Chinese repast. And feel free to rely on your waiter for advice. Restaurant staff appreciate the serious eater, the interested tourist, the demanding gourmand. Furthermore, the waiter knows the temperament and skill levels of the chefs on duty. Steamed fish, for example, takes a keen eye, a steady hand and close concentration. If the man at the fire is a great artiste but lacks discipline, you might take the waiter's advice and order the fried fish instead.

You can specify whether you want the various dishes to be served all together, one at a time in prescribed sequence, or as they are ready. If you opt for a prescribed sequence, which would be the norm at a banquet, the practice is to start with the lighter dishes (dumplings, cold dishes), then main dishes and soup, followed by rice or noodles, then dessert. We prefer the third (and most traditional) approach, though we always ask for plain rice to be served up-front so that we have it available with all courses (we never ask for fried rice, in spite of the fact that restaurants catering to foreigners seem always to provide it). And if you find that you and your party of hungry travellers have not ordered enough, just call for more. It's a common thing. Soups, roasts and barbecues will be ready immediately, stir fries take little time, and you'll have to wait for deep-fried or steamed dishes.

Braised Ching Yi fillets with green asparagus, black truffles and poached yabbies in a crustacean butter from Restaurant Pétrus, Hong Kong Island

A couple of caveats. Translations can be a bit confusing: 'fried' generally refers to stir fried, while 'pan fried' can mean grilled or sauteed. 'Soyed' means red cooked (see East China in the Culture of Hong Kong Cuisine chapter). And if you are in a Chinese but non-Cantonese restaurant a few differences in the structure of a meal prevail. For example, in a Beijing-style restaurant you need to remember that Peking duck by itself constitutes three courses. If you're eating at a northern-style or Mongolian-style restaurant, hotpot is the entire meal, less drinks and dessert (see North China in the Culture of Hong Kong Cuisine chapter). Same with the Hakka-style **poon choy** dinner (see the boxed text Hakka in the Culture of Hong Kong Cuisine chapter). And if you are dining Sichuan style you'll want most of your dishes to be rather spicy in order to make it authentic.

What to drink with your Chinese meal? Anything. Anything at all. As mentioned earlier, soup was traditionally the beverage of choice. Nowadays it is common to see people drinking tea, usually jasmine or green, with their meal. It cuts through fats and aids digestion. Beer is popular, and you will sometimes see both men and women drinking it at dinner. Curiously, younger women rarely imbibe. It seems to be the prerogative of those who have given birth. These days designer waters, such as Evian and local variants, are finding many fans. We see kids taking fruit juice with their meal, and teenagers enjoying fleecies (see the Drinks chapter). We also see people who are having noodle soup or juk taking no liquid at all. And then there is that sparkling universal constant: a cold Coca-Cola. Can't get away from it.

Most restaurants levy a 10% service charge. Tipping, as we think of it, is not customary. That is, tips are not expected to account for a significant part of serving staff's income. Still, the generous gesture is expected. Most people simply round the bill up to some comfortably even number. This generally results in a tip of 3-5%.

macau

Macau is a culinary retreat, a place that Hong Kongers visit for unique food, substantially lower prices, and an ambience that is therapeutic after the intensity of Hong Kong. And the food to make a pilgrimage here for, mainly, is Macanese. You can also find Portuguese. Though you can find that in Hong Kong as well, it's much better in Macau.

Superficially, Macau is very much like Hong Kong. A modern-looking city with a largely Cantonese population who were long under a foreign administration (Portugal since the 16th century), and now have a unique approach to business. But in Macau, the dollar is not the only driving force; it is not joined at the hip to profit. It's prosperous enough, but many Macau people cannot see what good money is if you have no time to spend it. This may sound a very un-Chinese attitude, but Macau was designed, built and then run by the Portuguese for five, count 'em, five centuries. They brought with them sound Mediterranean concepts such as really knowing how to live. And they always managed to get along better with Chinese governments (even the communists) than did the Johnny-come-lately Brits. This probably made it easier for Chinese people to adopt Portuguese ways. And vice versa. In a nutshell, the difference between Macau and Hong Kong is wine culture versus beer culture. Sensual, soft and slightly sinful versus bubbly, brawly and bawdy.

> To lie on this rock
> Is to lie on the back of a tiger,
> Listening to the waves below
> As they create a dragon's howl.
> And always close by,
> A bottle of wine
> And temple bells
>
> *Anonymous Macanese poet*

People

All Macau people are usually lumped together under the term, Macanese. But in Macau not everyone is Macanese, only those who are of both Portuguese and Asian ancestry. They also call themselves **Filhos da Terra** (Sons of the Earth). In addition to the Macanese, there are 100% ethnic-Chinese who have adopted Portuguese culture and even citizenship. Others are Portuguese expatriates who have lived in Macau so long that they have adopted it as their home. Most

St Fraceses Square, Macau

people born in Macau are Chinese, and call themselves **Ou Mun Yan** (Macau people). An estimated 60,000 Macanese live overseas, and fewer than 20,000 now live in central Macau among a total population in the territory of around 450,000. And of that population today the Portuguese number only in the hundreds.

Weighing fish at the Red Market, Macau

MACAU

Food of Macau

What with their language and number decreasing, the Macanese maintain a strong identity through their culinary arts. It is here that Portugal meets China, and introduces it to the rest of the world. This is the cuisine of an empire. Dishes like **tasho** (beef, pork, chicken and sausage stew), **capella** (pork and almonds) and the use of coconut milk as a sauce base are examples of the blending of ingredients and techniques collected during the European age of discovery. A favourite of the Macanese school, prepared by Portuguese cooks on the south coast of China is **Galinha Africana** (African Chicken; see the recipe). But perhaps the most easily recognisable ingredient of the Macanese flavour-blending tradition is **balichao** (fermented shrimp sauce; similar to Malaysian *blachan*). It is both subtle yet assertive, contrasting with rather than competing with the other flavours in a dish.

Galinha Africana (African Chicken)

Ingredients

1	chicken, divided into large pieces
1	medium-sized onion, minced
1	clove garlic, minced
1	bay leaf, crushed
1	chilli pepper, minced
1 cup	dry white wine
1 tsp	paprika
1 cup	coconut milk

Combine all the ingredients except the coconut milk and let stand for one hour. Grill the chicken over coals. While the chicken is grilling, cook the marinade in a saucepan with the coconut milk over medium heat for 10 minutes. Pour the sauce over the chicken and serve.
    Serves 4

The Hac Sa One workers market, Central Macau

Another of the signature dishes of Macau began as a Hong Kong speciality, but Macau stole it away: **pastéis de nata** (egg tartlets). Not that Hong Kong has gone without these little sweeties (Hong Kong produces and consumes them in prodigious number), but the Macau version is far superior; one taste and you will surely agree. And this is all due to the efforts of an Englishman. Not an Englishman who sold Hong Kong out, but an Englishman who set up shop in Macau and mastered the art of making egg tartlets. He is known as Lord Stowe. We don't know but Lord might be his name, it is certainly not his title, for he has none. At least none that Her Majesty would recognise. Unless, perhaps, she tasted his wares.

MACAU

Corner shop on Rua da Felicidade, Macau

MACAU

Pastéis de Nata (Egg Tartlets)

Ingredients
Puff Pastry
250g (½ lb)	all purpose flour
⅔ cup	water
175g (6oz)	margarine

Make the dough by mixing the flour and water. Let it rest for 10 minutes, then with a rolling pin roll it out to a thickness of 1½cm (½ inch). Put the margarine at the centre of the dough and wrap the dough around it. Roll the dough out again, fold it over, roll out, and repeat twice more. Roll it into a cylinder, wrap it in plastic and refrigerate for one hour. Roll out the dough and with a cookie cutter render it into rounds small enough to fit into small moulds.

Filling
½ cup	water
½kg (16oz)	sugar
75g (3oz)	plain flour
2 cups	cold milk
8	egg yolks

Mix sugar and water and bring to a simmer. Stir for three minutes or until you have a syrupy consistency. Remove from the heat. Mix the flour with ½ cup of the milk. Scald the remaining milk, then stir it into the first flour and milk mixture. Mix in the sugar syrup and let it cool to room temperature. Stir in the egg yolks and pour the mixture into the moulds. Bake in an oven preheated to 320°F (160°C) for eight minutes. Dust with cinnamon and powdered sugar.
    Makes 20

TASTES OF MACAU

I've never actually seen the Macanese lawyer and novelist Henrique de Senna Fernandes eat, but it was perhaps he who turned me onto Macanese food in the first place. An octogenarian who puffs incessantly on a pipe, he's from an old family and it shows in his charm and appreciation of things civilised. He talks of visits in Hong Kong, to English-style establishments where, he says reverently, "everyone spoke softly". I am a sucker for all this stuff. He can remember his youth, when each of his siblings had a maid for themselves, and how there would be one girl in the kitchen just to beat the eggs for all the complicated and time-consuming dishes (typical recipe: take 20 eggs ...). He tells me about **minchi**, the mincemeat and potato dish, his comfort food, and he also tells me how to distinguish between Macanese and Chinese. "They eat rice differently. The Macanese always put sauce on top."

Then he introduces me to his daughter, Marina, who is in her 40s. She shows me a pair of magnificent cookbooks she found after the death of her grandmother. The first is an 1890 book of Portuguese recipes, but it is the second by which we are most fascinated: it contains old, hand-written Macanese recipes, including dishes that even Marina hadn't heard of. "My grandmother died when I was in my 20s", she explains, "and then I was not interested in cooking. I really regret that." I've heard of another such book, passed on in a will, which lists ingredients not by weight but by price. Talk about a stable society.

Decorative windows on Rua da Felicidade, Macau

Shrimp curry with crab meat, Restaurant Litoral, Rua do Almirante Sergio, Macau

Marina is now fascinated by cooking, but struggles with some of the recipes. There's one for a sauce to put on top of rice, made with **balichao** (fermented shrimp sauce) and papaya flowers. Even balichao is difficult to find because it is made with a special kind of tiny shrimp that used to be found in the delta of the Pearl River, but which have now all but disappeared. And the second problem is that you can't find papaya flowers in Macau anymore. So Marina buys her balichao from one of a couple of old ladies who still make it, and uses other kinds of petals instead.

I have a younger Macanese friend, Isabel, who is in her 30s and equally passionate about Macanese food. I lament with her that there is no cookbook. Correction, there are two or three cookbooks but they're in Portuguese, and even if you can read Portuguese, they assume you know more than you probably do if you are to catch the secret of the dish. Another problem is that there is no single Macanese cuisine; every family would cook its **garilda caran guejo** (crab curry) or its **tasho** (beef, pork, chicken and sausage stew) a little differently. Recipes are passed down orally, and if Marina wasn't interested in her 20s, you'd certainly find few people in their 20s now who are interested in watching their forebears in the kitchen.

To me, Macanese cuisine is a fascinating and delicious cultural study. The key flavourings are ginger, turmeric, balichao and coconut milk, while the cooking techniques borrow heavily from the Portuguese kitchen. That it is the ultimate east-meets-west cuisine, now with 450 years of history, and that it works – unlike much of today's fusion non-sense – is equally fascinating.

Annabel Jackson has been a food & wine author, consultant and resident in Hong Kong for 12 years.

Drinks of Macau

Macau is also home to a wine culture. In Hong Kong the wine awakening took place in the current generation. In Macau it has been in place for 500 years. Even the small shops, as well as the supermarkets and groceries, carry wine. It is almost all Portuguese wine. Undemanding stuff, unchallenging to the palate, but comforting and reassuring. And cheap. **Vinho verde**, an almost spritzy white wine goes well with just about anything. There are almost too many Portuguese reds to keep track of, and we have never had a bad one. So we just buy another, and are satisfied. And there are a whole range of ports from which to choose when you want to sip an evening away.

Collection of Portuguese wines from Restaurant Litoral, Rua do Almirante Sergio, Macau

Tasting the wines of Macau

For a stronger solution, the head-boiling drink **aguardente** is available throughout Macau. Aguardente is like Cognac but without flavour. It is close to methyl alcohol, but it won't cure things. It is simply there to drive drinkers crazy.

Where to Eat & Drink in Macau

Now Macau is also known as place with a touch of sin. Okay, more than a touch. Okay a lot. One of the most famous streets in the city is Rua da Felicidade (Street of Happiness). This is where the prostitutes used to live, in gaily painted brothels. The prostitutes have gone elsewhere (you'll need a different book for that), but their former residences are as gaily painted as ever. And the chief articles of commerce here now are sweets. All up and down this lively lane are makers and sellers of all kinds of Chinese and Macanese sweets. You can smell them from a block away. So many sweets that some people call this Sweet Street. Considering its former commerce, we like to call it Tart Street. But we digress.

Market stalls at the laid-back Red Market, Macau

Macau is a good place for dining on the dark side. All those culinary culpas that have become hard to find in Hong Kong are out in the open in Macau. Here they never had the Brits to huff and puff about the impropriety of eating your neighbour's pets, or a buck's best. Hong Kong used to be a good place to enjoy cornfield worms. But with agriculture constantly shrinking, its by-products are shrinking, too.

Sea bass with vinegarette, Flamingo Restaurant

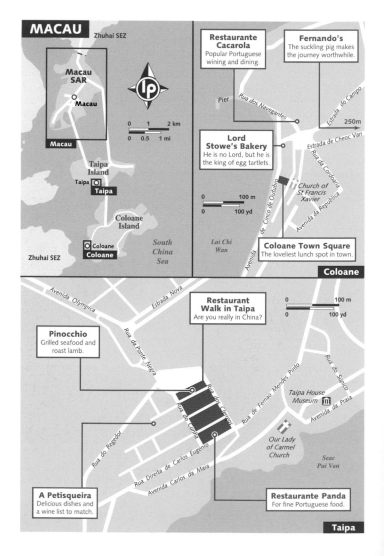

MACAU

Zhuhai SEZ

Macau SAR

Macau

Macau

Taipa Island

Taipa · Taipa

Coloane Island

Coloane · Coloane

Zhuhai SEZ

South China Sea

0   1   2 km
0   0.5   1 mi

Restaurante Cacarola
Popular Portuguese wining and dining.

Fernando's
The suckling pig makes the journey worthwhile.

Pier

Rua dos Navegantes

Estrada do Campo

Estrada de Cheoc Van

250m

Rua da Cordoaria

Lord Stowe's Bakery
He is no Lord, but he is the king of egg tartlets.

Church of St Francis Xavier

Avenida de Cinco de Outubro

Avenida da Republica

0   100 m
0   100 yd

Lai Chi Wan

Coloane Town Square
The loveliest lunch spot in town.

Coloane

Avenida Olympica

Estrada Nova

Restaurant Walk in Taipa
Are you really in China?

0   100 m
0   100 yd

Pinocchio
Grilled seafood and roast lamb.

Rua da Ponte Negra

Rua dos Clerigos

Rua do Cunha

Rua de Fernao Mendes Pinto

Rua do Sulpico

Taipa House Museum

Avenida da Praia

Rua do Regedor

Our Lady of Carmel Church

Seac Pai Van

Rua Direita de Carlos Eugenio

Avenida Carlos da Maia

A Petisqueira
Delicious dishes and a wine list to match.

Restaurante Panda
For fine Portuguese food.

Taipa

MACAU

Restaurante Riquexo
The soul of the Macanese kitchen.

Zhuhai Special
Economic Zone

Sun Yat-Sen
Memorial Park

Estrada Mareginal do Hipodromo

Ilha
Verde

Ave do Conselheiro Borja

Istmo Ferreira do Amaral

Ave de Venceslau de Morais

Sweets on Tart Street
Sugar hits found here and beyond.

Ave do Almirante Lacerda

Mong-Ha
Fortress

R da Ribeira du Patane

Luis de
Camoes
Museum

R de Francisco Xavier Pereira

R dos Lorchas

Camoes
Gardens

St Paul's
Façade

St Michael's
Cemetery

Monte
Fort

Grand
Prix
Track

Reservoir

Guia Hill

Inner
Harbour

R de Francisco Xavier Pereira

R do Campo

Guia
Lighthouse

Hong Kong-
Macau Ferry
Terminal

Ave de Almeida Ribeiro

St Dominic's
Church

R Nova à Guia

Ave da Amizade

St Augustine's
Church

Jetfoil
Pier

R da Praia do Bom Parto

Ave do Doutor Mario Soares

R do Almirante Sergio

St.
Larwence's
Church

Penha
Church

Baia da
Praia Grande

Ave de Sagres

Ponte de Amizade

Club Militar
Feast on the faded empire
at 975 Praia Grande.

Maritime
Museum

Ave da República

Ave Dr Sun Yat Sen

Nam Van
Lakes

Ponte Governador Nobre de Carvalho

Outer
Harbour

0   300 m
0   300 yd

Restaurante Litoral
The best African chicken in Macau.

Macau

MACAU

But things are different in Macau. People go to Macau to do all those things that they cannot do in Hong Kong because it is either illegal or impractical. They can gamble in Macau, and chase after (or be chased by) prostitutes. In Hong Kong what's left of these vices is strictly behind closed doors. In Macau they can eat anything they like. It's forbidden to eat dogs or other pet-like animals in Hong Kong, but not in Macau. In Macau you can eat anything. You can even order a worm pudding in many restaurants. The worms are about 3cm long and about as fat as a strand of spaghetti. They are mixed with eggs, seasoned with salt and pepper, topped with croutons and then baked. It's quite a rich dish, so a small portion is ample. The famous deer penis soup is also available in the same restaurants. The stag's instrument of continuity comes to the kitchen dried and resembling an old stick about 20cm long. As is usual with most non-human mammals there is a thin bone running through its length. The cook rehydrates the member, then slices it into thin rounds (bone and all). It is then cooked in herbal soup that tastes very, shall we say, herbaceous. And the little slices of life? Rather chewy, the bone not quite crunchy, and a rather gamey taste.

Fresh bread from the Cafe Bolo de Arroz Pastelaria, which serves a range of pastries, cheeses, cakes and coffees, just off Largo do Senado, Macau

Fabrica de Massas De Farinna VA Heng noodle-making shop in Macau

The area around Sweet Street is good for restaurants serving this exotic fare. But these dishes are virtually never on English-language menus. They are boldly posted on the walls of the dining rooms, but you'll need to read Chinese to know it. Of course you can always ask the waiter, provided he speaks English. Portuguese fare is fairly good at Club Militar, and one of the best expressions of Macanese cuisine in the city is found in the kitchens of Restaurante Litoral (261 Rua do Almirante Sergio).

MACAU

Chef from Restaurant Fresco Mediterasian Grill with African chicken, Mandarin Oriental Hotel

Outlying Islands

The best place to sample Macanese cuisine is on the outlying islands of Taipa and Coloane. Unlike in Hong Kong you will not take a ferry, for there is a causeway connecting them to the city. In Taipa Village and Coloane Village, if you closed one eye, you could convince yourself that you were in Portugal. Or is it Mozambique? Goa? Hmmm. Cobbled streets, whitewashed walls, Catholic churches, little tavernas. Where in blazes are we? We're in a charming little confluence of cultures. And about to have something good to eat.

If we opt for a Portuguese restaurant we might be served **bacalhau** (dried and salted cod; so integral to Iberian cookery), **caldo verde** (cabbage and potato stew) or **carne de porco à Algarvia** (braised pork with clams; don't knock it). And it will all be served in blessed calm. There are several places to find these dishes, but the most famous is Fernando's on Coloane Island's Hac Sa Beach. You won't need an address. Just tell your taxi driver, or anybody for that matter. Don't come here with credit cards. It's not that you can't use them in Macau, Fernando just doesn't like them. And while we're at it, he doesn't have any sympathy for vegetarians either. He just doesn't understand them. Oh well. If you don't want to eat Fernando's **leitão** (suckling pig), try A Petisqueira in Taipa Village (15 Rua Joao).

MACAU

a hong kong
banquet

So now you've been to Hong Kong, and you want to show what you've learned, share what you've eaten and experienced. You've got your basic Chinese kitchen equipment, you've got chopsticks and chopstick rests, and you've got a taste for the exotic. So now you're ready to throw a damned good party.

Of course virtually nobody in Hong Kong entertains at home. Nobody has the floor space. And it's simply not the custom. On the outlying islands expats might host a barbecue on the roof of their building, but generally entertaining is done in a restaurant. But let's prepare you to do both.

Whether at your spacious home or in a spacious restaurant, the seating arrangements are very important if you want to maintain the real feel of Hong Kong. As host, you will sit nearest the kitchen or service door – the least favoured position. This is where the waiter will lay the mark (meaning a set of serving utensils) and this is where all service will commence, so it will be a rather busy spot. Seating yourself here shows humility and a willingness to sacrifice your comfort for the sake of your honoured guests. Kudos to you!

In a proper Hong Kong fete there will be a seating priority based on seniority. Age is the first factor. If you are entertaining in Hong Kong, take into account the rankings of persons who work in the same company. Juniors go nearest the mark. Nowadays many Hong Kong hosts will seat themselves not at the mark, but near the guest of honour, especially if that guest is a foreigner. And speakers of the foreigner's tongue are seated nearby.

A proper Hong Kong banquet will show at least a bit of CC (conspicuous consumption). You can see to this obligation by serving horribly expensive dishes. But you can also discharge this duty by providing a bottle of cognac or scotch at each table. Make sure it is there before during and after, and replace if necessary. Guests should pour for each other. Same with tea and other beverages.

The most tender morsels, the juiciest cuts and the tastiest titbits are reserved for the guest of honour and are offered with no little aplomb. For example, when a fish is served, be sure that the platter holding the fish is laid on the table in such a way that the fish head points towards the guest of honour. You are honour bound to reserve the fish head for that esteemed person (after all it is the most nutritious part). To show real sophistication, offer the eyes and lips to the senior lady present. People will remark on the nice touch. (If you are ever the guest of honour and find that you cannot, with good grace, accept this honour, you should at least delegate the honour to the person on your left, or without speech turn the platter so that the fish head faces the host (see the recipe Steamed Whole Fish in the Celebrating with Food chapter).

What should you serve for your Fragrant Harbour Feast? In a restaurant, rely on the management to craft the dinner for you (just make sure they stay within budget). At home you need to put some thought into the matter, because you have learned the intricacies and concepts behind Chinese gastronomy, and Hong Kong flair.

The first course in any Hong Kong banquet is noise! Switch on the TV, turn up the stereo, encourage your guests to speak in a loud voice. Or you might decide that the better part of banquet is discretion. We will not speak ill of you if you do not provide the authentic audio portion of this program. And while you're at it you might as well take a few other liberties. You can dispense with the seating arrangements, and with the hot towels, and the fish heads, and the bottles of cognac (on second thoughts you should keep the cognac).

As your guests arrive, seat them in the living room and serve tea or white wine. Perhaps a few melon seeds or sesame crisps. Then bring out a couple of dim sum specialities: **ha gao** (shrimp bonnets) and **ju yug bao** (pork buns). You can make one of them vegetarian by substituting tofu for meat. You will probably have guests who cannot use chopsticks, so give them a special dispensation to use their hands. Almost any dim sum dish is easily made finger food.

Classic dim sum

Shrimp Bonnets & Pork Buns

Ha Gao (Shrimp Bonnets)

A culinary tale states that shrimp bonnets were originally made with riceflour. But one day the chef of the Imperial kitchens came to work roaring drunk. He began to make shrimp bonnets for the emperor, but in his altered state he used wheat starch instead of rice flour. No one could tell the difference until the bonnets were steamed and the prawns could be seen through the transparent dough. The emperor was delighted at this and rewarded the chef. It was several days, however, before the chef sobered up enough to realise his good fortune.

Ingredients
Dough

1 cup	wheat starch
²/₃ cup	tapioca starch
¹/₂ tsp	salt
1 cup	boiling water
2 tsp	oil

Filling

350g (12oz)	prawns, cleaned
³/₄ cup	bamboo shoots, minced
1	spring onion, minced
2¹/₂ Tbs	cornstarch
1 tsp	sesame oil
1 tsp	light soy sauce
¹/₂ tsp	white pepper
4 tsp	sugar
¹/₂ tsp	salt
¹/₄ cup	oil

Combine all the filling ingredients and refrigerate for three hours. Mix the dry dough ingredients thoroughly, then add the water and stir until a dough mixture forms. Cover and let it stand for 15 minutes. Knead the dough on an oiled surface for five minutes. Roll the dough out as thinly as possible and cut into rounds about 8cm (3 inches) in diameter. To make the bonnets, pinch each round at three evenly spaced points on the edge to form pleats, the result of which will produce a little pouch. Fill each pouch with a teaspoon of filling. Pinch the edge as many times as needed to make enough pleats to close the pouch. Place the bonnets in a lightly oiled cake or pie pan, pleats up, and then into a steamer for 15 minutes.

Ju Yug Bao (Pork Buns)

Use the same recipe for the dough as for the shrimp bonnets.

Filling
500g (1lb) pork butt, minced
12 water chestnuts, minced
1 spring onion, minced
4 Chinese black mushrooms, soaked and minced
1 Tbs sugar
1 tsp salt
1/4 tsp white pepper
1 Tbs cornstarch
2 tsp light soy sauce
2 Tbs sherry or rice wine
1 Tbs sugar

Heat a small amount of oil in a wok and fry the pork, mushrooms and chestnuts together until nearly cooked. Add the other ingredients and cook, stirring, until the sauce thickens. Set aside to cool before using it as a filling.

When it's time to call the guests to table, set out a winter melon soup that you have made ahead of time.

Dung Gua Tong (Winter Melon Soup)

This soup is not a chemical formula, but a variation on a theme. Perhaps no two cooks prepare it the same way.

Ingredients

100g (4oz)	cooked chicken, pork or duck
50g (2oz)	ham
2	chicken gizzards
2	chicken livers
4	shiitake mushrooms, softened in warm water
50g (2oz)	small shrimp
1 cup	sliced bamboo shoots
2	dry scallops
2	slices ginger
2 tsp	salt
2 tsp	rice wine or sherry
5 cups	chicken stock
1 tsp	sesame oil
1	winter melon, with one end cut off and the seeds removed in order to make the serving vessel. Steam it until soft (about 30 minutes).

Cut the mushrooms, chicken, shrimp, gizzards, livers and ham into bite-size pieces. Bring a pot of water to a rolling boil and blanch all the cut-up ingredients for 10 seconds, then drain. Soak the scallops in hot water then tear them into shreds. Place all the ingredients into the well of the softened winter melon. Place the melon in a bowl, then into a steamer basket and steam for 15 minutes. Before serving sprinkle the soup with sesame oil.
Serves 4

After serving the soup, excuse yourself to your guests, as you must prepare the dishes to follow. You will have already done the prep work, so it should not take you long to finish each one. It's okay to bring the dishes to the table one at a time as they are finished, but don't serve them in discreet courses as you would do at a western table. Be sure to include seafood or you will have had no Hong Kong feast (see the recipe Steamed Whole Fish in the Celebrating with Food chapter and Shrimp Bonnets earlier in this chapter).

Offer two or three vegetable dishes such as Asparagus in Black Bean Sauce or Water Spinach with Chilli & Tofu (see the recipes in the Staples & Specialities chapter). Asparagus is always a winner among Hong Kong diners. A true Hong Kong banquet should include something unexpected by the western palate. Try beef tongue. Even the timid diner should be able to essay this dish and say they were adventurous in doing so. Rice should be on the table all the time and everyone should have their own bowl. Once the guest of honour is served people can serve themselves.

Suan Jap Au Lei (Beef Tongue with Garlic)

Ingredients

1kg (2¼lb)	beef tongue
3	ginger slices
3	star anise
1	cucumber

Sauce

2 Tbs	light soy sauce
1	clove garlic, minced
1 tsp	Tabasco sauce
1 Tbs	vinegar
1 Tbs	sugar
1 Tbs	sesame oil

Place the beef tongue in boiling water for five minutes, then scrape and clean it. Place it in a pressure cooker with the ginger and anise, cover with water and cook for 15 minutes. Remove the tongue and let it cool for 20 minutes, then slice it into bite-size pieces. Arrange it on a serving platter in a circular pattern. Combine the sauce ingredients in a hot wok and cook for one minute. Pour the mixture over the meat.

Serves 4

For dessert, pretend you've gone to Lan Kwai Fong and have cheesecake, or offer some fresh tropical fruit. Or do both. Or dispense with both. A proper Chinese meal is so well balanced that sweets are not really necessary. But be sure to brew that special tea you purchased when you took lessons in tea mastery from the Mistress of Tea (see the boxed text The Tea Mistress in the Drinks chapter). A little more cognac won't hurt either.

The end of a formal banquet is a bit dicey. Strictly speaking, no one should rise until the guest of honour rises. You as the host, however, are authorised to discreetly suggest to the guest of honour that it is time to do so. If arrangements were made ahead of time in a restaurant, the serving of dessert or the distribution of hot towels would signal the end of the meal. In your home, you may party on as long as you like. But if you have guests from Hong Kong, make sure they know that or they will feel compelled to leave.

eat your words

language guide

Pronunciation

Cantonese is the oldest Chinese language with a history of over 2000 years. These days it is influenced by many other languages and popular culture and could be described as 'new Cantonese'. Many of these new influences are oral, and cannot be written in Chinese characters: a lot of slang and colloquial expressions have arisen that do not have written equivalents.

We follow the pronunciation of Cantonese used in Hong Kong. If you can't make yourself understood, the Chinese characters should help; there is usually no shortage of friendly Chinese people who will gladly assist you with the word or phrase you need.

Cantonese is a spoken language, and the Chinese characters included are written in what we call Traditional (or complex) Chinese and can, in fact, be understood by speakers of other dialects such as Mandarin and Shanghainese. Cantonese in Hong Kong differs slightly from Cantonese spoken in other locations (southern China, for example), however, most speakers of Cantonese, irrespective of their origin, will understand most pronunciations.

Consonants

Cantonese words and sounds ending in **-p**, **-t**, **-k** and **-m** are clipped, similar to words with a silent letter in English (like 'climb'). While these final consonants seem about to be voiced, they are cut off before a sound is made.

Most other consonants are pronounced similar to English, although '**x**' should be pronounced like 'see' in English.

Vowels
Short Vowels

a	as the 'a' in 'act'
e	as the 'e' in 'let'
oot	as the 'oot' in 'foot'
un	very short 'oo' + 'n'
ut	as the 'ut' in 'put'
ung	very short 'oo' + 'ng'
uk	as the 'ook' in 'cook'

Long Vowels

aam	as the 'arm' in 'farm'
aap	as the 'arp' in 'carp'
eng	as the 'eng' in 'length'
ei	as the 'ay' in 'pay'
euk	as the 'erk' in 'jerk'
i	as the 'ee' in 'me'
iu	'ee' + 'iu'
ou	as the long 'o' in 'go'
oh	as the 'or' in 'for'
u	as the 'ew' in 'few'
uen	as the 'ewn' in 'strewn'
uet	as the 'ute' in 'flute'
ui	as the 'oy' in 'toy' + long 'ee'

Tones
The other notable feature of Cantonese is the presence of tones. There are more than 10 tones in Cantonese, however, we have simplified them into six basic tones. These are denoted by the superscript number after each word and indicate whether the word should be pronounced at a high or low pitch; rising, falling or flat; clipped or lengthened. Pronunciation of tones sorts the good speakers from those who 'muddle along'. However, we should stress that if the context is clear, you will usually be understood even if the tone is incorrect or missing. Tones are the hardest aspect of Cantonese (or any Chinese dialect) to master.

Tone [1]	highest tone: words vary from being clipped, to long and lingering, or may even drop slightly
Tone [2]	a rising tone that starts about mid-pitch and rises to as high as Tone 1
Tone [3]	a level or flat tone at about mid-pitch. The sounds are both clipped and lingering.
Tone [4]	starts almost at the lowest pitch and drops to the lowest level
Tone [5]	starts at the same low level as Tone 4 and rises to the mid-level
Tone [6]	same low level as Tones 4 and 5, but is flat. Some words may also be clipped.

We hope this summary helps you negotiate your way around the gastronomic delights that Hong Kong has to offer.

Useful Phrases
Eating Out

restaurant
  chaan¹ goon²   餐館

cheap restaurant
  ping⁴ ga³ chaan¹ goon²   平價餐館

Can you help me, please?
  ng² goi¹ hoh⁵ yi⁵ bong¹ ngoh⁵ ma¹?   唔該可以幫我嗎?

Do you speak English?
  nei⁵ wui⁵ gong² ying¹ men⁴ ma¹?   你會講英文嗎?

Could you speak more slowly, please?
  ng² goi¹, hoh⁵ yi⁵ gong² maan⁶ di¹ ma¹?   唔該可以講慢地啲嗎?

Table for ..., please.
  ng² goi¹ ... wei⁶   唔該 ... 位

Do you accept credit cards?
  nei⁵ sau¹ sun³ yung⁶ ked¹ ma¹?   你收信用咭嗎?

Do you have a highchair for the baby?
  yau⁵ mou⁵ bei² b b co⁵ ge³ gou¹ yi² a¹?   有冇俾 B B 坐嘅高椅呀?

Can I smoke here?
  ngoh⁵ hoh⁵ yi⁵ hei⁶ ni¹ dou⁶ xig⁶ yin¹ ma¹?   我可以喺呢度食煙嗎?

Can I pay by credit card?
  ngoh⁵ hoh⁵ yi⁵ bei² sun³ yung⁶ ked¹ ma¹?   我可以俾信用咭嗎?

Just Try It!

What's that?
hei⁶ med¹ ye⁵ lei⁴ ga³? 係乜嘢㗎㗎?

What's the speciality here?
ni¹ dou⁶ yau⁵ med¹ ye⁵ deg⁶
bid⁶ hou² ge³ choi³ xig¹? 呢度有乜嘢特別好嘅菜式?

What do you recommend?
nei⁵ dou⁶ yau⁵ med¹ ye⁵ hou² gai³ xiu⁶? 呢度有乜嘢好介紹呀?

What are they eating?
kui⁵ dei⁶ xig⁶ gen² med¹ ye⁵? 佢哋食緊乜嘢?

I'll try what she/he's having.
ngoh⁵ seung² xi³ ha⁵ kui⁵ goh² di¹ ye⁵ 我想試下佢個啲嘢

The Menu

Can I see the menu please?
ng² goi¹ bei² goh³ chaan¹ pai⁴ ngoh⁵ tei²? 唔該俾個餐牌我睇?

Do you have a menu in English?
yau⁵ mou⁵ ying¹ men⁴ ge³ chaan¹ pai⁴? 有冇英文嘅餐牌?

What are today's specials?
gem¹ yud⁶ ge³ deg⁶ bid⁶
choi³ xig¹ hei⁶ med¹ ye⁵? 今日嘅特別菜式係乜嘢?

I'd like ...
ngoh⁵ seung² yiu³ ... 我想要 ...

I'd like the set menu, please.
ng² goi¹, ngoh⁵ seung² yiu³
tou³ chaan¹ chaan¹ pai⁴ 唔該我想要套餐餐牌

What does it include?
yau⁵ di¹ med¹ ye⁵ hei² lui⁶ min⁶ a¹? 有啲乜嘢係裡面呀?

Is service included in the bill?
jeung² daan¹ lui⁵ min⁶ hei⁶ ng²
hei⁶ bao¹ zo² fuk⁶ mou⁶ fei³? 帳單裡面喺唔係包咗服務費?

Does it come with salad?
hei⁶ ng² hei⁶ lin⁴ mai⁵ sa¹ lut⁶? 係唔係連埋沙律?

What's the soup of the day?
gem¹ yud⁶ ge³ chaan¹
tong¹ hei⁶ med¹ ye⁵? 今日嘅餐湯係乜嘢?

Throughout the Meal

What's in this dish?
ni¹ goh¹ sung³ yau⁵ di¹ med¹ ye⁵? 呢個餸有啲乜嘢?

Do you have sauce?
yau⁵ mou⁵ jap¹ a¹? 有冇汁呀?

Not too spicy please.
ng² goi¹ ng² hou² tai³ laat⁶ 唔該唔好太辣

210

Is that dish spicy?
ni¹ goh¹ sung³ laat⁶ ng² laat⁶?　　　　呢個餸辣唔辣?

I like it hot and spicy!
ngoh⁵ jung¹ yi³ yau⁶ laat⁶ yau⁶ heung¹!　　我鍾意又辣又香!

It's not hot. (temperature)
ng² yid⁶ a¹　　　　唔熱呀 (溫度)

I didn't order this.
ngoh⁵ mou⁵ giu⁵ ni¹ goh¹ sung³　　　我冇叫呢個餸

I'd like something to drink.
ngoh⁵ seung² yiu² di¹ yem² ben²　　我想要啲飲品

Can I have a (beer) please?
ng² goi¹ ngoh⁵ yiu³ yed¹ jun¹ (be¹ jau²)?　　唔該我要一樽 (啤酒)?

Please bring me ...	ng² goi¹ loh²... bei² ngoh	唔該攞 ... 俾我
an ashtray	goh³ yin¹ fun¹ jung¹	個煙灰盅
some bread	di¹ min⁶ bao¹	啲麵包
a cup	jek³ bui¹	隻杯
a fork	jek³ cha¹	隻叉
a glass	jek³ boh¹ lei¹ bui¹	隻玻璃杯
a knife	ba² dou¹	把刀
a napkin	tin⁴ chaan¹ gen¹	條餐巾
some pepper	di¹ wu⁴ jiu¹	啲胡椒
a plate	jek dib⁶	隻碟
some salt	di¹ yim⁴	啲鹽
a spoon	jek³ chi⁴ geng¹	隻匙羹
a teaspoon	jek³ cha⁴ chi⁴	隻茶匙
a toothpick	ji¹ nga⁴ chim¹	枝牙籤
some water	di¹ sui²	啲水
some wine	di¹ jau²	啲酒

This food is ...	ni¹ di¹ xig⁶ med⁶ hei⁶ ...	呢啲食物係 ...
cold	dung¹ ge³	凍嘅
burnt	xiu¹ jiu¹	燒焦
spoiled	bin³ wai⁶ zo²	變壞咗
stale	ng² sen¹ xin¹	唔新鮮
undercooked	ju⁴ deg¹ ng² gau³ sug⁶	煮得唔夠熱

Thank you, that was delicious.
doh¹ je⁶ nei⁵, hou² hou² xig⁶ a¹　　多謝你, 好好食呀

Please pass on our compliments
to the chef.
ng² goi¹ tung⁴ goh³ dai⁶ chue⁴ gong²,　　唔該同個大廚講, 我哋讚佢好手勢
ngoh⁵ dei⁶ jaan³ kui⁵ hou² sau² sei³

The bill, please.
ng² goi¹ mai⁴ dan¹　　　　唔該埋單

You May Hear

Anything else?
jung⁶ yau⁵ med¹ ye⁵ a¹?　　　　重有乜嘢呀?

We have no ... today.
ngoh⁵ dei⁶ gem¹ yud⁶ mou⁵ ...　　我哋今日冇...

Family Meals

You're a great cook!
nei⁵ ju² sung³ zen¹ hou² ye⁵!　　你煮餸真好嘢!

This is brilliant!
hou² leng³ hou² hou² mei⁶ dou⁶!　　好靚好好味道!

Is this a family recipe?
ni¹ goh³ hei⁶ ng² hei⁶ ga¹ ting⁴ xig⁶ pou²?　　呢個係唔係家庭食譜?

If you ever come to (Australia)
I'll cook you a local dish.
yu⁴ guo² nei⁵ lei⁴ (o³ jau¹),　　如果你嚟澳洲,
ngoh⁵ wui⁶ ju² yed¹ goh³ boon²　　我會煮一個本地菜式俾你食
dei⁶ choi³ xig¹ bei² nei⁵ xig⁶

Thanks very much for the meal.
hou² doh¹ je⁶ nei⁵ ni¹ yed¹ chaan¹ fan⁶　　好多謝你呢一餐飯

I really appreciate it.
ngoh⁵ zen¹ hei⁶ hou² yen¹　　我真係好欣賞好多謝
seung hou² doh¹ je⁶

Vegetarian & Special Meals

I'm a vegetarian.
ngoh⁵ hei⁶ xig⁶ sou³ ge³　　我係食素嘅

I'm a vegan, I don't eat meat
or dairy products.
ngoh⁵ xig⁶ sou³ ge³,　　我食素嘅,
ngoh⁵ ng² xig⁶ yug⁶ lui⁶ wag⁶　　我唔食肉類或者奶類產品
je² nai⁵ lui⁶ chaan² ben²

I don't eat ...	ngoh⁵ ng⁴ xig⁶ ...	我唔食 ...
chicken	gei¹	雞
fish	yu⁴	魚
meat	yug⁶ lui⁶	肉類
pork	ju¹ yug⁶	豬肉
poultry	ga¹ kem⁴	家禽
seafood	hoi² xin¹	海鮮

Do you have any vegetarian dishes?
yau⁵ mou⁵ sou³ xig⁶ choi³ xig¹ a¹?　　有冇素食菜式呀?

Can you recommend a
vegetarian dish, please?
    ng² goi¹ nei⁵ gai³ xiu⁶ yed¹ goh³
    sou³ choi³ bei² ngoh⁵ hou² ma¹?

唔該你介紹一個
素菜俾我好嗎?

Does this dish have meat?
    ni¹ goh³ sung³ yau⁵ mou⁵ yug⁶ lui⁶?

呢個餸有冇肉類?

Can I get this without the meat?
    ni¹ goh³ sung³ hoh⁵ yi² ng² yiu³ yug⁶ lui⁶ ma¹?

呢個餸可以唔要肉類嗎?

Is the sauce meat-based?
    ni¹ goh³ jap¹ hei⁶ ng² hei⁶
    yong⁶ yug⁶ lui⁶ jo⁶ ga³?

呢個汁係唔係用肉類做㗎?

Does it contain eggs/dairy products?
    ni¹ goh³ sung³ lui⁵ min⁶ yau⁵ mou⁵
    gei¹ dan⁶/ nai⁵ lui⁶ jai³ ben²?

呢個餸裡面有冇
雞蛋 / 奶類製品?

Does this dish have gelatine?
    ni¹ goh³ sung³ lui⁵ min⁶
    yau⁵ mou⁵ yu⁴ gao¹?

呢個餸裡面有冇魚膠?

I'm allergic to ...
    ngoh⁵ dui³ ... men⁵ gem²

我對 ... 敏感

Is it ...?	ni¹ di¹ hei⁶ ng² hei⁶ ...?	呢啲係唔係 ...?
gluten-free	mou⁶ gao¹ dan⁶ baak⁶	冇膠蛋白
lactose-free	mou⁵ yu⁵ tong⁴	冇乳糖
salt-free	mou⁵ yim⁴	冇鹽
sugar-free	mou⁵ tong⁴	冇糖
wheat-free	mou⁵ siu² meg⁶	冇小麥
yeast-free	mou⁵ hao¹ mou⁵	冇酵母

I'd like a kosher meal.
    ngoh⁵ seung² yiu³ yed¹ di¹ yau⁴
    tai³ gao³ ge³ xig⁶ med⁶

我想要一啲猶太教嘅食物

Is this kosher?
    ni¹ di¹ hei⁶ ng² hei⁶ yau⁵ tai³
    gao³ gei¹ xig⁶ med⁶?

呢啲係唔係猶太教嘅食物?

Is this organic?
    ni¹ di¹ hei⁶ ng² hei⁶ yau⁵ gei¹ xig⁶ med⁶?

呢啲係唔係有機食物?

At the Market

Where's the nearest (market)?
    Lei⁴ ni¹ dou⁶ jui³ gen⁶ ge³
    (gai¹ si⁵) hei⁶ bin¹ chue³?

離呢度最近嘅
(街市) 喺邊處?

Where can I find the (sugar)?
    hei² bin¹ chue³ hoh⁵ yi⁵ mai⁵ dou³ (tong⁴)?

喺邊處可以買到 (糖)?

Can I have a ...?	ngoh⁵ seung² yiu³ yed¹ ...?	我想要一 ...?
bottle	jun¹	樽
box	heb⁶	盒
can	goon³	罐
packet	bao¹	包
sachet/bag	sei³bao¹/doi⁶	細包 / 袋
tin of ...	tit³ goon³...	鐵罐 ...

How much?
gei² doh¹ chin⁴? 幾多錢？

Do you have anything cheaper?
yau⁵ mou⁵ kei⁴ ta¹ ping⁴ di¹ ga³? 有冇其他平啲㗎?

Give me a kilo, please.
ng² goi¹ bei² yed¹ gung¹ gen¹ 唔該俾一公斤

I'd like (six) slices of (ham).
ngoh⁵ seung² yiu³ (luk⁶) pin³ (foh² tui²) 我想要（六）片（火腿）

I don't want to buy anything.
ngoh⁵ ng² hei⁶ seung² mai⁵ ye⁵ 我唔係想買嘢

I'm just looking.
ngoh⁵ jing⁶ hei⁶ tei² ha⁵ 我淨係睇下

Can I taste it?
ngoh⁵ hoh⁵ yi⁵ xi³ xig⁶ ma¹? 我可以試食嗎?

Is this the best you have?
ni¹ di¹ hei⁶ ng² hei⁶ jui³ hou² ge³? 呢啲係唔係最好嘅?

What's the local speciality?
boon¹ dei⁶ ge³ deg⁶ bid⁶ choi³ 本地嘅特別菜式係乜嘢?
xig¹ hei⁶ med¹ ye⁵?

I'd like some ...	ngoh⁵ seung² yiu³ yed¹ di¹ ...	我想要一啲 ...
bread	min⁶ bao¹	麵包
butter	ngau⁴ yau⁴	牛油
cheese	ji¹ si²	芝士
chocolate	ju¹ gu² lig⁶	朱古力
eggs	gei¹ dan⁶	雞蛋
flour	min⁶ fen²	麵粉
frozen foods	laang⁵ chong⁴ xig⁶ med⁶	冷藏食物
fruit & vegetables	seng¹ guo² soh¹ choi³	生果蔬菜
ham	joh² tiu²	火腿
honey	med⁶ tong⁴	蜜糖
margarine	yen⁴ jo³ ngau⁴ yau⁴	人造牛油
milk	ngau⁴ nai⁵	牛奶
pepper	wu⁴ jiu¹	胡椒
rice	mai⁵	米
salt	yim⁴	鹽
sugar	tong⁴	糖

At the Bar

Shall we go for a drink?
ngoh⁵ dei⁶ hui³ yem² bui¹ jau² hou² ma¹? 　我哋去飲杯酒好嗎?

I'll buy you a drink.
ngoh⁵ ching² nei⁵ yem² bui¹ jau² 　我請你飲杯酒

Thanks, but I don't feel like it.
doh¹ je⁶, dan⁶ hei⁶ ngoh⁵ ng² seung² yem² 　多謝, 但係我唔想飲

I don't drink (alcohol).
ngoh⁵ ng² yem² (jau²) 　我唔飲 (酒)

What would you like?
nei⁵ seung² yem² med¹ ye⁵? 　你想飲乜嘢?

I'll have ...
ngoh⁵ yiu³ ... 　我要 ...

It's on me.
gem¹ chi³ ngoh⁵ bei² zo² chin⁴ 　今次我俾咗錢

It's my round.
gem¹ chi³ lun⁴ dou² ngoh⁶ ching² 　今次輪到我請

I'm next.
ngoh⁵ hei⁶ ha⁶ yed¹ wai² 　我係下一位

Excuse me.
dui² ng² ju⁶ 　對唔住

I'll have (a) ...	ngoh⁵ yiu³ ...	我要 ...
beer	be¹ jau²	啤酒
brandy	baak⁶ lan⁴ dei² jau²	白蘭地酒
champagne	heung¹ ben¹	香檳
cocktail	gei¹ mei⁵ jau²	雞尾酒
rum	lem¹ jau²	冧酒
whisky	wei¹ xi⁶ gei²	威士忌

Cheers!
yem² xing³! 　飲勝!

No ice.
ng² yiu³ bing¹ 　唔要冰

Can I have ice, please?
ng² goi¹ bei² di¹ bing¹ ngoh⁵? 　唔該俾啲冰我?

Same again, please.
ng² goi¹ jiu³ yeung⁶ joi³ lei⁴ yed¹ fen⁶ 　唔該照樣再嚟一份

Is food available here?
ni¹ dou⁶ yau⁵ mou⁵ xig⁶ med⁶ gung¹ ying³ a¹? 　呢度有冇食物供應呀?

This is hitting the spot.
ni¹ di¹ jing³ hei⁶ ngoh⁵ seung² yiu³ ge³ 　呢啲正係我想要嘅

Where's the toilet?
chi³ soh² hei² bin¹ dou⁶ a¹? 　廁所喺邊度呀?

I'm a bit tired, I'd better get home.
    ngoh⁵ yau⁵ di¹ gooi⁶ seung² faan¹ uk¹ kei⁵　　我有啲累想返屋企
I'm feeling drunk.
    ngoh⁵ gog³ deg¹ yau⁵ di¹ jui³　　我覺得有啲醉
I'm pissed.
    ngoh⁵ jui³ la³　　我醉啦
I feel ill.
    ngoh⁵ gog³ deg¹ ng² xu¹ fug⁶　　我覺得唔舒服
I want to throw up.
    ngoh⁵ seung² au²　　我想嘔
S/he's passed out.
    kui⁵ yi⁵ ging¹ jui³ dou¹ bed¹ xing² yen⁴ xi⁶　　佢已經醉到不省人事
I'm hung over.
    ngoh⁵ yau⁵ di¹ jui³ hau⁶ tau⁴ tung³　　我有啲醉後頭痛
So, do you come here often?
    gem², nei⁵ hei⁶ ng² hei⁶ si⁴ si⁴ lei⁴ ni¹ dou⁶?　　咁, 你係唔係時時嚟呢度?
I really, really love you.
    sen¹ ge³, hgoh⁵ zen¹ hei⁶ hou² oi³ nei⁵　　真嘅, 我真係好愛你
What did I do last night?
    zog⁶ maan⁵ ngoh⁵ jo³ zo² med¹ ye⁵?　　昨晚我做咗乜嘢?

Wine

May I see the wine list, please?
    ng² goi¹ bei² goh³ jau⁴ pai⁴ ngoh⁵ tei²?　　唔該俾個酒牌我睇?
What is a good year?
    bin¹ yed¹ nin⁴ di¹ jau² bei² gao³ hou²?　　邊一年啲酒比較好?
May I taste it?
    ngoh⁵ hoh¹ yi⁵ xi³ yem² ma¹?　　我可以試飲嗎?
Which wine would you recommend
with this dish?
    nei⁵ wui⁵ gai³ xiu⁶ bin¹ jung² jan²　　你會介紹邊種酒嚟配呢個餸?
    lei⁴ pui³ ni¹ goh¹ sung³?

I'd like a glass/	**ngoh⁵ seung² yiu³ yed¹ bui¹/**	我想要一杯 /
bottle of ... wine	**jun¹ ... jau²**	樽 .. 酒
red	**hung⁴**	紅
rose	**miu⁴ gwai³ hung⁴**	玫瑰紅
sparkling	**hei³**	汽
white	**baak⁶**	白

This is brilliant!
    hou² leng³ hou² hou² mei⁶ dou⁶!　　好靚好好味道!
This wine has a nice/bad taste.
    ni¹ di¹ jau² mei⁶ dou⁶ hou² hou²/ng² hou²　　呢啲酒味道好好 / 唔好

English – Cantonese Glossary

A

abalone	bao¹ yu⁴	鮑魚
acid (acetic)	cho³ suen¹	醋酸
additive	tim¹ ga¹ jai¹	添加劑
agar-agar (jelly)	dai⁶ choi³ go¹	大菜糕(瓊脂)
a la carte	xan³ chaan¹	散餐
ale	nung⁴ be¹ jau²	濃啤酒
alfalfa shoots	xiu² meg⁶ cho⁴	小麥草(苜蓿)
allspice	doh¹ heung¹ guo²	多香果
almond	heng⁵ yen⁴	杏仁
anchovy	fung⁶ mei⁵ yu⁴	鳳尾魚
anise	baat³ goh³	八角
aniseed	wui⁴ ken⁴ ji²	茴芹子
apple	ping⁴ guo²	蘋果
apricot	wong⁴ mui⁴	黃梅
asparagus	lou⁶ sen²	蘆筍
aspic	yug⁶ dung³	肉凍
aubergine	ngei² gua¹	矮瓜
avocado	ngau⁴ yau⁴ guo²	牛油果

B

bacon	yin¹ yug⁶	煙肉
to bake	hung³	烘
baking powder	faat³ fen¹	發粉
baking soda	xig⁶ yung⁶ sou¹ da²	食用蘇打
bamboo leaves	juk¹ yip⁶	竹葉
bamboo shoots	juk¹ sen²	竹筍
pickled	suen¹ sen²	酸筍
salted	haam⁴ sen²	鹹筍
banana	heung¹ jiu¹	香蕉
barbecue	xiu¹ hao²	燒烤
basil	lop⁴ lak⁶	羅勒
to baste	tou⁴ yau⁴ hao²	塗油烤
batter	min⁶ wu⁴	麵糊
bean	deo⁶	豆
black	hak¹ deo⁶	黑豆
black, salted	lou⁵ chau¹	老抽
broad	chaam⁴ deo⁶	蠶豆
fava	chaam⁴ deo⁶	蠶豆
fermented	deo⁶ xi⁶	豆豉
kidney	choi³ deo⁶	菜豆
red	hung⁴ deo⁶	紅豆

red, puree	hung³ deo⁶ sa¹	紅豆沙
sweetened	deo⁶ sa¹	豆沙
cakes	deo⁶ beng²	豆餅
curd (tofu)	deo⁶ fu⁶	豆腐
green	cheng¹ dou¹ deo⁶	青刀豆
long	dou¹ deo⁶	刀豆
paste, red	hung⁴ deo⁶ sa¹	紅豆沙
paste, yellow	min⁶ xi⁶ jeung³	麵豉醬
paste, brown	deo⁶ xi⁶ jeung³	豆豉醬
runner	hung⁴ fa¹ choi³ deo⁶	紅花菜豆
sauce, black	xi⁶ jap⁴	豉汁
sauce, brown	jeung³ yeo⁴	醬油（老抽）
sauce, hot	deo⁶ baan⁶ jeung³	豆瓣醬
sprouts	nga⁴ choi³	芽菜
string	deo⁶ gok³	豆角
threads	fen² xi¹	粉絲
beef	ngau⁴ yug⁶	牛肉
beer	be¹ jau²	平均
beetroot	hung⁴ choi³ tau⁴	紅菜頭
berry	jeung¹ guo²	漿果
beverage	yem² liu⁶	飲料
bird's nest	yin³ woh¹	燕窩
basket	jeuk³ cao⁴	雀巢
soup	yin³ woh¹ tong¹	燕窩湯
sweetened	yin³ woh¹ tong⁴ sui²	燕窩糖水
to blanch	cheuk³	焯
blood	hung⁴	紅
to boil	ju²	煮
boiling	gwan²	滾
bok choy	baak⁶ chu³	白菜
botulism	yug⁶ dug⁶ jung¹ dug⁶	肉毒中毒
brains	nou⁵	腦
to braise	hung⁴ xiu¹	紅燒
brandy	baak⁶ lan⁴ dei² jau²	白蘭地酒
brawn	yug⁶ dung³	肉凍
bread	min⁶ bao¹	麵包
breadcrumbs	min⁶ bao¹ hong¹	麵包糠
breakfast	zou² chaan¹	早餐
breast	hung¹ yug⁶	胸肉
to brew	yeung⁶ zou³/chung¹ pao³	釀造 / 沖泡
brine	yim⁴ sui²	鹽水
broccoli	sai¹ lan⁴ fa¹	西蘭花
Chinese	gai³ laan⁴ tau⁴	芥蘭頭

218

broth	ching¹ tong¹	清湯
brown	hao²	烤
brunch	zou² ng⁵ chaan¹	早午餐
brussels sprout	ye⁴ choi³ zei²	椰菜仔
buffet	ji⁶ joh⁶ chaan¹	自助餐
bun	yuen⁴ ying⁴ min⁶ bao¹	圓形麵包
burger	hon³ bou² bao¹	漢堡包
butcher	yug⁶ fan³	肉販
butter	ngau⁴ yau⁴	牛油

C

cabbage	choi³	菜
Chinese	dai⁶ baak⁶ choi³	大白菜
dried	choi³ gon¹	菜乾
flowering	choi³ sem¹	菜心
mustard	gai³ choi³	芥菜
palm	yeung⁴ gai³	洋薊
pickled	pao³ choi³	泡菜
preserved	haam⁴ suen¹ choi³	鹹酸菜
salted	haam⁴ choi³	鹹菜
cafe	ga³ fe¹ sed¹	咖啡室
cafe au lait	ngau⁴ nai⁵ ga³ fe¹	牛奶咖啡
cake	sai¹ beng²	西餅
calorie	ka¹ lou⁶ lei⁵	卡路里
can	goon³ tau⁴	罐頭
to can	yeb⁶ goon³	入罐
candy	tong⁴ guo²	糖果
cantaloupe	jau³ pei⁴ gua¹	皺皮瓜
canteen	dai⁶ choi³	大菜
capon	gei¹	雞
capsicum	sai¹ jiu¹	西椒
caramel	jiu¹ tong⁴	焦糖
to caramelise	ju² xing⁴ jiu¹ tong⁴	煮成焦糖
carbonate	yi⁶ yeung⁵ fa³ taan³	二氧化碳
cardamon	xiu² deo⁶ kau³	小豆蔻
carrot	hung⁴ loh⁴ baak⁶	紅蘿蔔
cashew nut	yiu¹ guo²	腰果
casserole	mun⁶	燜
to cater	bao¹ baan⁶ jau² jig⁶	包辦酒席
cauliflower	ye⁴ choi³ fa¹	椰菜花
caviar	yu⁴ ji² jeung³	魚子醬
cayenne pepper	laat⁶ jiu¹ fen²	辣椒粉
celery	ken⁴ choi³	芹菜
cereal	meg³ pin³	麥片

cheese	ji¹ xi²	芝士
chef	dai⁶ chue⁴	大廚
cherry	che¹ lei⁴ ji²	車厘子
chestnut	lut⁶ ji²	栗子
dried	lut⁶ ji² gon¹	栗子干
chicken	gei¹	雞
feet	fung⁶ zao² (gei¹ geuk³)	鳳爪 (雞腳)
liver	fung⁶ gon¹	鳳肝
spring	tung⁴ ji² gei²	童子雞
testicles	gei¹ ji²	雞子
wings	gei¹ yik⁶	雞翼
chicory	fu² baak⁶ choi³	苦白菜
chilli	laat⁶ jiu¹	辣椒
Chinese	hung⁴ laat⁶ jiu¹	紅辣椒
chip	sue⁴ tiu⁴	薯條
chives	gau² choi³	韭菜
yellow	gau² wong⁴	韭黃
chocolate	ju¹ gu² lig⁶	朱古力
chop (meat)	ju¹ pai⁴	豬排
to chop	deuk³	剁
chopsticks	fai³ ji²	筷子
cilantro	yuen⁴ sai¹	芫茜
cinnamon	yug⁶ guei³	肉桂
citrus	gem¹ gued¹	柑橘
clam	hin²	蜆
clove	ding¹ heung¹	丁香
clover, Chinese	sug⁶ cho²	蓿草
Coca Cola	hoh² heo² hoh² lok⁶	可口可樂
cocktail	gei¹ mei⁵ jau²	雞尾酒
coconut	ye⁴ ji²	椰子
coffee	ga³ fei¹	咖啡
cognac	gon¹ yeb¹	干邑
cold	dung³	凍
condiment	tiu⁴ mei ben²	調味品
confectionery	tong⁴ guo² go¹ beng² dim³	糖果糕餅店
congee	juk¹	粥
consomme	ching¹ den⁶ yug⁶ tong¹	清炖肉湯
continental breakfast	au¹ luk⁶ xig¹ zou² chaan¹	歐陸式早餐
convenience food	fong¹ bin⁶ xig⁶ ben²	方便食品
cook	chue⁴ xi¹	廚師
to cook	ju²	煮
cookbook	pang¹ yem⁵ xu¹	烹飪書
cooker	lou⁴ gui⁶	爐具
cordial	mung⁴ suk¹ guo² jap¹	濃縮果汁

coriander	yuen⁴ sai¹	芫茜
corkage	hoi¹ ping⁴ fei³	開瓶費
corn	sug¹ mei⁵	粟米
cornflour	saang¹ fen²	生粉
cos lettuce	saang¹ choi³	生菜
course	choi³ xig¹	菜式
crab	hai⁵	蚧
cracker	bog⁶ chui³ beng² gon¹	薄脆餅乾
crackers (prawn)	ha¹ pin³	蝦片
crackling	chui³ pei⁴	脆皮
crayfish	xiu² lung⁴ ha¹	小龍蝦
cream	nai⁵ yau⁴	奶油
cress	sui² ken⁴	水芹
crisp	chui³	脆
crouton	ja³ min⁶ bao¹ neb¹	炸麵包粒
crumb	min⁶ bao¹ hong¹	麵包糠
cumquat	gem¹ gued¹	金橘
crustaceans	gab³ hok³ lui⁶	甲殼類
cucumber	cheng¹ gua¹/wong⁴ gua¹	青瓜／黃瓜
pickle	yim¹ wong⁴ gua¹	醃黃瓜
cuisine	fung¹ mei⁶ choi³	風味菜
cumin	xiu² wui¹ heung¹	小茴香
curd	ying⁴ yu⁵	凝乳
to cure	yin¹ fen¹	煙薰
curry	ga³ lei¹	咖哩
powder	ga³ lei¹ fen²	咖哩粉
custard	daan⁶ nai⁵ dung³	蛋奶凍
custard apple	faan¹ lai⁶ ji¹	蕃荔枝
to cut	chit³	切
cutlet	heo⁵ pin³	厚片
cuttlefish	meg⁶ yu⁴	墨魚
dried	meg⁶ yu⁴ gon¹	墨魚干

D

daikon	dai⁶ gen¹	大根
date, red	hung⁴ jo²	紅棗
deep fry	ja³	炸
deer	luk⁶	鹿
dehydrate	tuet³ sui²	脫水
delicatessen	sug⁶ xig⁶ dim³	熟食店
dessert	tim⁴ ben²	甜品
to dice	chit³ neb¹	切粒
diet	xin⁶ xig⁶	膳食
dim sum	dim² sem¹	點心

dinner	maan⁵ chaan¹	晚餐
dip	jeung³ jap¹	醬汁
done (cooked)	sug⁶	熟
dough	min⁶ tuen⁴	麵團
dressing	sa¹ lut⁶ yau⁴	沙律油
dried	gon¹	干
drink	yem² liu⁶	飲料
to drink	yem²	飲
drumsticks	gei² tui²	雞腿
duck	ab³	鴨
feet	ab³ geuh³	鴨腳
liver sausage	yun⁶ cheung⁴	潤腸
preserved	ab³ beng²	鴨餅
pressed	lab⁶ ab³	臘鴨
salted	haam⁴ ab³	鹹鴨
tongues	ab³ lei⁶	鴨唎
duckling	nuen⁶ ab³	嫩鴨
dumpling	tong¹ yuen³	湯圓
durian	lau⁴ lin⁴	榴槤

E

eel	xin⁶	鱔
eggs	daan⁶	蛋
duck	ab³ daan⁶	鴨蛋
preserved/century	pei⁴ daan⁶	皮蛋
quail	em¹ chun¹ daan⁶	鵪鶉蛋
roll	daan⁶ guen³	蛋捲
eggplant	ngei² gua¹	矮瓜
endive	gug¹ gui⁶	菊苣
entree	chin⁴ choi³	前菜
extract	nung⁴ suk¹	濃縮
eye (fillet)	yug⁶ ngan⁵	肉眼

F

fast food	fai³ chaan¹	快餐
fatty	ji¹ fong¹	脂肪
fennel	wui⁴ heung¹	茴香
seeds	wui⁴ heung¹ ji²	茴香籽
fermentation	faat³ hao¹	發酵
fig	mou⁴ fa¹ guo²	無花果
fillet	lau⁵ yug⁶	柳肉
filling	haam⁶	餡
fish	yu⁴	魚
dried	haam⁴ yu⁴ gon¹	鹹魚干

balls	yu⁴ daan⁶	魚旦
lips	yu⁴ sen⁴	魚唇
maw	yu⁴ tou⁵	魚肚
salted	haam⁴ yu⁴	鹹魚
sauce	yu⁴ lou⁶	魚露
fish cake	yu⁴ beng²	魚餅
flavour (n)	mei⁶ dou⁶	味道
flavouring	tiu⁴ mei⁶	調味
flour	min⁶ fen²	麵粉
food	xig⁶ med⁶	食物
fortune cookies	chim¹ beng²	簽餅
fowl	ga¹ kem⁴	家禽
to freeze	bing¹ dung³	冰凍
fresh	sen¹ xin¹	新鮮
fried rice	cao² fan⁶	炒飯
fritter	ja³ haam⁶ beng²	炸餡餅
frog	tin⁴ gei²	田雞
fat	suet³ geb³ go¹	雪蛤糕
fruit	saang¹ guo²	生果
to fry	cao²/ja³	炒 / 炸

G

garlic	suen³ tau⁴	蒜頭
garnish	jong¹ xig¹ choi³	裝飾菜
gel	guo² dung³/yug⁶ dung³	果凍 / 肉凍
gelatine/gelatin	ming⁴ gao¹	明膠
gherkin	xiu² wong⁴ gua¹	小黃瓜
giblets	ga¹ kem⁴ noi⁶ jong⁶	家禽內臟
ginger	geung¹	薑
candied	tong⁴ geung¹	糖薑
pickled	suen¹ geung¹	酸薑
powder	sa¹ geung¹ fen²	沙薑粉
preserved	med⁶ jin³ geung¹	蜜餞薑
red	hung⁴ geung¹	紅薑
root	geung¹ gen¹	薑根
stem	geung¹ ging³	薑莖
ginkgo nuts	baak⁶ guo²	白果
ginseng	yen⁴ sem¹	人參
gizzards	zen¹	肫
glucose	pou⁴ tou⁴ tong⁴	葡萄糖
gluten	min⁶ gen¹	麵筋
goat	saan¹ yeung⁴	山羊
goose	ngoh⁴	鵝
gooseberry	ngoh⁴ mui⁴	鵝莓

gosling	yau³ ngoh⁴	幼鵝
gourd	wu⁴ lou⁴	葫蘆
grain	gug¹ med⁶	穀物
grape	pou⁴ tei⁴ ji²	葡提子
grapefruit	sai¹ yau²	西柚
to grate	moh⁴ xi¹	磨絲
gravy	nung⁴ yug⁶ jap¹	濃肉汁
green	saang¹	生
grill	hao¹ ga³	烤架
to grill	hao¹	烤
guava	faan¹ seg⁶ lau⁴	番石榴

H

ham	foh² tui²	火腿
hamburger	hon³ bo² bao¹	漢堡包
hard-boil	ju² lou⁵	煮老
health food	gin⁶ hong¹ xig⁶ med⁶	健康食物
heart	sem¹	心
hen	mou⁵ gei²	母雞
herbal	heung¹ cho²	香草
high tea	ha⁶ ng² cha⁴	下午茶
hock	ju¹ sau²	豬手
homogenised	guen¹ zed¹	均質
honey	med⁶ tong⁴	蜜糖
hors d'oeuvre	lang⁵ poon⁴	冷盤
horseradish	laat⁶ gen¹	辣根
hotpot	da² bin¹ lou⁴	打邊爐
husk	guo² hok³	果殼

I

ice	bing¹	冰
ice cream	suet³ go¹	雪糕
icing	tong⁴ yi¹	糖衣
instant	chuk¹ yung⁴	速溶

J

jackfruit	boh¹ loh⁴ med⁶	菠蘿蜜
jam	guo² jeung³	果醬
jasmine	moot⁶ lei⁶ cha⁴	茉莉茶
jellyfish	hoi² jid³	海蜇
dried	gon¹ hoi² jid³	乾海蜇
jerky	fung¹ gon¹	風干
juice	guo² jap¹	果汁
junk food	lab⁶ sab³ xig⁶ med⁶	垃圾食物

K

kale/kail	gai³ laan⁴	芥蘭
kebab	xiu¹ yeung⁴ yug⁶	燒羊肉
ketchup	ke⁴ jap¹	茄汁
kid (goat)	saan¹ yeung⁴ zei² yug⁶	山羊仔肉
kidney	yiu¹	腰
kiwi fruit	kei⁴ yi⁶ guo²	奇異果
knuckle	ju¹ geuk³	豬腳
kumquat	gem¹ gued¹	金橘

L

lamb	yeung⁴ yug⁶	羊肉
lean	sau³ yug⁶	瘦肉
leek	cheng¹ suen³	青蒜
leftover	xing⁶ choi³	剩菜
legume	deo⁶ lui⁶ soh¹ choi³	豆類蔬菜
lily buds	lin⁴ ji²	蓮子
lily bulb petals	baak³ heb⁶	百合
lemon	ning⁴ mung¹	檸檬
leaves	ning⁴ mung¹ yip⁶	檸檬葉
sauce	ning⁴ mung¹ jeung³	檸檬醬
lemongrass	heung¹ mao⁴	香茅
lemonade	ning⁴ mung¹ sui²	檸檬水
lettuce	saang¹ choi³	生菜
Chinese	tong⁴ saang¹ choi³	唐生菜
lime	cheng¹ ning⁴	青檸
liquor	lid⁶ jau²	烈酒
liver	gon¹	肝
sausage	gon¹ nai⁴ heung¹ cheung⁴	肝泥香腸
lobster	lung⁴ ha¹	龍蝦
loin	lei⁵ jek³ yug⁶	里脊肉
longans	lung⁴ ngan⁵	龍眼
loquat	pei⁶ pa⁴ guo²	枇杷果
lotus flower	lin⁴ fa¹	蓮花
leaves	lin⁴ yip⁶	蓮葉
nuts (or seeds)	lin⁴ ji²	蓮子
root	lin⁴ ngeo⁵	蓮藕
lunch	ng⁵ chaan¹	午餐
lychee	lai⁶ ji¹	荔枝

M

maize	sug¹ mei⁵	粟米
malt	meg⁶ nga⁴	麥芽
mandarin	gem¹	柑
peel	cen⁴ pei⁴	陳皮

mangetout (sugar pea)	nuen⁶ woon² deo⁶	嫩豌豆
mango	mong¹ guo²	芒果
mangosteen	dou² nim³ ji²	倒捻子
marinade	yim¹ pao³ jap¹	醃泡汁
to marinade	yim¹ pao³	醃泡
mayonnaise	baak⁶ jap¹	白汁
meal	chaan¹	餐
meat	yug⁶ lui⁶	肉類
red	hung⁴ yug⁶	紅肉
white	baak⁶ yug⁶	白肉
meatball	yug⁶ yuen²	肉丸
melon	gua¹	瓜
bitter	fu² gua¹	苦瓜
seeds	gua¹ ji²	瓜子
winter	dung¹ gua¹	冬瓜
menu	chaan¹ pai⁴	餐牌
milk	ngau⁴ nai⁵	牛奶
pudding	ngau⁴ nai⁵ bou³ ding¹	牛奶布丁
shake	nai⁵ xig⁶	奶昔
millet	sug¹ mei⁵	粟米
mince	yug⁶ sui³	肉碎
to mince	gao² sui³	鉸碎
mineral water	kong³ chuen⁴ sui²	礦泉水
mint	bog⁶ hoh⁴	薄荷
to mix	tiu⁴ boon⁶	調拌
mollusc	yuen⁵ tei² dung⁶ med⁶	軟體動物
monosodium glutamate (MSG)	mei⁶ jing¹	味精
mousse	muk⁶ xi¹ (nai⁵ yau⁴ dung³)	木司 (奶油凍)
mung bean	luk⁶ deo⁶	綠豆
sprouts	luk⁶ deo⁶ nga⁴ choi³	綠豆菜芽
mushrooms	gu¹ lui⁶	菇類
abalone	bao¹ yu⁴ gu¹	鮑魚菇
black	dung¹ gu¹	冬菇
black, dried	gon¹ dung¹ gu¹	乾冬菇
button	moh⁴ gu¹	磨菇
champignon	dung¹ gu¹	冬菇
cloud ear	wen⁴ yi⁵	雲耳
enokitake	gem¹ gu¹	金菇
grass	cho² gu¹	草菇
oyster	hou⁴ gu¹	蠔菇
shiitake	dung¹ gu¹	冬菇
snow ear	suet³ gu¹	雪菇

straw	cho² gu¹	草菰
white	suet³ gu¹	雪菰
winter	dung¹ gu¹	冬菰
wood ear	muk⁶ yi⁵	木耳
mussel	cheng¹ hau²	青口
dried	daam⁶ choi³	淡菜
mustard	baat⁶ gai³	白芥
yellow	wong⁴ gai³ laat⁶	黃芥辣
mustard greens	cheng¹ gai³ laat⁶	青芥辣
mutton	yeung⁴ yug⁶	羊肉

N

nectarine	tou⁴ bog³ lei⁵	桃駁李
nightcap	sui⁶ chin⁴ jau²	睡前酒
noodles	min⁶	麵
egg	daan⁶ min⁶	蛋麵
beanstarch	fen² xi¹	粉絲
cellophane	fen² xi¹	粉絲
rice-flour	mai⁵ fen²	米粉
seaweed	hoi² toi⁴ xi¹	海苔絲
slippery rice	hoh⁴ fen²	河粉
transparent noodles	fen² xi¹	粉絲
udon	kiu⁴ meg⁶ min⁶	蕎麥麵
wheat-flour	meg⁶ min⁶	麥麵
won ton	wen¹ ten¹ min⁶	雲吞麵
nut	gin¹ guo²	堅果
nutmeg	yug⁶ deo⁶ keo³	肉豆蔻

O

octopus	jeung¹ yu⁴	鱆魚
offal	ju¹/ngau⁴/yeung⁴ jaap⁶	豬牛羊雜
oil	yau⁴	油
corn	sug¹ mei⁵ yau⁴	粟米油
olive	gem² laam⁵ yau⁴	橄欖油
peanut	fa¹ seng¹ yau⁴	花生油
red chilli	hung⁴ laat⁶ jiu¹ yau⁴	紅辣椒油
rose oil	mui⁴ guei³ yau⁴	玫瑰油
safflower	hung⁴ fa¹ yau⁴	紅花油
sesame	ma⁴ yau⁴	麻油
soybean	deo⁶ yau⁴	豆油
sunflower	kwai⁴ fa¹ ji² yau⁴	葵花籽油
okra	chau¹ kwai⁴	秋葵
olive	gam² laam⁵	橄欖
omelette	um¹ lit⁶ (jin¹ daan⁶ guen²)	奄列（煎蛋卷）

onion	yeung⁴ chung¹	洋蔥
Chinese	dai⁶ chung¹	大蔥
orange	cang⁴	橙
organic	yau⁵ gei¹	有機
oven	guk⁶ lou⁴	焗爐
ox	ngau⁴	牛
oyster	hou⁴	蠔
dried	ho⁴ xi⁶	蠔豉
sauce	hou⁴ yau⁴	蠔油

P

pancake	baan¹ gik¹ (bog⁶ beng²)	班戟 (薄餅)
papaya	muk⁶ gua¹	木瓜
parsley	yeung³ yeun⁴ sai¹	洋芫茜
Chinese	yuen⁴ sai¹	芫茜
parsnip	au¹ zeo¹ fong⁴ fung¹	歐洲防風
paste	jeung³	醬
pastry	sou¹ pei⁴	酥皮
flaky	sou¹ pei⁴	酥皮
pawpaw	muk⁶ gua¹	木瓜
pea	woon² deo⁶	豌豆
bean	goon² deo⁶	豇豆
pods	cheng¹ deo⁶	青豆
shoots	deo⁶ miu⁴	豆苗
peach	tou⁴	桃
peanut	fa¹ seng¹	花生
butter	fa¹ seng¹ jeung³	花生醬
oil	fa¹ seng¹ yau⁴	花生油
pear	lei⁴	梨
peel	guo² pei⁴	果皮
pepper	wu⁴ jiu¹	胡椒
bell	deng¹ lung⁴ jiu¹	燈籠椒
black	heg¹ wu⁴ jiu¹	黑胡椒
red	hung⁴ jiu¹	紅椒
white	baak⁶ wu⁴ jiu¹	白胡椒
to pepper/season	wu⁴ jiu¹ fen²	胡椒粉
peppercorn	wu⁴ jiu¹ neb¹	胡椒粒
Pepsi Cola	baak³ xi⁶ hoh² lok⁶	百事可樂
periwinkle	hoi² loh²	海螺
persimmon	chi⁵	柿
pickle (n)	suen¹ pao³ choi³	酸泡菜
pickle/pickled	yim¹ pao³	醃泡
ginger	suen¹ geung¹	酸薑
melon	suen¹ pao² wong⁴ gua¹	酸泡黃瓜

228

mustard, green	suen¹ pao³ gai³ choi³	酸泡芥菜
vegetables	pao³ choi³	泡菜
pie	pai¹ (haam⁶ beng²)	批（餡餅）
pig	ju¹	豬
pigeon	baak⁶ geb³	白鴿
pineapple	boh¹ loh⁴	菠蘿
pine nut	chung⁴ ji²	松子
pith	sui⁵	髓
plum	mui⁴	梅
sour	suen¹ mui⁴	酸梅
sauce	mui⁴ ji² jeung³	梅子醬
to poach	sui² ju²	水煮
pod	deo⁶ gaap³	豆莢
polyunsaturated	doh¹ bed¹ bao² woh⁴ ji¹ fong¹	多不飽和脂肪
pomegranate	seg⁶ lau⁴	石榴
pomelo	lug¹ yau⁴	碌柚
pork	ju¹ yug⁶	豬肉
belly	ju¹ nam⁵ yug⁶	豬腩肉
dried	ju¹ geuk³ gen¹ gon¹	豬腳筋乾
potato	sue⁴ zei²	薯仔
chip	sue⁴ tiu⁴/sue⁴ pin³	薯條 / 薯片
poultry	ga¹ kem⁴	家禽
prawn	dai⁶ ha¹	大蝦
crackers	ha¹ pin³	蝦片
preservative	fong⁴ fu⁶ jai¹	防腐劑
to preserve, preserve (n)	bou² chuen³ xig⁶ med⁶	保存食物
prickly pear	xin¹ yen⁴ kau⁴	仙人球
prime (cut of meat)	xig⁶ bao²	食飽
prune	sai¹ mui⁴	西梅
pudding	bou³ ding¹	布丁
puff	so¹ pei⁴ beng²	酥皮餅
pastry	so¹ pei⁴	酥皮
puree	nei⁴	泥

Q

quail	em¹ chun¹	鵪鶉
quince	saan¹ ja¹	山楂

R

rabbit	tou³ yug⁶	兔肉
radish	hung⁴ loh⁴ baak⁴	紅蘿蔔
rapeseed	choi³ ji²	菜籽
rare	boon³ saang¹	半生
raw	saang⁶	生

ray	yiu⁴	鰩
recipe	xig⁶ pou²	食譜
red	hung³	紅
to reduce	ju² nung⁴	煮濃
refrigerator	suet³ guei²	雪櫃
restaurant	chaan¹ goon²	餐館
rib	pai⁴ gued¹	排骨
rice	mai⁵/fan⁶	米 / 飯
boiled	fan⁶	飯
flour	mai⁵ fen²	米粉
flour, glutinous	noh⁶ mai⁵ fen²	糯米粉
fried	cao² fan⁶	炒飯
glutenous	noh⁶ mai⁵	糯米
long-grain	jim¹ mai⁵	粘米
noodles, glutinous	seung⁶ hoi² nin⁴ go¹	上海年糕
paper	mai⁵ ji²	米紙
red-coloured	hung⁴ mai⁵	紅米
short-grain	zen¹ ju¹ mai⁵	珍珠米
starchy	noh⁶ mai⁵	糯米
steamed	jing¹ fan⁶	蒸飯
stick	gon¹ hoh⁴ fen²	乾河粉
sweet	tim⁴ mai⁵	甜米
vinegar, black	heg¹ cho³	黑醋
vinegar, red	hung⁴ cho³	紅醋
vinegar, white	baak⁶ cho³	白醋
wine	mai⁵ jau²	米酒
wine, glutinous	noh⁶ mai⁵ jau²	糯米酒
wine, yellow	fa¹ diu¹ jau²	花雕酒
rind	guo² pei⁴	果皮
ripe	sug⁶	熟
roast	xiu¹ hao¹	燒烤
duck	xiu¹ ab³	燒鴨
lobster	seg⁶ lung⁴ ha¹	石龍蝦
pig	xiu¹ ju¹	燒豬
pork	xiu¹ yug⁶	燒肉
sugar	bing¹ tong⁴	冰糖
rockmelon	jau³ pei⁴ gua¹	皺皮瓜
roe	yu⁴ ji²	魚子
shrimp (prawn)	ha¹ ji²	蝦子
roll (bread)	min⁶ bao¹ guen³	麵包卷
rooster	gung¹ gei²	公雞
root	faai³ gen¹	塊根
rosemary	mai⁴ did⁶ heung¹	迷迭香
rose water	mui⁴ guei³ fa¹ jing¹	玫瑰花精
rump	ngau⁴ lem¹ yuk⁶	牛䐑肉

S

saccarin	tong⁴ jing¹	糖精
safflower	hung⁴ fa¹	紅花
sago	sai¹ mai⁵	西米
salad	sa¹ lut⁶	沙律
dressing	sa¹ lut⁶ jeung³	沙律醬
salmonella	sa¹ moon⁴ xi⁶ kuen²	沙門氏菌
salt	yim⁴	鹽
pork	haam⁴ ju¹ yug⁶	鹹豬肉
to salt/season	yim⁴ yim¹	鹽醃
sandwich	saam¹ men⁴ ji⁶	三文治
sardine	sa¹ din² yu⁴	沙甸魚
satay	sa¹ de¹	沙嗲
sauce	sa¹ de¹ jeung³	沙嗲醬
sauce	jeung³	醬
black	xi⁶ jap⁴	豉汁
brown	jeung³ yeo⁴	醬油（老抽）
chilli	laat⁶ jiu¹ jeung³	辣椒醬
eight-treasure hot	baat³ bou² laat⁶ jeung³	八寶辣醬
fish	yu⁴ lou⁶	魚露
hot	deo⁶ baan⁶ jeung³	豆瓣醬
lemon	ning⁴ mung¹ jeung³	檸檬醬
oyster	hou⁴ yau⁴	蠔油
plum	mui⁴ ji² jeung³	梅子醬
red simmering	hung⁴ xiu¹ jeung³	紅燒醬
satay	sa¹ de¹ jeung³	沙嗲醬
soy	jeung³ yau⁴	醬油
sweet & sour	tim⁴ suen¹ jeung³	甜酸醬
sweet bean	tim⁴ min⁶ jeung³	甜麵醬
sweet chilli	tim⁴ laat⁶ jiu¹ jeung²	甜辣椒醬
ten-flavoured sauce	sab⁶ mei⁶ jeung³	十味醬
Worcestershire	laat⁶ xi⁶ yau⁴	辣豉油
yellow	min⁶ xi⁶ jeung³	麵豉醬
sausage	heung¹ cheung⁴	香腸
to saute	cao²	炒
savoury	hoi¹ wei⁶ choi³	開胃菜
scallion	dai⁶ chung¹	大蔥
scallop	dai³ ji²	帶子
to scramble	cao² daan⁶	炒蛋
sea cucumber/slug	hoi² sem¹	海參
seafood	hoi² xin¹	海鮮
to season	tiu⁴ mei⁶	調味
seasoning	tiu⁴ mei⁶ liu⁶	調味料
sea urchin	hoi² daam²	海膽

seaweed	hoi² cho²	海草
dried	hoi² dai³	海帶
seed	heung¹ ji²	香籽
serving	seung⁵ choi³	上菜
sesame	ji¹ ma⁴	芝麻
oil	ma⁴ yau⁴	麻油
paste	ji¹ ma⁴ jeung³	芝麻醬
shallots	xiu² chung¹	小蔥
shark	sa¹ yu⁴	鯊魚
fin	yu⁴ chi³	魚翅
sharp (taste/smell)	chi³ bei⁶	刺鼻
sheep	yeung⁴	羊
shell	hok³	殼
to shell	hui³ hok³	去殼
sherry	se¹ lei⁶ jau²	些利酒
shrimps	ha¹ zei²	蝦仔
chips	ha¹ pin²	蝦片
dried	ha¹ mai⁵	蝦米
paste	ha¹ jeung³	蝦醬
side dish	pui³ choi³	配菜
to sift	sei¹	篩
to simmer	men¹	炆
skin	pei⁴	皮
smoke (n), to smoke	yin¹ fen¹	煙薰
smokehouse	fen¹ lou⁴	薰爐
snack	xiu² xig⁶	小食
snow cabbage	suet³ choi³	雪菜
soft drink	yuen⁵ yem² ben²	軟飲品
sommelier	yem² liu⁶ jung² goon²	飲料總管
sorghum	go¹ leung⁴	高粱
sorrel	cou³ jeung³ cho²	酢漿草
soup	tong¹	湯
sour	suen¹	酸
soybean	wong³/dai⁶ deo⁶	黃 / 大豆
fresh	sen¹ xin¹ wong⁴ deo⁶	新鮮黃豆
green	mou⁴ deo⁶	毛豆
milk	deo⁶ nai⁵	豆奶
paste	deo⁶ jeung³	豆醬
sprouts	dai⁶ deo⁶ nga⁴	大豆芽
soy sauce	jeung³ yau⁴	醬油
dark	lou⁵ chau¹/heg¹ jeung³ yau⁴	老抽 / 黑醬油
Japanese	yed⁶ boon² jeung² yau⁴	日本醬油
light	saang¹ chau¹ (xi⁶ yau⁴)	生抽（豉油）
mushroom	cho² gu¹ lou⁵ chau¹	草菇老抽

spam	goon³ tau⁴ foh² tui²	罐頭火腿
sparerib	pai⁴ gued¹	排骨
spatchcock	saang¹ cao² gei² ding¹	生炒雞丁
spices	heung¹ liu⁶	香料
split pea	gon¹ woon² deo⁶	干豌豆
spring onion	chung¹	蔥
spring roll	chun¹ guen³	春捲
spud	sue⁴ zei²	薯仔
squab	yug⁶ gei²	肉雞
squash	xiu² nam⁴ gua¹	小南瓜
star anise	baat³ goh⁵	八角
star apple/star fruit	yeung⁴ tou⁴	楊桃
starchy	fen²	粉
steak	ngau⁴ pa⁴	牛扒
steam (n), to steam	jing¹	蒸
steaming baskets	jing¹ lung⁴	蒸籠
to stew	den⁶	炖
stir-frying	cao²	炒
stock	seung⁶ tong¹	上湯
to strain	lui⁶	濾
strawberry	xi⁶ doh¹ be¹ lei⁴ (cho² mui⁴)	士多啤梨（草莓）
stuffing	haam⁶ liu⁶	餡料
suckling	yu⁵ ju¹	乳豬
sugar, brown	wong⁴ tong⁴	黃糖
sugar cane	gem¹ je³	甘蔗
sugar cane juice	je³ jap¹	蔗汁
sugar, caster	yau³ sa¹ tong⁴	幼砂糖
sunflower oil	kwai⁴ fa¹ ji² yau⁴	葵花籽油
sunflower seeds	kwai⁴ fa¹ ji²	葵花籽
supper	xiu¹ ye⁶	宵夜
sweet	tim⁴	甜
sweet & sour sauce	tim⁴ suen¹ jeung³	甜酸醬
sweet potato	faan¹ sue⁴	番薯
syrup	tong⁴ jeung¹	糖漿

T

takeaway	ngoi⁶ mai⁶	外賣
tamarind	loh⁴ mong⁶ ji²	羅望子
tangelo	gem¹ yau²	柑柚
tangerine	gem¹	柑
tapioca	muk⁶ sue⁴ fen²	木薯粉
tart (pie)	tad³	撻
taste	mei⁶ dou⁶	味道

tea	cha⁴	茶
bag	cha⁴ bao¹	茶包
black	hung⁴ cha³	紅茶
dragon well	lung⁴ jeng² cha⁴	龍井茶
green	luk⁶ cha⁴	綠茶
gunpowder	ju¹ cha⁴	珠茶
leaf	cha¹ yip⁶	茶葉
melon	cha⁴ gua¹	茶瓜
oolong	wu¹ lung⁴ cha⁴	烏龍茶
souchong	xiu² jung² cha⁴	小種茶
tiger lilies	baak³ heb⁶	百合
tin	tid ³ goon³	鐵罐
tinned	goon³ jong¹	罐裝
toast (bread)	doh¹ xi² (hung³ min⁶ bao¹)	多士 (烘麵包)
toffee-apple	bed⁶ xi¹ ping⁴ guo²	拔絲蘋果
tofu	deo⁶ fu⁶	豆腐
deep fried	deo⁶ fu⁶ buk¹	豆腐卜(豆腐泡)
dried	ji¹ juk¹	枝竹
fermented	fu⁶ yu⁵	腐乳
fresh	xin¹ deo⁶ fu⁶	鮮豆腐
pressed	deo⁶ fu⁶ gon¹	豆腐干
red	nam⁴ yu⁵	南乳
skins	fu⁶ juk¹	腐竹
sticks	ji¹ juk¹	枝竹
stinky	ceo³ deo⁶ fu⁶	臭豆腐
watery	deo⁶ fu⁶ fa¹	豆腐花
tongue	lei⁶	唎
tripe	ngau⁴ tou⁵	牛肚
trotter	ju¹ geuk³	豬腳
turnip	dai⁶ tau⁴ choi³	大頭菜
Chinese	loh⁴ baak⁶	蘿蔔
dried	loh³ baak⁶ gon¹	蘿蔔干
turtle	bid³	鱉

U

underdone	nuen⁶ jin¹	嫩煎

V

vegetable	soh¹ choi³	蔬菜
marrow	gua¹	瓜
salted	haam⁴ choi³	鹹菜
vegetarian	sou³ xig⁶	素食
venison	luk⁶ yug⁶	鹿肉
vinegar	cho³	醋
vitamin	wei⁴ ta¹ ming⁶	維他命

W

waiter/waitress	xi⁶ ying³	侍應
walnut	heb⁶ tou⁴	核桃
English	wu⁴ tou⁴	胡桃
water, carbonated	hei³ sui²	汽水
water, drinking	yem² yung⁶ sui²	飲用水
water chestnut	ma⁵ tei⁴	馬蒂
watercress	sai¹ yeung⁶ choi³	西洋菜
water-lily root	lin⁴ ngeo⁵	蓮藕
watermelon skin	sai¹ gua¹ pei⁴	西瓜皮
water spinach	ngung² choi³	蕹菜
well-done (cooked)	sug⁶ tau³	熟透
wheat	xiu² meg⁶	小麥
starch	meg⁶ fen²	麥粉
to whip	da²	打
whisky	wai¹ xi⁶ gei⁶	威士忌
wholefood	yuen⁴ xig⁶ med⁶	原食物
wholemeal	chuen⁴ meg⁶	全麥
wine	jau²	酒
bar	jau² ba¹	酒吧
fortified	ga¹ dou⁶ jau²	加度酒
red	hung³ jau²	紅酒
rice	mai⁵ jau²	米酒
white	baak⁶ jau²	白酒
wing	yig⁶	翼
wok	wok⁶	鑊
won ton	wen⁴ ten¹	雲吞
skins	wen⁴ ten¹ pei⁴	雲吞皮

Y

yam	faan¹ sue⁴	番薯
yeast	hao¹ mou⁵	酵母
yolk	daan⁶ wong⁴	蛋黃

Z

zest	gem¹ pai⁴	柑皮
zucchini	yi³ dai⁶ lei⁶ cheng¹ gua¹	意大利青瓜

Hong Kong Culinary Dictionary

This dictionary follows standard alphabetical order, however the numerical tone marks *(see page 209)* also affect the order. For example, baak³ heb⁶ comes before baak⁶ cheuk³ ha¹

A

ab³   鴨
  duck

ab³ beng²   鴨餅
  salted, boned and pressed duck immersed in peanut oil then steamed

ab³ geuk³   鴨腳
  duck feet

ab³ lei⁶   鴨喇
  duck tongue, available fresh or dried, prepared as an entree

ab³ yun⁶ cheung⁴   鴨潤腸
  duck-liver sausage, made from pork and duck liver. Served sliced with rice.

ab³ yun⁶ gon¹   鴨潤干
  duck liver, cured, soaked, chopped and wrapped in cured duck web (feet)

B

baak³ heb⁶   百合
  tiger lilies; lily buds *(see lin⁴ ji²)*

baak⁶ cheuk³ ha¹   白灼蝦
  fresh whole prawns, poached then simmered and served with a peanut oil and soy sauce dip

baak⁶ cho³   白醋
  white rice vinegar

baak⁶ choi³   白菜
  Chinese white cabbage

baak⁶ gai³   白芥
  white mustard

baak⁶ geb³   白鴿
  pigeon

baak⁶ guo²   白果
  ginkgo nuts, olive shaped with white flesh

baak⁶ wu⁴ jiu¹   白胡椒
  white pepper

baak⁶ xin⁶   白鱔
  white eel

baak⁶ yug⁶   白肉
  white meat

baat³ bou² laat⁶ jeung³   八寶辣醬
  eight-treasure hot sauce made from pressed tofu and chilli

baat³ goh³   八角
  star anise

baat³ gok³ fen²   八角粉
  weihsion powder, made from ground star anise

bak¹ ging¹ ja³ dai⁶ ha¹   北京炸大蝦
  whole prawns, first sauteed then quickly braised in chicken stock, rice wine, sugar and salt.

bak¹ ging¹ tin⁴ ab³   北京填鴨
  Peking Duck *(see Peking Duck in the Staples & Specialities chapter)*

bao¹ yu⁴   鮑魚
  abalone

bao¹ yu⁴ gu¹   鮑魚菇
  abalone mushrooms; also called oyster mushrooms

bid³   鱉
  turtle

bid³ kwan⁴   鱉裙
  calipash; edible substance found under turtle shell

bog⁶ hoh⁴   薄荷
  mint

boh¹ choi³   菠菜
  spinach

boh¹ loh⁴ med⁶   菠蘿蜜
  jackfruit

boon³ saang¹   半生
  rare

bou² chuen³ xig⁶ med⁶   保存食物
  preserve

bou² wei⁴ yi⁵ ngau⁴ yug⁶ jap¹   保衛爾牛肉汁
  beef stock

bou³ ding¹   布丁
  pudding

C

cang⁴ mei⁶ baak⁶ hou⁴　　橙味白毫
　orange pekoe tea

cao²　　炒
　fry; stir fry; saute

cao² daan⁶　　炒蛋
　scrambled egg

cao² fan⁶　　炒飯
　fried rice

cao² fen²　　炒粉
　flat rice noodle dish with shredded meat
　and vegetables

cao² min⁶　　炒麵
　chow mein; fried egg noodles with
　meat, seafood or vegetables

cao² seung⁶ so³　　炒上素
　vegetarian stir-fry dish of mushrooms, lotus
　root, ginkgo nuts and fresh vegetables

cei⁵ choi³　　薺菜
　shepherd's purse; watercress-like
　vegetable

cen⁴ pei⁴　　陳皮
　mandarin or tangerine peel used as a
　flavouring; ages well

ceo³ deo⁶ fu⁶　　臭豆腐
　stinky tofu; tofu fermented in cabbage
　juice

cha¹ xiu¹　　叉燒
　barbecued sweet roast pork (see Pork
　Dishes in the Staples & Specialities
　chapter)

cha¹ xiu¹ bao¹　　叉燒包
　barbecued pork bun; diced barbecued
　sweet roast pork and seasoning steamed
　in dough

cha⁴　　茶
　tea

cha⁴ bao¹　　茶包
　tea bag

cha⁴ gua¹　　茶瓜
　tea melon; melon preserved in honey
　and spices and used as flavouring

cha⁴ yip⁶　　茶葉
　tea leaf

chaam⁴ deo⁶　　蠶豆
　broad beans

chaan¹ cheuk³ yim⁴　　餐桌鹽
　table salt

chaan¹ goon²　　餐館
　restaurant

chaan¹ pai⁴　　餐牌
　menu

cham¹ yu⁴　　參魚
　trevally

chau¹ kwai¹　　秋葵
　okra; used in stir fries and soup

cheng¹ deo⁶　　青豆
　pea pods

cheng¹ gai³ laat⁶　　青芥辣
　mustard greens

cheng¹ gua¹　　青瓜
　cucumber

cheng¹ hau²　　青口
　mussels

cheng¹ loh⁴ baak⁶　　青蘿蔔
　oriental radish

cheng¹ ning⁴　　青檸
　lime

cheuk³　　焯
　scald/blanch

cheung⁴ fen²　　腸粉
　rice noodle roll; shrimp, pork or beef
　filling encased by rice noodles to form
　a soft roll that is steamed and served
　with soy sauce and sesame oil

chi⁴ gu¹　　茨菇
　arrowhead; a root vegetable

chi⁵　　柿
　persimmon

chim¹ beng²　　簽餅
　fortune cookies

chin⁴ choi³　　前菜
　entree

ching¹ den⁶ yug⁶ tong¹　　清炖肉湯
　consomme

ching¹ tong¹　　清湯
　broth

ching¹ yi¹　　青衣
　maori wrasse; fish of the whiting
　family

chit³　　切
　to cut

chit³ neb¹   切粒
to dice

cho¹ fen²   粗粉
rice noodle

cho² gu¹   草菇
grass (or straw) mushrooms; name
derived from being cultivated on straw.
Available in dried form.

cho² gu¹ lou⁵ chau¹   草菇老抽
mushroom soy sauce

cho³   醋
vinegar

choi³ gon¹   菜乾
dried cabbage (see gai³ choi³ tau⁴)

choi³ sem¹   菜心
Chinese flowering cabbage

choi³ xig¹   菜式
course

chue⁴ xi¹   廚師
chef

chue⁵ hau⁴ jeung³   柱侯醬
sweet sauce used in meat dishes

chui³   脆
crisp

chui³ pei⁴   脆皮
crackling

chui⁴ jau¹ lou⁵ sui² ngoh⁴   潮州鹵水鵝
Chui Chow soyed goose; goose stewed
in rich sauce, served with garlic and vinegar
dip (Shantou)

chui⁴ jau¹ yi¹ min⁶   潮州伊麵
thin egg noodles pan fried until crunchy,
served with chives, sugar and vinegar
(Shantou)

chui⁴ jau¹ yu⁴ tong¹   潮州魚湯
aromatic fish soup; sliced fish (usually
pomfret), squid, celery, mushrooms
and rice cooked in chicken stock and
sprinkled dried fish pieces (Shantou)

chui⁴ ji²   廚子
to cook

chun¹ guen³   春捲
spring roll; deep-fried pancake stuffed
with a mixture that can include
vegetables, chicken, pork, prawns,
mushrooms, sprouts and noodles.
Served as an entree or finger food.

chun¹ guen³ pei⁴   春捲皮
egg roll skins made of flour and water;
sold in sheet form

chun¹ sen²   春笋
spring bamboo shoots; large vegetable
with fuzzy outer leaves

chung¹   蔥
spring onion; green onion

chung¹ jap¹   蔥汁
spring onion sauce

chung¹ yau⁴ beng²   蔥油餅
onion cakes; fried pastries filled with
spring onion

chung⁴ ji²   松子
pine nuts

chung⁴ pei⁴ hai⁵   重皮蚧
hairy legged crab; can be fried, braised,
steamed and made into fritters.
Available in autumn.

chung⁴ xu² yu⁴   松鼠魚
squirrel fish; fish scored so that when
coated with batter and fried, a squirrel
pattern appears. Served with tomato-
based sweet & sour sauce and garnished
with peas, shrimp and pine nuts.

D

da²   打
to whip

da² bin¹ lou⁴   打邊爐
hotpot; Cantonese steamboat; raw
ingredients including chicken, pork,
seafood and vegetables are placed around
a vessel containing boiling broth. Diners
cook their own ingredients in the broth.

daam⁶ choi³   淡菜
dried mussels used in soups

daan⁶   蛋
eggs

daan⁶ fa¹ tong¹   蛋花湯
egg flower soup

daan⁶ min⁶   蛋麵
egg noodles; sold dried or fresh

daan⁶ tad³   蛋撻
egg tart; baked puff pastry with egg
custard filling

daan⁶ wong⁴   蛋黃
  yolk

dai³ ji²   帶子
  scallop

dai⁶ baak⁶ choi³   大白菜
  Chinese cabbage

dai⁶ cho³ go¹   大菜糕(瓊脂)
  agar-agar

dai⁶ chung¹   大蔥
  scallions; green onions

dai⁶ deo⁶   大豆
  soybean

dai⁶ gen¹   大根
  daikon

dai⁶ ha¹   大蝦
  prawn

dai⁶ leung⁴ cao² xin¹ nai⁵   大良炒鮮奶
  fried milk; made by frying milk or cream, egg whites and crab meat. Can be battered and deep fried or served over rice noodles

dai⁶ meg⁶ jau²   大麥酒
  barley wine

dai⁶ tau⁴ choi³   大頭菜
  turnip; preserved parsnips (see dung¹ choi³)

dam¹ dam¹ min⁶   擔擔麵
  bon-bon noodles; egg noodles served with chilli-hot meat sauce

den⁶   炖
  to stew

den⁶ ben²   炖品
  slow-cooked meat & vegetables

deng⁶ min⁶   澄麵
  Chinese flour; wheat flour used to make delicate and translucent dough for dumpling skins

deo⁶   豆
  bean

deo⁶ baan⁶ jeung³   豆瓣醬
  hot bean sauce made from chillies, oil and soybeans

deo⁶ beng²   豆餅
  bean cakes (see deo⁶ fu⁶)

deo⁶ fu⁶   豆腐
  tofu; bean curd; highly nutritious ingredient made from pureed, coagulated soybeans

deo⁶ fu⁶ buk¹   豆腐卜
  deep-fried fresh tofu cakes

deo⁶ fu⁶ fa¹   豆腐花
  soft tofu floating in sweetened syrup. Eaten as a snack or dessert.

deo⁶ fu⁶ gon¹   豆腐干
  pressed tofu; fresh tofu with the liquid pressed out. Can be shredded, cubed or left whole.

dco⁶ fu⁶ pei⁴   豆腐皮
  bean sheets

deo⁶ fu⁶ pci⁴ dan⁶   豆腐皮蛋
  diced preserved eggs scattered over tofu squares and topped with ginger & onion dressing

deo⁶ gok³   豆角
  string beans

deo⁶ jeung³   豆醬
  soybean paste

deo⁶ lui⁶ soh¹ choi³   豆類蔬菜
  legumes

den⁶ min⁴   豆苗
  pea shoots

deo⁶ sa¹   豆沙
  sweet black beans; used as filling

deo⁶ sue⁴   豆薯
  jicama

deo⁶ xi⁶   豆豉
  fermented black beans (see xi⁶ jap⁴)

deo⁶ xi⁶ jeung³   豆豉醬
  brown bean sauce (see jeung³ yeo⁴)

deo⁶ yau⁴   豆油
  soybean oil

deuk³   剁
  to chop

dim² sem¹   點心
  dim sum (see Yum Cha & Dim Sum in the Culture of Hong Kong Cuisine chapter)

ding¹ heung¹   丁香
  clove

doh¹ bed¹ bao² woh⁴ ji¹ fong¹   多不飽和脂肪
  polyunsaturated

dou¹ deo⁶   刀豆
  long beans

dou² nim³ ji²　　倒捻子
　mangosteen
dui³ ha¹　　對蝦
　king prawn
dun⁶ geb³ tong¹　　燉鴿湯
　double-boiled pigeon soup; restorative
　soup
dung¹ boh¹ yug⁶　　東坡肉
　rich casserole with belly pork, including
　skin and fat. Named after the poet, Su
　Dung Boh.
dung¹ choi³　　冬菜
　preserved turnips; finely chopped
　turnip that is steamed, salted then dried.
　Seasons soup, fish and pork dishes.
dung¹ gu¹　　冬菇
　black mushrooms; only the caps are
　eaten. Available fresh or dried. Also
　called shiitake or winter mushrooms.
dung¹ gua¹　　冬瓜
　winter melon
dung¹ gua¹ tong¹　　冬瓜湯
　winter melon soup (see recipe in the
　Hong Kong Banquet chapter)
dung¹ sen²　　冬筍
　bamboo shoots
dung³　　凍
　cold

E

em¹ chun¹　　鵪鶉
　quail
em¹ chun¹ daan⁶　　鵪鶉蛋
　quail egg
eng¹ goh¹ lei⁵　　鸚哥鯉
　parrot fish

F

fa¹ diu² jau²　　花雕酒
　glutinous rice wine; yellow rice wine
　used as flavouring
fa¹ jiu¹　　花椒
　anise pepper
fa¹ saang¹ yau⁴　　花生油
　aranchis oilê
fa¹ seng¹　　花生
　peanut

fa¹ seng¹ yau⁴　　花生油
　peanut oil
faai³ gen¹　　塊根
　root
faan¹ ke⁴　　蕃茄
　tomato
faan¹ lai⁶ ji¹　　蕃荔枝
　custard apple
faan¹ seg⁶ lau⁴　　番石榴
　guava
faan¹ sue⁴　　番薯
　sweet potato; yam
faat³ choi³　　髮菜
　black seaweed with hair-like appearance.
　Also called seaweed hair and maidenhair.
faat³ fen¹　　發粉
　baking powder
faat³ hao¹　　發酵
　fermentation
fai³ chaan¹　　快餐
　fast food
fai³ ji²　　筷子
　chopsticks
fan¹ ke⁴ ngau⁴　　蕃茄牛肉湯
yug⁶ tong¹
　tomato and beef soup
fan⁶　　飯
　boiled rice
fei¹ sui²　　飛水
　par boil
fei² chui¹ nung⁴ tong¹　　翡翠濃湯
(yuen¹ yueng¹ tong¹)　　(鴛鴦湯)
　thick soup sometimes called Yin &
　Yang soup because of the white chicken
　breast and dark-green spinach leaves
fei² chui¹ wu¹　　翡翠烏龍茶
lung⁴ cha⁴
　jade oolong tea, drunk to aid digestion
fen¹ lou⁴　　薰爐
　smoke house
fen²　　粉
　starchy
fen² xi¹　　粉絲
　bean starch noodles. Also called bean
　threads, cellophane or glass noodles.
foh² tui²　　火腿
　Chinese ham

fong¹ bin⁶ ng⁵ chaan¹ 方便午餐
fork luncheon; a midday buffet meal eaten while standing

fong¹ bin⁶ xig⁶ ben² 方便食品
convenience food

fu² baak⁶ choi³ 苦白菜
chicory

fu² gua¹ 苦瓜
bitter melon with corrugated skin. Softer ones are more bitter. Made palatable by blanching and adding sugar.

fu⁴ yung⁴ gei¹ 芙蓉雞
deep-fried chicken breast and egg whites simmered in wine stock

fu⁶ juk¹ 腐竹
dried yellow sticks made from soy milk

fu⁶ pei⁴ 腐皮
thin sheets of dried soft tofu used to make rolls

fu⁶ pei⁴ guen³ 腐皮卷
crispy tofu roll; tofu sheets wrapped around a filling made of shredded, stir-fried mushrooms, bean sprouts, carrot and celery. The rolls are pan-fried and sliced for serving.

fu⁶ yu⁵ 腐乳
fermented tofu cubes, dried, steamed, then bottled with wine. Has a Camembert-like taste and texture.

fuk⁶ mou⁶ fei³ 服務費
cover charge

fung¹ gon¹ 風乾
hang; term used to describe how game is suspended to allow flavour and texture to develop

fung⁶ cao⁴ 鳳巢
phoenix nest (see jeuk³ cao⁴)

fung⁶ gon¹ 鳳肝
chicken liver

fung⁶ zao² (gei¹ geuk³) 鳳爪 (雞腳)
chicken feet

G

ga¹ dou⁶ jau² 加度酒
fortified wine

ga¹ jau¹ mai⁵ 加州米
short-grain rice

ga¹ kem⁴ 家禽
fowl/poultry

ga¹ kem⁴ noi⁶ jong⁶ 家禽內臟
giblets

ga¹ tong⁴ 加糖
to sweeten

ga³ fe¹ 咖啡
coffee

ga³ fe¹ sed¹ 咖啡室
cafe

ga³ lei¹ 咖哩
curry

ga³ lei¹ fen² 咖哩粉
curry powder

gab³ hok⁶ lui⁶ 甲殼類
crustacean

gai³ choi³ tau⁴ 芥菜頭
dried, pressed and salted mustard cabbage. Used to flavour stews, soups and pork.

gai³ laan⁴ 芥蘭
kale/kail

gai³ laan⁴ tau⁴ 芥蘭頭
Chinese broccoli; leafier and longer than normal broccoli

gao¹ sen² 茭筍
wild rice shoots

gao² ji² 餃子
steamed or boiled meat dumplings; usually stuffed with pork and cabbage. Can also be fried then steamed and eaten with ginger & vinegar dip. Shanghai dumplings are larger than Cantonese ones.

gao² sui³ 鉸碎
to mince

gao² wen⁴ 攪勻
to toss

gau² choi³ fa¹ 韭菜花
flowering garlic chives

gau² gei² 枸杞
box thorn; similar in texture and nutritional value to spinach

gau² wong⁴ 韭黃
yellow chives

gei¹ 雞
chicken

gei¹ ji²　　　　雞子
  rooster testicles; a delicacy

gei¹ yik⁶　　　　雞翼
  chicken wings

gei² tui²　　　　雞腿
  drumsticks

gem¹　　　　柑
  mandarin, orange or tangerine

gem¹ goon¹ ping⁴ guo²　金冠蘋果
  golden delicious; sweet apple with
  greenish-yellow skin

gem¹ gu¹　　　　金菰
  enokitake mushrooms; often used in
  soup and noodle dishes

gem¹ gued¹　　　　柑橘
  citrus

gem¹ je³　　　　甘蔗
  sugar cane

gem¹ lam⁴　　　　甘藍
  brassica; generic name for plants of
  the mustard family

gem¹ pei⁴　　　　柑皮
  zest

gem¹ yau²　　　　柑柚
  tangelo

gem¹ zem¹　　　　金針
  golden needles; lily buds (see lin⁴ ji²)

gem² laam⁵ yau⁴　　橄欖油
  olive oil

geng² yug⁶　　　　頸肉
  neck

geung¹　　　　薑
  ginger

geung¹ chung¹ hai⁵　薑葱蚧
  ginger crab; whole crab is chopped,
  fried then braised with ginger and
  spring onion

geung¹ gen¹　　　　薑根
  ginger root

geung¹ ging³　　　　薑莖
  ginger stem

gin¹ guo²　　　　堅果
  nut

go¹ leung⁴　　　　高粱
  sorghum

gon¹　　　　肝
  liver

gon¹ bao¹ yu⁴　　　干鮑魚
  dried abalone

gon¹ dung¹ gu¹　　乾冬菰
  dried black mushrooms

gon¹ gam² laam⁵　　乾橄欖
  cured, dried and halved olives, used to
  flavour dishes

gon¹ hoh⁴ fen²　　　乾河粉
  rice sticks (see mai⁵ fen²)

gon¹ hoi² jid³　　　乾海蜇
  dried jellyfish, used for texture

gon¹ nai⁴ heung¹　　肝泥香腸
cheung⁴
  liver sausage

gon¹ pin¹ ngau⁴ yug⁶　乾煸牛肉
pui³ ngen⁴ xi¹ guen³　配銀絲卷
  shredded beef deep fried then tossed
  with chillies. Served with buns or rice.

gon¹ pin¹ sei³　　　乾煸四季豆
guei³ dao⁶
  deep-fried snake beans stir fried with
  garlic, ginger and shrimps. Served with
  soy sauce, wine, vinegar and sesame oil.
  (Sichuan)

gon¹ woon² deo⁶　　干豌豆
  split pea

goon³ tau⁴ foh² tui²　罐頭火腿
  spam

got² gen¹　　　　葛根
  kudzu; large root vegetable with coarse
  skin and sweet, white flesh. Used to
  make soup.

gu¹ lui⁶　　　　菰類
  generic name for fungi

gua¹　　　　瓜
  melon; vegetable marrow

gua¹ ji²　　　　瓜子
  melon seeds

gued¹ sui⁵　　　　骨髓
  marrow

guen³ sam¹ choi³　　卷心菜
  cabbage

guen³ sem¹ gai³ choi³　捲心芥菜
  savoy cabbage

guen³ yib⁶ gem¹ laam⁴　卷葉甘藍
  curly kale (cabbage)

gueng¹ chung¹ bak⁶ chit³ gei¹　　薑蔥白切雞
chicken poached with ginger, spring onion and salt. Sliced and served with ginger and spring onion dip.

gug¹ gui⁶　　菊苣
endive

gug¹ med⁶　　穀物
grain

guk¹ fa¹　　菊花
chrysanthemum; similar to lettuce. Accompanies dishes such as hotpots and snake.

gung¹ bou² gei¹ ding¹　　宮保雞丁
marinated chicken cubes stir fried with chillies and peanuts, seasoned with sweet bean sauce

gung¹ fu¹ cha⁴　　工夫茶
congou; black tea

gung¹ gei²　　公雞
rooster

guo² dung³　　果凍
fruit jelly

guo² dung³/yug⁶ dung³　　果凍 / 肉凍
gel (meat jelly)

guo² hok³　　果殼
husk

guo² jap¹　　果汁
juices

guo² pei⁴　　果皮
peel/rind

guo² yen⁴　　果仁
pip

gwai³ fa¹　　桂花
cassia flowers

gwan²　　滾
boiling

gwong² dung¹ lab⁶ cheung⁴　　廣東臘腸
cured pork sausage

H

ha¹ gao²　　蝦餃
bonnet-shaped prawn dumpling with translucent dough (see recipe in the Hong Kong Banquet chapter)

ha¹ jeung³　　蝦醬
shrimp paste; very pungent and salty flavouring

ha¹ ji²　　蝦子
prawn roe

ha¹ mai⁵　　蝦米
dried shrimps; used in stews, slow-cooked soups and to add flavour to stuffings for some dumplings

ha¹ pin³　　蝦片
prawn crackers; expand and crispen when deep fried. Eaten as a snack or used as garnish.

ha¹ zei²　　蝦仔
shrimps

ha⁶ ng² cha⁴　　下午茶
high tea

ha⁶ sen²　　夏筍
summer bamboo shoots; small variety common to China

haam⁴ ab³　　鹹鴨
preserved duck, sun dried and used as flavouring

haam⁴ ab³ daan⁶　　鹹鴨蛋
egg, salted and preserved in charcoal dust. Before eating, the egg is washed and hard boiled or steamed.

haam⁴ choi³　　鹹菜
preserved vegetables; salted and stored in an earthenware jar

haam⁴ daan⁶　　鹹蛋
duck eggs soaked in brine, causing the yolks to become firm. Used as flavouring.

haam⁴ ning⁴ mung¹ ab³ tong¹　　鹹檸檬鴨湯
duckling and salted lime soup

haam⁴ ju¹ tou⁵　　鹹豬肚
sowbelly

haam⁴ ju¹ yug⁶　　鹹豬肉
fat pork cured in salt or brine

haam⁴ sen²　　鹹筍
bamboo shoots; dried, salted, washed, shredded and sauteed

haam⁴ suen¹ choi³　　鹹酸菜
dried mustard cabbage (see gai³ choi³ tau⁴)

haam⁴ yu⁴　　鹹魚
fish, such as flounder, haddock, sole and salmon, preserved by salting. Can

be steamed with ginger, sliced, dry fried
and served as an appetiser.

haam⁶ 餡
filling

haam⁶ liu⁶ 餡料
stuffing

**haan⁴ yu⁴ jing¹ 鹹魚蒸豬肉
ju¹ yug⁶**
small amounts of salted fish mixed
through seasoned minced pork, then
steamed

hai⁵ 蚧
crab

hai⁵ ji² yu⁴ chi³ tong¹ 蚧子魚翅湯
shark's fin soup with crab roe sauce (see
Shark in the Staples & Specialities
chapter)

hai⁵ kim⁴ 蚧箝
crab claw

**hai⁵ yug⁶ choi³ 蟹肉菜膽雞
daam² gei¹**
steamed chicken and ham slices served
with crab meat sauce

hai⁵ yug⁶ pa⁴ lou⁶ sen² 蚧肉扒露筍
crab meat sauce served over sauteed
asparagus

hak¹ deo⁶ 黑豆
black beans

ham⁴ suen¹ choi³ 鹹酸菜
mustard cabbage fermented in brine.
Adds tang to soup, noodle, beef and
pork dishes. Can be stir fried or
steamed.

hao¹ 烤
to grill

hao¹ ga³ 烤架
grill

hao¹ mou⁵ 酵母
to ferment; yeast

hao² ab³ choi³ tong¹ 烤鴨菜湯
roast duck, cabbage and mushroom
soup; the carcass left over from Peking
Duck is the soup base

heb⁶ tou⁴ gei¹ ding¹ 合桃雞丁
boned chicken meat in bite-size pieces,
marinated and stir fried with vegetables
and walnuts

hed¹ yi⁴ gei¹ 乞兒雞
beggar's chicken (see Fowl in the Staples
& Specialities chapter)

heg¹ cho³ 黑醋
black rice vinegar

**heg¹ jiu¹ jap¹ pa⁴ 黑椒汁扒蘆筍
lou⁶ sen²**
asparagus in black bean sauce

heg¹ muk⁶ yi⁵ 黑木耳
black fungi (see wen⁴ yi⁵)

heg¹ tim⁴ cho³ 黑甜醋
sweet dark vinegar; thick, dark-brown
vinegar sold in jars and used to make
Cantonese pork and pig's feet stew

heg¹ wu⁴ jiu¹ 黑胡椒
black pepper

hei¹ chun¹ cha⁴ 熙春茶
hyson; Chinese green tea

hei³ woh¹ 汽鍋
Yunnan pot; red clay pot from Yunnan
Province made with an inverted air-
funnel rising from the base. Used for
steaming special soups.

hem⁵ zem¹ yu⁴ 頜針魚
garfish

heng⁵ yen⁴ 杏仁
almonds

heng⁶ yen⁴ jeung³ 杏仁醬
almond paste; sweetened, ground
almonds used in desserts and pastry
fillings

heung¹ cheung⁴ 香腸
sausage

heung¹ cho² 香草
herbal

heung¹ gua¹ 香瓜
muskmelon; sweet, edible melon with
a musky odour

heung¹ mao⁴ 香茅
lemongrass

heung¹ pin³ cha⁴ 香片茶
jasmine tea

hin² 蜆
clam

hin² gon¹ 蜆干
dried clams

ho⁴ xi⁶   蠔豉
dried oysters; added to stews or minced then sauteed or steamed

ho⁴ yau⁴ bao¹ pin³   蠔油鮑片
thinly sliced abalone, stir fried, seasoned in rich oyster sauce then served over braised greens

ho⁴ yau⁴ ngau⁴ yug⁶   蠔油牛肉
slices of tender beef stir fried and seasoned with oyster sauce

hoh¹ laan¹ deo⁶   荷蘭豆 (雪豆)
(suet³ deo⁶)
snow peas

hoh² heo² hoh² lok⁶   可口可樂
Coca-Cola

hoh⁴ bao¹ gei¹   荷包雞
purse chicken; small omelette-like pancake wrapped around a variety of minced ingredients, including chicken to resemble a purse (Shantou)

hoh⁴ fen²   河粉
slippery rice noodles; thin, round (like spaghetti) or flat

hoi¹ ping⁴ fei³   開瓶費
corkage

hoi¹ wei⁶ choi³   開胃菜
savoury

hoi¹ wei⁶ xiu² xig⁶   開胃小食
appetiser

hoi² baak⁶ choi³   海白菜
sea lettuce

hoi² cho²   海草
seaweed (see **kuen¹ bou³**)

hoi² daam²   海膽
sea urchin

hoi² dai³   海帶
dried seaweed (see **kuen¹ bou³**)

hoi² jid³   海蜇
jellyfish sold in sheets and packed in salt; served shredded

hoi² loh²   海螺
periwinkle

hoi² sem¹   海參
spiny black mollusc is soaked to become soft and gelatinous. Also known as sea cucumber, sea slug or trepang.

hoi⁴ toi⁴ xi¹   海苔絲
seaweed noodles; transparent, thread-like noodles made from seaweed. Used in cold dishes such as salads. Also called cellophane noodles or vermicelli

hoi² tong⁴ guo²   海棠果
crab apple; haw fruit from the hawthorn bush, thinly sliced and used as confectionery

hoi² xin¹   海鮮
seafood

hoi² xin⁶   海鱔
moray eel; a delicacy

hou⁴   蠔
oyster

hou⁴ gu¹   蠔菇
oyster mushrooms; also called abalone mushrooms

hou⁴ yau⁴   蠔油
oyster sauce (see Sauces & Flavourings in the Staples & Specialities chapter)

hui³ hok³   去殼
to shell

hung³   烘
bake/toast

hung³ deo⁶ sa¹   紅豆沙
red bean puree

hung³ cha⁴   紅茶
black tea

hung⁴ cho³   紅醋
red rice vinegar

hung⁴ deo⁶   紅豆
red mung beans

hung⁴ deo⁶ sa¹   紅豆沙
red bean paste; used in desserts and pastry fillings

hung⁴ fa¹ choi³ deo⁶   紅花菜豆
runner bean; string bean

hung⁴ fa¹ yau⁴   紅花油
safflower oil

hung⁴ geung¹   紅薑
red ginger

hung⁴ jiu¹   紅椒
red pepper

hung⁴ jo²   紅棗
red dates; small, red fruits with dry skin; adds sweetness to soups, stews, fish and chicken

hung⁴ laat⁶ jiu¹　　紅辣椒
Chinese red pepper; seasoning made from red pepper flakes

hung⁴ laat⁶ jiu¹ yau⁴　　紅辣椒油
red chilli oil

hung⁴ loh⁴ baak⁴　　紅蘿蔔
radish

hung⁴ loh⁴ baak⁶　　紅蘿蔔
carrot

hung⁴ mai⁵　　紅米
red-coloured rice; used for desserts and meat dishes

hung⁴ xiu¹　　紅燒
braise

hung⁴ xiu¹ baat³ bou² ab³　　紅燒八寶鴨
braised eight-jewelled duck (see Fowl in the Staples & Specialities chapter)

hung⁴ xiu¹ jeung³　　紅燒醬
red simmering sauce

hung⁴ xiu¹ju¹ sau²　　紅燒豬手
red simmered knuckle of pork (see Pork Dishes in the Staples & Specialities chapter)

hung⁴ xiu¹ pai⁴ gued¹　　紅燒排骨
braised spareribs (see Pork Dishes in the Staples & Specialities chapter)

hung⁴ xiu¹ yu⁴ chi³　　紅燒魚翅
braised shark's fin (see Shark in the Staples & Specialities chapter)

hung⁴ yug⁶　　紅肉
red meat

J

ja³　　炸
deep fry

ja³ choi³　　榨菜
kohlrabi preserved in salt and chilli powder (Sichuan)

ja³ choi³ yug⁶ xi¹　　榨菜肉絲
shredded pork with pickled vegetables

ja³ dai⁶ cheung⁴　　炸大腸
deep-fried intestines (Hakka)

ja³ ji² gei¹　　炸子雞
crispy skin chicken (see Fowl in the Staples & Specialities chapter)

ja³ saang¹ hou⁴　　炸生蠔
fresh oysters dipped in light batter and deep fried. Served with salt & pepper dip.

jau² ba¹　　酒吧
wine bar

jau² jo¹　　酒糟
semi-dried sediment remaining from the making of glutinous rice wine. Popular flavouring for Beijing and Shanghai dishes.

je³ jap¹　　蔗汁
sugar cane juice

jeuk³ cao⁴　　雀巢
bird's nest basket; phoenix nest; potato or yam straws shaped to resemble a nest, that is deep fried to make an edible, crisp basket. Filled with seafood, vegetables and/or chicken.

jeung¹ cha⁴ ab³　　樟茶鴨
duck smoked in camphor tea (see Fowl in the Staples & Specialities chapter)

jeung¹ yu⁴　　鱆魚
octopus

jeung³　　醬
paste

jeung³ jap¹　　醬汁
dip

jeung³ yau⁴　　醬油
soy sauce (see Sauces & Flavourings in the Staples & Specialities chapter). Also brown bean sauce made with fermented soybeans; used to flavour stews and braised dishes

ji¹ fong¹　　脂肪
fatty

ji¹ juk¹　　枝竹
cream-coloured sticks of dried tofu with an enamel-like surface and a nutty flavour. They soften with soaking. Generally used in fish, vegetarian and soup dishes. Some glazed tofu skin varieties, are made into stiff sheets and used for pastries and wrappings. Also known as tofu sticks.

ji¹ ma⁴　　芝麻
sesame

ji¹ ma⁴ beng² 芝麻餅
sesame cakes made from flour, lard, yeast, and coated with sesame seeds. Baked until crisp and golden then split in the centre to make a pouch, and a mixture of ground beef and pickled vegetables is spooned inside. The Chinese answer to the hamburger.

ji¹ ma⁴ jeung³ 芝麻醬
sesame paste

ji² bai⁴ gei¹ 紙包雞
small pieces of marinated chicken wrapped in greaseproof paper and deep fried. Very tasty and surprisingly free of oil.

ji² choi³ 紫菜
red seaweed, often boiled, flattened and fried; dried sheets of seaweed, eaten raw or added to soups

ji⁶ joh⁶ chaan¹ 自助餐
buffet

jid³ cho³ 浙醋
Chin Kiang vinegar; used to flavour soups, sauces, noodles, seafood and meat. Available in three types: white (for sweet and pungent dishes); red (for boiled crab); and black (for braised dishes and as dip).

jid³ gua¹ 節瓜
fuzzy melon; green, cylindrical vegetable covered with fine fur. Peeled, the melon is used in soups but can be stir fried or braised. Also known as fuzzy squash or summer melon.

jik⁶ wei⁶ 席位
cover

jim¹ mai⁵ 粘米
rice (see Rice in the Staples & Specialities Chapter)

jim¹ mei⁵ 占米
oriental rice; similar to long-grain rice

jin¹ dui¹ zei² 煎堆仔
deep-fried dumpling made from glutinous rice flour with a savoury filling

jin¹ hou⁴ beng² 煎蠔餅
oyster omelette made with oysters, spring onion and coriander

jing¹ 蒸
steam

jing¹ fan⁶ 蒸飯
steamed rice

jing¹ hei³ toi⁴ 蒸汽檯
steam table

jing¹ lau⁶ sui² 蒸餾水
still water

jing¹ lung⁴ 蒸籠
steaming basket

jing¹ saam¹ xin¹ 蒸三鮮
steamed three shredded meats; shredded ham, chicken and pork packed into a bowl with bamboo shoots, and steamed until set. The bowl is then inverted and the food moistened with chicken consomme. The three meats symbolise a family reunion. (Shanghai)

jing¹ sui² daan⁶ 蒸水蛋
water egg; eggs beaten with water and steamed

jing¹ woh¹ 蒸鍋
steamer

jing¹ yu⁴ 蒸魚
whole fish steamed and served with ginger, spring onion and soy sauce

jiu¹ si¹ fu⁶ yu⁵ tung¹ choi³ 椒絲腐乳通菜
water spinach with chilli and tofu

jiu¹ yim¹ 椒鹽
peppery salt; condiment made from roasted salt and ground pepper. Also called prickly ash.

jiu¹ yim⁴ yau⁴ yu⁴ 椒鹽魷魚
cooked squid tossed in a wok with roasted salt and pepper

jo² 棗
jujubes (see hung⁴ jo²)

jong¹ xig¹ 裝飾
to garnish

jong¹ xig¹ choi³ 裝飾菜
garnish

ju¹ 豬
pig; offal

ju¹ cha⁴ 珠茶
gunpowder tea

ju¹ geuk³ 豬腳
knuckle; trotter

ju¹ gu² lig⁶　　　朱古力
  chocolate

ju¹ hung⁴　　　豬紅
  pig's blood, salted, steamed, and cubed.
  Added to soup after poaching.

ju¹ min⁶ yug⁶　　豬麵肉
  jowl

ju¹ nam⁵ yug⁶　　豬腩肉
  belly pork

ju¹ pai⁴ gued¹　　豬 排骨
  chop (cut of meat); sparerib

ju¹ sau²　　　豬手
  hock

ju¹ yau⁴　　　豬油
  lard

ju¹ yug⁶　　　豬肉
  pork

ju¹ yug⁶ bao¹　　豬肉包
  pork buns (steamed; see the recipe in
  the Hong Kong Banquet chapter)

ju¹ yug⁶ pei⁴　　豬肉皮
  pork rind

ju²　　　　煮
  to cook/to boil

ju² nung⁴　　　煮濃
  reduce

ju² xing⁴ jiu¹ tong⁴　煮成焦糖
  caramelise

jui³ gei¹　　　醉雞
  drunken chicken; chicken poached, then
  marinated in the poaching broth and rice
  wine. Served chilled as an appetiser.

juk¹　　　　粥
  rice porridge; rice cooked in chicken
  broth to make a thick, savoury porridge

juk¹ gai³ choi³　　竹芥菜
  bamboo mustard cabbage; long, thin
  variety of mustard cabbage with
  serrated leaf·edges

juk¹ sang¹　　　竹笙
  bamboo pith/fungus; dry, lacey fungus
  derived from bamboo plants. Has a
  musty, earthy flavour and crunchy
  texture.

juk¹ sen²　　　竹筍
  bamboo shoots

juk¹ yip⁶　　　竹葉
  bamboo leaves; long, dried, green leaves
  used as a wrapping

juk⁶　　　　濁
  cloudy

jung²　　　　粽
  Chinese tamale

K

kau⁴ ging³ gem¹ lam⁴　球莖甘藍
  kohlrabi; variety of cabbage

ken⁴ choi³　　　芹菜
  celery

kiu⁴ meg⁶　　　蕎麥
  buckwheat

kiu⁴ meg⁶ min⁶　　蕎麥麵
  udon; thick Japanese noodle

kong³ chuen⁴ sui²　礦泉水
  mineral water

kuen¹ bou³　　　昆布
  purple laver; dark-purple seaweed
  available in sheets. Has a tangy, sea-
  sweet taste and is used in soups.

kwai¹ fa¹ ji²　　葵花籽
  sunflower seeds

kwai⁴ fa¹ ji² yau⁴　葵花籽油
  sunflower oil

L

laam⁵ yen⁴　　　欖仁
  olive nuts; kernel of the Chinese olive
  used for its nutty texture

laat⁶ gen¹　　　辣根
  horseradish

laat⁶ jap¹ ha¹ lug¹　辣汁蝦碌
  whole prawns are fried then braised in
  garlicky tomato sauce

laat⁶ jiu¹　　　辣椒
  chilli

laat⁶ jiu¹ fen²　　辣椒粉
  cayenne pepper

laat⁶ jiu¹ hai⁵　　辣椒蟹
  chilli crab

laat⁶ jiu¹ jeung³　　辣椒醬
  very hot sauce made from chilli, garlic,
  lemon and apricots. Used as seasoning
  especially in pickled vegetables.

laat⁶ xi⁶ yau⁴   辣豉油
Worcestershire sauce; pungent sauce
made from soy sauce, vinegar and spices

lab⁶ ab³   臘鴨
flattened, salted and dry-cured duck.
Sold whole or in large pieces. Also called
pressed duck.

lab⁶ cheung   臘腸
Chinese sausage (see gwong² dung¹ lab⁶
cheung⁴)

lab⁶ sab³ xig⁶ med⁶   垃圾食物
junk food

lab⁶ yug⁶   臘肉
dry-cured pork

lai⁶ ji¹   荔枝
lychee

lai⁶ ji¹ gon¹   荔枝干
lychee nuts; dried lychees with a
smokey, sweet flavour; eaten like nuts
or candy

lai⁶ tong¹   例湯
Chinese cabbage soup; usually pork and
a green vegetable such as cabbage or
watercress simmered in a light broth

lau⁴ lin⁴   榴槤
durian

lau⁵ yug⁶   柳肉
fillet

lei⁴   梨
pear

lei⁵ jek³ yug⁶   里脊肉
loin

lei⁵ yu⁴   鯉魚
carp

lei⁶   唎
tongue

leng⁴ yu⁴   鯪魚
dace; fish prepared with black beans
and generally served steamed with rice
as a snack

leung⁴ xig⁶ baak⁶ jau⁴   糧食白酒
samshou; alcoholic liqueur distilled
from rice or millet

lig⁶ giu¹/tim⁴ lou⁶ jau²   力嬌 / 甜露酒
liqueur

lin⁴ ji²   蓮子
lily buds; musky tasting, highly
nutritious vegetable used to flavour fish,
pork and poultry. The petals are used in
desserts. Also name for lotus nuts (or
seeds); olive-sized seeds of the lotus plant
used in desserts; a symbol of fertility.

lin⁴ ngeo⁵   蓮藕
lotus root; the tuber stem of the water
lily. Can be stuffed with rice and steamed,
stir fried, or used in soups and stews.

lin⁴ yip⁶   蓮葉
leaves of the water lily. When fresh they
impart a straw-like flavour, when dried
(after soaking) they are used as
wrapping for rice, meat and sweet
steamed rolls

lin⁴ yung⁴ bao¹   蓮蓉包
lotus seed dumpling; sweet bun filled
with mashed lotus seeds

lin⁶ nai⁵   煉奶
condensed milk

ling⁴ yu⁴   鯪魚
dace; fish of the carp family

loh³ baak⁶ gon¹   蘿蔔干
dried turnip; popular with pork and
snow peas

loh⁴ baak⁶ gon¹   蘿蔔干
preserved parsnips (see dung¹ choi³)

loh⁴ hon³ jai¹   羅漢齋
Lo Han in claypot; grand vegetarian
stew. Classically includes wood ear
fungus and lily bud stems, but there are
many variations.

loh⁴ lak⁶   羅勒
sweet basil

loh⁴ mong⁶ ji²   羅望子
tamarind

lop⁴ lak⁶   羅勒
basil

lou⁴ yu⁴   鱸魚
perch

lou⁵ chau¹   老抽
salted black beans (see xi⁶ jap⁴)

lou⁵ chau¹   老抽（黑醬油）
(heg¹ jeung³ yau⁴)
dark Chinese soy sauce; made from
soybean extract, flour, salt, sugar and
caramel

lou⁵ sui² jap¹   鹵水汁
marinade of salt, pepper, soy sauce, fennel seeds, star anise, cinnamon, cloves and licorice root. Used for meat and fish.

lou⁵ xu² baan¹   老鼠斑
barramundi cod

lou⁶ sen²   蘆筍
asparagus

lug¹ yau⁶   碌柚
pomelo

luk⁶   鹿
deer

luk⁶ cha⁴   綠茶
green tea

luk⁶ deo²   綠豆
green mung beans. When not harvested for their sprouts, mung beans are cooked with water and sugar and made into a paste for filling desserts.

luk⁶ deo⁶ nga⁴ choi³   綠豆芽菜
mung bean sprouts

luk⁶ gab⁵ hoi² guei¹   綠甲海龜
green turtle; large sea turtle

luk⁶ yug⁶   鹿肉
venison

lung⁴ jeng² cha⁴   龍井茶
dragon well tea; the aristocrat of green teas

lung⁴ ngan⁵   龍眼俱
dragon's eyes; longan

lung⁴ so¹ choi³   龍鬚菜
seaweed hair (see faat³ choi³)

lut⁶ ji²   栗子
chestnut

M

ma⁴ poh⁴ deo⁶ fu⁶   麻婆豆腐
'pock-marked grandmother's tofu'; fresh tofu combined with pork or beef, garlic, chilli, bean paste, soy sauce, rice wine, Sichuan peppercorn and spring onion. Also known as Sichuan braised tofu. (Sichuan)

ma⁴ yau⁴   麻油
sesame oil

ma⁵ lai¹ gou¹   馬拉糕
steamed egg sponge cake

ma⁵ ngei⁵ seung⁵ xu⁶   螞蟻上樹
'ants climbing a tree' bean-thread noodles braised with seasoned minced pork

mai⁴ did⁶ heung¹   迷迭香
rosemary

mai⁵   米
rice

mai⁵ fen²   米粉
rice-flour noodles; brittle and opaque noodles. Can be boiled, deep fried or steamed. Or slippery rice noodles; thin, round (like spaghetti) or flat.

mai⁵ jau²   米酒
yellow rice wine used with fish and duck dishes

mai⁵ ji²   米紙
rice paper; used as confectionery wrapping

man⁵ chaan¹   晚餐
dinner

mao⁴ toi⁴ jau²   茅台酒
extremely potent alcohol distilled from sorghum

med⁶ gem¹   蜜柑
satsuma

med⁶ jin³ geung¹   蜜餞薑
preserved ginger

meg⁶ fen²   麥粉
wheat starch (see deng⁶ min⁶)

meg⁶ min⁶   麥麵
wheat-flour noodles

meg⁶ nga⁴   麥芽
malt

meg⁶ nga⁴ tong⁴   麥芽糖
maltose

meg⁶ yu⁴   墨魚
cuttlefish; inkfish (see yau⁴ yu⁴)

meg⁶ yu⁴ gon¹   墨魚干
dried cuttlefish

mei⁶ dou⁶   味道
flavour; taste

mei⁶ jing¹   味精
monosodium glutamate (MSG)

men¹   炆
simmer

min⁶　　　麵
narrow 'cluster' noodles that can be made from egg, rice or even seaweed

min⁶ bao¹　　　麵包
bread

min⁶ bao¹ guen³　　　麵包卷
bread roll

min⁶ bao¹ hong¹　　　麵包糠
breadcrumbs

min⁶ fen²　　　麵粉
flour

min⁶ gen¹　　　麵筋
gluten made from dough. Used in braised vegetarian dishes.

min⁶ gen¹ kau⁴　　　麵筋球
gluten balls made from dough that is washed so only gluten remains. The gluten is fashioned into balls and deep fried. Has a meaty texture and is used mostly in vegetarian cooking.

min⁶ wu⁴　　　麵糊
batter

min⁶ xi⁶ jeung³　　　麵豉醬
yellow bean paste; pungent soybean product used as a flavouring as well as to preserve food. Also called yellow sauce.

ming⁴ gao¹　　　明膠
gelatin

moh⁴ gu¹　　　磨菇
button mushrooms; used in stir fries and soups

moh⁴ xi¹　　　磨絲
grated

mong¹ guo²　　　芒果
mango

mong¹ guo² bou³ ding¹　　　芒果布丁
mango pudding; fresh mangoes pureed and set in a smooth mousse-like dessert

moot¹ lei⁶ cha⁴　　　茉莉茶
jasmine

mou¹ deo⁶　　　毛豆
green soybeans; green and chewy beans usually braised and eaten when cooled (Shanghai)

mou⁴ fa¹ guo²　　　無花果
fig

mug⁶ sug⁶ cho²　　　苜蓿草
Chinese clover; similar to watercress (Shanghai)

mui⁴　　　梅
plum

mui⁴ choi³　　　梅菜
salt-cured cabbage; tightly wrapped bundles of cured, salty, moist cabbage. Used to flavour steamed pork and fish.

mui⁴ choi³ kau³ yug⁶　　　梅菜扣肉
double-cooked steamed pork with pickled salted cabbage

mui⁴ guei³ yau⁴　　　玫瑰油
rose oil

mui⁴ ji² jeung³　　　梅子醬
plum sauce; thick, chutney-like sauce made from plums, apricots, vinegar, sugar and chilli. Used as a condiment or with roast dishes.

muk⁶ gua¹　　　木瓜
papaya/pawpaw

muk⁶ sue¹ fen²　　　木薯粉
tapioca

muk⁶ sui¹ yug⁶　　　木須肉
shredded meat (usually pork) stir fried with eggs and vegetables, including black mushrooms and lily flowers. The mix is then spooned into a pancake and rolled up.

muk⁶ yi⁵　　　木耳
wood ear fungus; used in stir fried, braised and steamed dishes. Sold in dried form.

mung⁴ gu² hao² yug⁶　　　蒙古烤肉
Mongolian barbecued beef

N

nai⁵ xig⁶　　　奶昔
milk shake

nai⁵ yau⁴　　　奶油
cream

nai⁵ yau⁴ hin²　　　奶油蜆
butter clam

nam⁴ gua¹　　　南瓜
Chinese squash; green marrow with yellow stripes. Usually cooked with beef, ham or fish, but can be stir fried on its own.

nam⁴ yu⁵   南乳
red tofu; sweet and crumbly tofu fermented in salt, sugar, alcohol and red colouring, used to flavour meat dishes

nam⁴ yu⁵   南乳
Chinese red cheese; canned, pressed tofu cubes fermented in salt, spices and rice wine. Very pungent seasoning used with pork and poultry.

neb¹   粒
dice

nei⁴   泥
puree

ng² heung¹ fen²   五香粉
five spice powder; combination of star anise, anise pepper, fennel, cloves and cinnamon

ng⁵ chaan¹   午餐
lunch

ng⁵ chaan¹ cha⁴ dim²   午餐茶點
tiffin; light meal taken at midday

ng⁵ chaan¹ yug⁶   午餐肉
popular luncheon meat eaten with bread

nga⁴ choi³   芽菜
bean sprouts (see luk⁶ deo⁶)

nga⁴ dai³   牙帶
pike; used primarily for making fish balls and fish cakes

ngang⁶ wed⁶ guo²   硬核果
stone fruit

ngau⁴   牛
ox

ngau⁴ hung¹ yug⁶   牛胸肉
brisket

ngau⁴ lem¹ yuk⁶   牛臄肉
rump

ngau⁴ mei⁵   牛尾
oxtail

ngau⁴ nai⁵ bou³ ding¹   牛奶布丁
milk pudding

ngau⁴ nai⁵ ga³ fe¹   牛奶咖啡
cafe au lait; cafe latte

ngau⁴ pa⁴   牛扒
steak

ngau⁴ tou⁵   牛肚
omasum; cow's third stomach

ngau⁴ yau⁴   牛油
butter

ngau⁴ yau⁴ guo²   牛油果
avocado; 'butter fruit'

ngau⁴ yug⁶   牛肉
beef

ngei² gua¹   矮瓜
aubergine/eggplant

ngen⁴ hou⁴   銀毫
silver tips tea (very rare)

ngen⁴ nga⁴   銀芽
mung bean sprouts with heads and roots removed

ngen⁴ yu⁴ zei²   銀魚仔
whitebait

ngeo⁴ gwat¹ sui⁵   牛骨髓
beef bone marrow

ngeo⁵ fen²   藕粉
lotus flour; made from lotus nuts, used as thickening agent

ngoh⁴   鵝
goose

ngoh⁴ mui⁴   鵝莓
gooseberry

ngung² choi³   蕹菜
water spinach

ning⁴ mung¹   檸檬
lemon

ning⁴ mung¹ gei¹   檸檬雞
lemon chicken (see Fowl in the Staples & Specialities chapter)

ning⁴ mung¹ hei³ sui²   檸檬汽水
lemon squash

ning⁴ mung¹ jeung³   檸檬醬
lemon sauce, used to make lemon chicken. Also eaten with roast pork or barbecued duck.

ning⁴ mung¹ sui²   檸檬水
lemonade

ning⁴ mung¹ yip⁶   檸檬葉
lemon leaves used as flavouring

noh⁶ mei⁵   糯米
glutinous rice; also known as sticky rice or sweet rice

noh⁶ mei⁵ gei¹   糯米雞
sticky rice dumpling; glutinous rice steamed in lotus leaves with such ingredients as pork or chicken

nou⁵   腦
  brains
nuen⁶ ab³   嫩鴨
  duckling
nuen⁶ jin¹   嫩煎
  underdone
nuen⁶ ju²   嫩煮
  soft boil
nuen⁶ woon² deo⁶   嫩豌豆
  mangetout (sugar pea)
nuen⁶ yeung⁶ chung¹   嫩洋蔥
  green onions
nui⁵ sen⁴ geb³   女神蛤
  giant clam

P

pao³ choi³   泡菜
  vegetables that are shredded and pickled
  in soy sauce. Eaten with noodles, soups
  and congee.
pei⁴   皮
  skin (of meat)
pei⁴ daan⁶   皮蛋
  preserved eggs (see Eggs in the Staples
  & Specialities chapter)
pei⁶ pa⁴ guo²   枇杷果
  loquat; small, yellow fruit
ping¹/ping² poon⁴   拼／拚盤
  combination of foods in one dish
pou² lei¹   普洱
  Pu-erh tea (black jasmine)
pui³ choi³   配菜
  side dish

S

sa¹ de¹   沙嗲
  satay; pieces of meat, poultry or prawns,
  grilled on a skewer
sa¹ de¹ jeung³   沙嗲醬
  satay sauce; thick sauce made from
  peanuts and chilli served with satay
sa¹ geung¹ fen²   沙薑粉
  ginger powder
sa¹ lut⁶   沙律
  salad
sa¹ lut⁶ jeung³   沙律醬
  salad dressing

sa¹ moon⁴ xi⁶ kuen²   沙門氏菌
  salmonella
sa¹ woh¹   沙窩
  casserole
sa¹ yu⁴   鯊魚
  flake (shark meat)
saam¹ men⁴ yu⁴   三文魚
  salmon
saan¹ ja¹   山楂
  quince
saan³ tau⁴ gai³ choi³   汕頭芥菜
  mustard cabbage; used mainly in soup
  (Shantou)
saan⁴ choi³   潺菜
  Ceylon spinach; leafy vegetable that is
  used mainly in soups. Also called
  slippery vegetable due to its mild
  laxative effect.
saang¹ cao² gei¹ ding¹   生炒雞丁
  spatchcock
saang¹ chau¹ (xi⁶ yau⁴)   生抽（豉油）
  light soy sauce used to flavour dishes
  such as clear soups and stir-fry dishes.
  Also used as a condiment.
saang¹ guo²   生果
  fruit
saang⁶   生
  raw
sab⁶ mei⁶ jeung³   十味醬
  ten-flavoured sauce; spicy sauce made
  from soybeans, spices, garlic, chilli and
  sugar. Used in cooking and as a
  condiment for prawns, pork and
  poultry.
sai¹ gua¹   西瓜
  watermelon
sai¹ lan⁴ fa¹   西蘭花
  broccoli
sai¹ mai⁵   西米
  sago
sai¹ mui⁴   西梅
  prune
sai¹ yau²   西柚
  grapefruit
sai¹ yeung⁶ choi³   西洋菜
  watercress

san³ yeung⁴ yug⁶　　　涮羊肉
Mongolian lamb hotpot; do-it-yourself meal cooked at the table in a flame-heated hotpot holding broth. Sliced meat is cooked in the broth. When the meat is finished, cabbage and noodles are added to make a soup.

sau³ yug⁶　　　瘦肉
lean

se¹ lei⁶ jau²　　　些利酒
sherry

seg⁶ lau⁴　　　石榴
pomegranate

seg⁶ lung⁴ ha¹　　　石龍蝦
rock lobster

sei³ chuen¹ kau⁴ ging³ gem¹ lam⁴　　　四川球莖甘藍
Sichuan kholrabi

sei³ chuen¹ laat⁶ jiu¹　　　四川辣椒
Sichuan peppercorn

sei³ chuen¹ laat⁶ jiu¹ yau⁴　　　四川辣椒油
Sichuan peppercorn oil

sei³ chuen¹ pou³ choi³　　　四川泡菜
vegetables such as cucumbers, radish and peppers pickled in brine and vinegar, and served chilled as an appetiser. Tart and spicy. (Sichuan)

sem¹　　　心
heart

sen¹ xin¹　　　新鮮
fresh

sen¹ xin¹ wong⁴ deo⁶　　　新鮮黃豆
fresh soybeans

seung⁶ hoi² nin⁴ go¹　　　上海年糕
combination of glutinous rice flour and water set in moulds to make slabs of rice cake. Slabs are sliced, soaked and sauteed or cooked in soup.

seung⁶ tong¹　　　上湯
stock

siu² xin³ bui³　　　小扇貝
pipi

so¹ pei⁴　　　酥皮
puff pastry

so³ xig⁶　　　素食
vegetarian

soh¹ choi³　　　蔬菜
vegetable

sou¹ da² sui²　　　蘇打水
soda water

sou¹ pei⁴　　　酥皮
pastry

sou³ xig⁶　　　素食
vegetarian

sou³ yug⁶　　　素肉
vegetable steak; soybean product used as a meat substitute

suan³ jap¹ au⁴ lei⁶　　　蒜汁牛唎
beef tongue with garlic sauce (see the recipe in the Hong Kong Banquet chapter)

sue⁴ pin³　　　薯片
potato chip

sue⁴ tiu⁴　　　薯條
potato chip

sue⁴ zei²　　　薯仔
potato

suen¹　　　酸
sour

suen¹ gai³ choi³　　　酸芥菜
whole mustard cabbages packed in brine and fermented; used as a tangy flavouring

suen¹ geung¹　　　酸薑
young, pink ginger, sliced and pickled with sugar and vinegar

suen¹ laat⁶ tong¹　　　酸辣湯
hot & sour soup with pepper, chillies and vinegar. A warming winter dish that traditionally included solidified chicken blood is added, but is usually omitted. (Sichuan, north China)

suen¹ mui⁴　　　酸梅
sour plums

suen¹ pao² wong⁴ gua¹　　　酸泡黃瓜
pickled melon; yellow cucumber similar to sweet pickle. Used in soup and sweet & sour sauces.

suen¹ pao³ choi³　　　酸泡菜
pickle

suen¹ pao³ gai³ choi³　　　酸泡芥菜
green pickled mustard

suen¹ sen² 酸筍
pickled bamboo shoots; impart a salty, sour taste to steamed pork and beef dishes

suen³ sem¹ 蒜心
flowering garlic shoots; related to flowering garlic chives (see **gau² choi³ fa¹**), but thicker, with buds on the stems.

suen³ tau⁴ 蒜頭
garlic

suen³ wong⁴ 蒜黃
blanched garlic chives; also garlic chives grown in the dark, traditionally under woven straw cylinders. The yellow, limp, flat leaves have a much stronger garlic flavour than garlic chives.

suet³ choi³ 雪菜
preserved snow cabbage

suet³ dau² ma⁵ tei² dung¹ gu¹ cao² dai³ ji² 雪豆、馬蒂、冬菇炒帶子
stir-fried scallops with snow peas, water chestnuts and shiitake mushrooms

suet³ geb³ go¹ 雪蛤糕
frog fat; medicinal ingredient supposedly removed from the unsuspecting frog while it hibernates

suet³ go¹ 雪糕
ice cream

suet³ saan¹ guo² poon⁴ 雪山果盤
fresh fruit and ice chunks artfully arranged on a bed of ice

suet³ yi⁵ 雪耳
snow ear fungus; white fungus that is crunchy when cooked

sug¹ fen² 粟粉
cornstarch

sug¹ mei⁵ 粟米
corn; maize; millet

sug¹ mei⁵ yau⁴ 粟米油
corn oil

sug⁶ 熟
done (cooked); ripe

sug⁶ tau³ 熟透
well done (cooked)

sui¹ jing¹ ha¹ kau⁴ 水晶蝦球
prawns marinated in eggwhite and cornflour, wok-tossed with minced ginger and garlic

sui² ju² 水煮
poach

sui² ken⁴ 水芹
cress

sui⁶ chin⁴ jau² 睡前酒
nightcap

sung¹ daan⁶ go¹ 鬆蛋糕
sponge cake

sung¹ nuen⁶ 鬆嫩
tenderise

T

tab³ sa¹ (lung⁴ lei⁶) 鰨沙（龍喇）
sole; mainly brought in from Macau. Excellent for steaming.

tad³ 撻
tart/pie

tam⁵ lin⁶ nai⁵ 淡煉奶
evaporated milk

tid³ goon³ 鐵罐
tin

tim¹ ga¹ ying⁴ yeung⁵ 添加營養
enrich

tim⁴ 甜
sweet

tim⁴ ben² 甜品
dessert

tim⁴ choi³ tau⁴ 甜菜頭
sugar beet

tim⁴ choi³ yip⁶ 甜菜葉
spinach beet

tim⁴ gen¹ 甜根
sweet root

tim⁴ laat⁶ jiu¹ jeung² 甜辣椒醬
sweet chilli sauce

tim⁴ mai⁵ 甜米
sweet rice

tim⁴ min⁶ jeung³ 甜麵醬
Hoisin sauce; thick, sweet, spicy sauce made from soybeans, red beans, sugar, garlic, vinegar, chilli, sesame oil and flour

(tim⁴) noh⁶ mai⁵ jau² （甜）糯米酒
glutinous sweet rice wine; used as a flavouring

tim⁴ suen¹ hung⁴ 　　甜酸紅燒蝦球
xiu¹ ha¹ kau⁴
deep-fried shrimp balls with sweet & sour sauce

tim⁴ suen¹ jeung³ 　　甜酸醬
sweet & sour sauce made with vinegar and sugar. The basis of sweet & sour pork and sweet & sour fish.

tim⁴ suen¹ pai⁴ gued¹ 　　甜酸排骨
sweet & sour pork *(see* Pork Dishes in the Staples & Specialities chapter)

tim⁴ suen¹ yu⁴ 　　甜酸魚
sweet & sour fish

tim⁴ sug¹ mai⁵ 　　甜粟米
sweet corn

tin⁴ gei² 　　田雞
frog

tiu⁴ boon⁶ 　　調拌
to mix

tiu⁴ mei⁶ ben² 　　調味品
condiment

tiu⁴ mei⁶ 　　調味
flavouring

tiu⁴ mei⁶ fen² 　　調味粉
monosodium glutamate (MSG)

tiu⁴ mei⁶ liu⁶ 　　調味料
seasoning

tong¹ 　　湯
soup

tong¹ yuen³ 　　湯圓
glutinous rice-flour balls

tong⁴ fen² 　　糖份
icing sugar

tong⁴ geung¹ 　　糖薑
candied ginger

tong⁴ guo² 　　糖果
candy

tong⁴ guo² go¹ 　　糖果糕餅店
beng² dim³
confectionery

tong⁴ jeung¹ 　　糖漿
syrup

tong⁴ jing¹ 　　糖精
saccarin

tong⁴ saang¹ choi³ 　　唐生菜
Chinese lettuce *(see* wong⁴ nga⁴ baak⁶)

tong⁴ sui² 　　糖水
sweet soup (Hakka)

tong⁶ bou¹ 　　湯煲
stockpot

tou³ yug⁶ 　　兔肉
rabbit

tou⁴ 　　桃
peach

tou⁴ yau⁴ hao² 　　塗油烤
baste

tuet³ sui² 　　脱水
dehydrate/dessicate

tung⁴ guo² go¹ beng² 　　糖果糕餅
confection

tung⁴ hou¹ 　　茼蒿
white wormwood; a three-pointed leafy vegetable with a long, reddish-purple leaf stalk and no stem. Used to make a tonic soup and can also be deep fried. Has a bitter taste.

W

wed⁶ tou⁴ 　　核桃
pecan

wei⁴ ta¹ ming⁶ 　　維他命
vitamin

wen⁴ mou⁶ cha⁴ 　　雲霧茶
cloud mist tea; grown high on the mountain cliffs of Jiangxi, where it is said monkeys are trained to harvest it

wen⁴ nam⁴ foh² tui² 　　雲南火腿
ham from Yunnan; reputedly the best ham in China

wen⁴ ten¹ 　　雲吞
won ton/wuntun; dumplings stuffed with mince pork, seafood or vegetables and either boiled in soup or deep fried and served with a dipping sauce

wen⁴ ten¹ pei⁴ 　　雲吞皮
won ton skins; pre-packaged egg flour skins or wrappings. Shanghai won tons are made with flour and water, Cantonese won tons are made from high-gluten flour.

wen⁴ ten¹ tong¹ 　　雲吞湯
won tons in chicken broth

wen⁴ yi⁵ 雲耳
cloud ear fungus; black fungus with a crunchy texture

wok⁶ 鑊
wok

wong³ deo⁶/dai⁶ deo⁶ 黃豆 / 大豆
soy

wong³ deo⁶/dai⁶ deo⁶ 黃豆 / 大豆
soybean

wong⁴ deo⁶ fen² 黃豆粉
ground powder from the yellow bean used to dust Chinese desserts

wong⁴ fa¹ yu⁴ 黃花魚
yellow croaker fish

wong⁴ gai³ laat⁶ 黃芥辣
yellow mustard

wong⁴ gua¹ 黃瓜
yellow cucumber; heavy melon with a similar skin to cantaloupe. Mature melons are chopped into chunks and boiled in soups with the flesh, peel and seeds used to make stock. Also known as yellow torpedo.

wong⁴ jau² 黃酒
yellow wine (see xiu⁶ hing¹ mai⁵ jau²)

wong⁴ muk⁶ yi⁵ 黃木耳
brown fungi (see muk⁶ yi⁵)

wong⁴ nga⁴ baak⁶ 黃芽白
celery cabbage; pale cabbage with a mellow flavour. Also called napa cabbage and Chinese lettuce.

wong⁴ tong⁴ 黃糖
brown sugar

wong⁴ xin⁴ 黃鱔
yellow eel

woon² deo⁶ 豌豆
pea

wu¹ gei² 烏雞
silkie; small chicken with dark meat. High in nutritional value.

wu¹ lung⁴ cha⁴ 烏龍茶
oolong tea

wu⁴ 糊
to cream (ingredients)

wu⁴ jiu¹ 胡椒
chilli/pepper

wu⁴ jiu¹ neb¹ 胡椒粒
peppercorn

wu⁴ lou⁴ 葫蘆
gourd/squash

wu⁴ lou⁴ gua¹ 葫蘆瓜
bottle squash; green marrow that is peeled, sliced and used in soup and stir-fried dishes

wu⁶ fen² 芋粉
taro starch

wu⁶ gok³ 芋角
deep-fried dumpling made of mashed and grated taro, filled with sweet pork mixture

wu⁶ tau⁴ 芋頭
eddoe; red-budded taro

wu⁶ tau⁴ 芋頭
taro root; brown root vegetable with a white flesh flecked with purple. Tastes like sweet potato.

wui⁴ heung¹ 茴香
fennel

wui⁴ heung¹ ji² 茴香籽
fennel seeds

X

xi¹ gua¹ 絲瓜
sponge luffa; dark-green melon with rough skin and dark stripes. Used in soups and washing sponges.

xi¹ ji² tau⁴ 獅子頭
stewed large meatball (see Pork Dishes in the Staples & Specialities chapter)

xi⁴ choi³ hung⁴ xiu¹ deo⁶ fu² 時菜紅燒豆腐
braised tofu with vegetables

xi⁶ doh¹ be¹ lei⁴ (cho² mui⁴) 士多啤梨 (草莓)
strawberry

xi⁶ jap⁴ 豉汁
black bean sauce; garlic, soy sauce, sugar and chilli added to fermented salted black beans and mashed into a paste

xi⁶ jap¹ fung⁶ zao² 豉汁鳳爪
deep-fried, steamed chicken feet in black bean and chilli sauce

xi⁶ jap¹ lung⁴ ha¹ 豉汁龍蝦
lobster (with shell) chopped in sections, deep fried then stir fried with black beans, ginger and garlic. Chicken stock is added and the lobster is braised.

xi⁶ jap¹ jing³ pai⁴ gwat¹ 豉汁蒸排骨
pork spareribs chopped into bite-size pieces, marinated then steamed with the sauce

xi⁶ jiu¹ cao² yug⁶ ding¹ 豉椒炒肉丁
diced belly pork stir fried with capsicums and chillies, seasoned with sauce of soybean paste, wine and soy sauce

xi⁶ jui¹ cao² pai⁴ gued¹ 豉椒炒排骨
marinated rib pieces and sliced onion and capsicum sauteed in black bean sauce

xi⁶ ying³ 侍應
waiter/waitress

xi⁶ ying³ ling⁵ baan¹ 侍應領班
headwaiter

xig⁶ med⁶ 食物
food

xig⁶ pou² 食譜
recipe

xin¹ deo⁶ fu⁶ 鮮豆腐
fresh tofu

xin⁵ 鱔
eel; can be smoked or braised

xing⁶ choi³ 剩菜
leftover

xiu¹ ab³ 燒鴨
roast duck (see Fowl in the Staples & Specialities chapter)

xiu¹ beng² 燒餅
flat bread topped with sesame seeds (north China)

xiu¹ hao¹ 燒烤
barbecue/roast

xiu¹ ju² 燒豬
roast pig

xiu¹ mai⁶ 燒買
steamed dumpling; won ton wrappers filled pork, prawns, water chestnuts and bamboo shoots then steamed

xiu¹ ngoh⁴ 燒鵝
roast goose; Hong Kong speciality with extremely tender meat and rich, crisp skin

xiu¹ yeung⁴ yug⁶ 燒羊肉
kebab (see sa¹ de¹)

xiu¹ yu⁵ ju¹ 燒乳豬
whole, marinated suckling pig roasted over hot coals resulting in rich, sweet meat and golden crackling skin. Can be served on its own, or with small pancakes or buns. Usually ordered for special occasions, but also sold in pieces at Cantonese restaurants.

xiu¹ yug⁶ 燒肉
roast pork

xiu² deo⁶ kau³ 小豆蔻
cardamom

xiu² jung² cha⁴ 小種茶
souchong tea

xiu² lung⁴ ha¹ 小龍蝦
crayfish

xiu² maan⁴ yu⁴ 小鰻魚
grig; freshwater eel

xiu² meg⁶ cho⁴ 小麥草
alfalfa shoots

xiu² wui¹ heung¹ 小茴香
cumin

xiu² xig⁶ 小食
snack/nibbles

xiu⁶ hing¹ mai⁵ jau² 紹興米酒
Shaohsing wine; glutinous rice wine used in marinades. Quality varieties are drunk.

Y

yau³ tiu⁴ min⁶ 幼條麵
vermicelli

yau⁴ 油
oil

yau⁴ yu⁴ 魷魚
squid/calamari

yau⁴ yu⁴ gon¹ 魷魚干
dried squid; used in stir fries and soups

ye⁴ choi³ 椰菜
Chinese flat cabbage; head cabbage

ye⁴ ji²　　　　　椰子
coconut

ye⁶ heung¹ fa¹　　　夜香花
night-fragrant flower; vegetable with a cluster of yellow flowers. Requires only light cooking and has a flavour similar to peas.

yed⁶ boon² foh² woh¹ 日本火鍋
sukiyaki; sliced meat, tofu and vegetables cooked with saki, sugar and soy sauce (Japan)

yed⁶ boon² jeung² yau⁴ 日本醬油
malt soy sauce (Japan)

yem² cha¹　　　　　飲茶
yum cha (see Yum Cha & Dim Sum in the Culture of Hong Kong Cuisine chapter)

yem² liu⁶ jung² goon² 飲料總管
sommelier

yem² yung⁶ sui²　　　飲用水
drinking water

yen⁴ sem¹　　　　　人參
ginseng, prized as a tonic and aphrodisiac

yeung⁴　　　　　　羊
sheep

yeung⁴ chung¹　　　洋蔥
onion

yeung⁴ gai³　　　　洋薊
palm cabbage; buds from the palm tree (not a cabbage)

yeung⁴ jek³ yug⁶　　羊脊肉
rack of lamb

yeung⁴ tou⁴　　　　楊桃
star apple/star fruit

yeung⁴ yug⁶　　　　羊肉
lamb/mutton

yeung⁶ fu² gua¹　　　釀苦瓜
minced shrimp and pork stuffed into melon rings, pan fried, then served with black bean sauce

yi¹ min⁶　　　　　伊麵
deep-fried egg noodles

yi³ dai⁶ lei⁶ cheng¹ gua¹ 意大利青瓜
zucchini

yig⁶　　　　　　　翼
wing

yim¹ pao³　　　　　醃泡
marinade/pickle

yim¹ wong⁴ gua¹　　醃黃瓜
cucumber pickle (see cha⁴ gua¹)

yim⁴　　　　　　　鹽
salt

yim⁴ guk⁶ gei¹　　　鹽焗雞
salt-baked chicken (see Fowl in the Staples & Specialities chapter)

yim⁴ sui²　　　　　鹽水
brine

yin¹ fen¹　　　　　煙薰
smoke/cure

yin³ woh¹　　　　　燕窩
bird's nest; swiftlets gather fish, and other food, and bind them with their saliva to form a nest.

yin³ woh¹ geng¹　　　燕窩羹
bird's nest soup; cleaned and soaked bird's nests cooked with minced chicken and egg whites in a superior chicken broth

yin³ woh¹ tong⁴ sui²　燕窩糖水
bird's nest soup sweetened with sugar, served as a dessert

yin⁶ choi³　　　　　莧菜
Chinese spinach; wild species with a strong flavour. The red leaf variety is more prized. Used in stir fries and soups.

ying⁴ yu⁵　　　　　凝乳
curd

yiu¹ deo⁶　　　　　腰豆
butter bean

yiu¹ guo²　　　　　腰果
cashew nut/acajou

yiu¹ chue⁵　　　　　瑤柱
dried scallops; used in soups and omelettes

yu⁴ beng²　　　　　魚餅
fishcake; minced fish mixed with salt water and formed into cakes that are fried and sliced into stir-fried dishes and soups.

yu⁴ chi³　　　　　魚翅
shark's fin (see Shark in the Staples & Specialities chapter)

yu⁴ daan⁶ 魚旦
fish balls; white fish shaped into balls.
Used in soups and stir fries.

yu⁴ heung¹ ke⁴ ji² 魚香茄子
shredded eggplant in a fish-flavoured
sauce of vinegar, wine, garlic, ginger,
pepper, spring onions and bean paste
(no fish)

yu⁴ lou⁶ 魚露
fish sauce

yu⁴ sen⁴ 魚唇
fish lips; sold in dried form. Once
soaked they have a much admired
gelatine-like texture.

yu⁴ tou⁵ 魚肚
fish's maw; dried fish stomach lining,
used in soups

yuen⁴ sai¹ 芫茜
Chinese parsley; cilantro; coriander

yuen⁴ ying⁴ min⁶ bao¹ 圓形麵包
bun

yuen⁵ tei² dung⁶ med⁶ 軟體動物
mollusc

yuen⁵ tong⁴ 軟糖
jelly (candied jubes)

yug⁶ deo⁶ keo³ 肉豆蔻
nutmeg

yug⁶ dung³ 肉凍
brawn/aspic

yug⁶ gei² 肉雞
squab

yug⁶ guei³ 肉桂
cinnamon

yug⁶ gwai³ pei⁴ 肉桂皮
Cassia bark

yug⁶ ngan⁵ 肉眼
eye (cut of meat)

yug⁶ yuen² 肉丸
meatball

Z

zab⁶ gem² jeung³ choi³ 雜錦醬菜
condiment of preserved ginger, peel and
fruits in a heavy syrup

zab⁶ gem² lang⁵ poon⁴ 雜錦冷盤
platter of food (four to six different
small portions) served as a first course

zab⁶ sui³ 雜碎
chop suey; American-Chinese dish of
shredded meat and vegetables, served
with rice and soy sauce

zab⁶ wui⁶ cao² min⁶ 雜會炒麵
fried combination noodles; thin egg
noodles pan fried until crunchy, topped
with stir-fried meat (or seafood) and
vegetables

zab⁶ wui⁶ juk¹ 雜會粥
assorted meat congee

zen¹ baak⁶ 津白
cabbage with long, white stems and
large leaves. The heart is delicate and
tender. Used for stir frying. Also known
as white vegetable.

zen¹ ju¹ pong⁵ 珍珠蚌
expensive mollusc cooked like abalone.
Available in dried form.

zen¹ ju² chung¹ 珍珠蔥
pearl onion

zou¹ leo⁶ yu⁴ pin³ 糟溜魚片
fish mixed with egg white and cornflour
and deep fried. Wood ear fungus is
sauteed and combined with the fish in a
sauce made of rice wine, chicken stock,
salt and sugar.

zou² chaan¹ cha⁴ 早餐茶
breakfast tea; a black tea

Recommended Reading

Chang, K C *Food in Chinese Culture,* (Yale University Press 1977)

Dahlen, Martha *A Cook's Guide to Chinese Vegetables,* (Hong Kong Guidebook Company Ltd 1992)

Habbeger & O'Reilly *Travelers' Tales: Hong Kong,* (Traveler's Tales Inc. 1996)

Hom, Ken *Fragrant Harbor Tastes,* (California Books 1989)

Lai, T C *At the Chinese Table,* (Oxford Images of Asia Series 1990)

Li & Wei *Culture Shock,* (Graphic Arts Center Publishing Company October 1994)

Mark, William *The Chinese Gourmet,* (Thunder Bay Press October 1994)

Perkins *Hong Kong and China Gas Company Chinese Cookbook,* (Northwest International Trading August 1982)

Welsh, Frank *A History of Hong Kong,* (Kodansha International July 1996)

Wine & Dine Magazine, published monthly by Panpac Media.com Ltd (Singapore); Hong Kong edition published by Wine & Dine Ltd

Contacts

Cecilia J Au-Yeung
Chopsticks Cooking Centre
8A Soares Avenue
Kowloon, Hong Kong
Tel: 852/2336-8433
Fax: 852/2338-1462

Hong Kong Tourist Association
Events and Tours Department
Tel: 852/2987-6390

Macau Government Tourist Office
Level 5, 17 Bridge Street
Sydney, NSW 2000
Tel: 1300 300 236

Photo Credits

Oliver Strewe Front cover, p1, p5, p8, p9 top, p10, p11, p13, p14, p15, p16, p18, p19, p20, p21, p25, p27, p31, p32, p33, p35, p36, p37, p38, p39, p41, p42, p44, p45, p48, p50, p52, p54, p55, p57, p58, p59, p60, p61, p64, p65, p66, p67, p69, p70, p72, p74, p77, p80, p82, p83 top, bottom right, p84, p85, p86, p87, p89, p90, p91, p92, p93, p96, p98, p99, p100, p101, p102, p103, p104, p105, p106, p107, p108, p110, p111, p115, p118, p119, p121 top, p122, p124, p126, p127, p128, p129, p131, p132, p134, p135, p136, p137, p138, p139, p140, p142, p143, p144, p147, p148, p149, p151, p152, p159, p160, p161, p167, p168 bottom, p169, p170, p171, p172, p173, p174, p175, p176, p178, 180, p183, p184, p185, p186, p187, p188, p189, p190, p191, p192, p193, p196, p197, p199, p201, p202, p207, back cover.

Richard I'Anson p9 bottom right, p56, p83 bottom left, p116, p121 bottom.

Glenn Beanland p9 bottom left, p168 top.

Chris Mellor p205

Di Mayfield p24.

Jerry Alexander p63

More World Food Titles

Brimming with cultural insight, the World Food series takes the guesswork out of new cuisines and provide the ideal guides to your own culinary adventures. The books cover everything to do with food and drink in each country – the history and evolution of the cuisine, its staples & specialities, and the kitchen philosophy of the people. You'll find definitive two-way dictionaries, menu readers and useful phrases for shopping, drunken apologies and much more.

The essential guides for travelling and non-travelling food lovers around the world, look out for the full range of World Food titles.

Out to Eat Series

Packed with independent, unstuffy opinion on hundreds of hand-picked restaurants, bars and cafes in each city, Lonely Planet's Out to Eat guides take food seriously but offer a fresh approach. Along with reviews, each Out to Eat identifies the best culinary cul-de-sacs, explores favourite ethnic cuisines, and the food trends that define each city. They also serve up the nitty-gritty on dish prices, wheelchair access and other useful facts with each review, and all include useful quick-scan indexes.

Updated annually, Out to Eat titles cover:
Melbourne, Sydney, London, Paris & San Francisco

Planet Talk

Our FREE quarterly printed newsletter is full of tips from travellers and anecdotes from Lonely Planet guidebook authors. Every issue is packed with up-to-date travel news and advice, and includes:

- a postcard from Lonely Planet co-founder Tony Wheeler
- a swag of mail from travellers
- a look at life on the road through the eyes of a Lonely Planet author
- topical health advice
- prizes for the best travel yarn
- news about forthcoming Lonely Planet events
- a complete list of Lonely Planet books and other titles

To join our mailing list, residents of the UK, Europe and Africa can email us at go@lonelyplanet.co.uk; residents of North and South America can do so at info@lonelyplanet.com; the rest of the world can email talk2us@lonelyplanet.com.au, or contact any Lonely Planet office.

The Lonely Planet Story

Lonely Planet published its first book in 1973 in response to the numerous 'How did you do it?' questions Maureen and Tony Wheeler were asked after driving, bussing, hitching, sailing and railing their way from England to Australia. Written at a kitchen table and hand collated, trimmed and stapled, *Across Asia on the Cheap* became an instant local bestseller.

Eighteen months in South-East Asia resulted in their second guide, *South-East Asia on a Shoestring*, which they put together in a backstreet Chinese hotel in Singapore in 1975. The 'yellow bible', as it quickly became known to backpackers around the world, soon became the guide to the region. It has sold well over ¾ million copies and is now in its 10th edition, still retaining its familiar yellow cover.

Today there are over 400 titles, including travel guides, walking guides, language kits & phrasebooks, travel atlases & maps, diving guides, restaurant guides, first time travel guides, condensed guides, illustrated pictorials and travel literature. The company is the largest independent travel publisher in the world.

The emphasis continues to be on travel for independent travellers. Tony and Maureen still travel for several months of each year and play an active part in the writing, updating and quality control of Lonely Planet's guides.

They have been joined by over 120 authors and over 400 staff at our offices in Melbourne (Australia), Oakland (USA), London (UK) and Paris (France). Travellers themselves also make a valuable contribution to the guides through the feedback we receive in thousands of letters each year and on our web site.

The people at Lonely Planet strongly believe that travellers can make a positive contribution to the countries they visit, both through their appreciation of the countries' culture, wildlife and natural features, and through the money they spend. In addition, the company makes a direct contribution to the countries and regions it covers. Since 1986 a percentage of the income from each book has been donated to ventures such as famine relief in Africa; aid projects in India; agricultural projects in Central America; Greenpeace's efforts to halt French nuclear testing in the Pacific.

Lonely Planet Offices

Australia
Locked Bag 1, Footscray, Victoria, 3011
☎ 03 9819 1877
fax 03 9819 6459
email: talk2us@lonelyplanet.com.au

USA
150 Linden St, Oakland, CA 94607
☎ 510 893 8555   TOLL FREE: 800 275 8555
fax 510 893 8572
email: info@lonelyplanet.com

UK
10a Spring Place, London NW5 3BH
☎ 020 7428 4800
fax 020 7428 4828
email: go@lonelyplanet.co.uk

France
1 rue du Dahomey, 75011 Paris
☎ 01 55 25 33 00
fax 01 55 25 33 01
email: bip@lonelyplanet.fr